Gender and Sexuality in Latin American Horror Cinema

Gustavo Subero

Gender and Sexuality in Latin American Horror Cinema

Embodiments of Evil

Gustavo Subero
Birkbeck College
University of London
London
United Kingdom

ISBN 978-1-137-56494-8   ISBN 978-1-137-56495-5   (eBook)
DOI 10.1057/978-1-137-56495-5

Library of Congress Control Number: 2016940831

© The Editor(s) (if applicable) and The Author(s) 2016
The author(s) has/have asserted their right(s) to be identified as the author(s) of this work in accordance with the Copyright, Designs and Patents Act 1988.
This work is subject to copyright. All rights are solely and exclusively licensed by the Publisher, whether the whole or part of the material is concerned, specifically the rights of translation, reprinting, reuse of illustrations, recitation, broadcasting, reproduction on microfilms or in any other physical way, and transmission or information storage and retrieval, electronic adaptation, computer software, or by similar or dissimilar methodology now known or hereafter developed.
The use of general descriptive names, registered names, trademarks, service marks, etc. in this publication does not imply, even in the absence of a specific statement, that such names are exempt from the relevant protective laws and regulations and therefore free for general use.
The publisher, the authors and the editors are safe to assume that the advice and information in this book are believed to be true and accurate at the date of publication. Neither the publisher nor the authors or the editors give a warranty, express or implied, with respect to the material contained herein or for any errors or omissions that may have been made.

Printed on acid-free paper

This Palgrave Macmillan imprint is published by Springer Nature
The registered company is Macmillan Publishers Ltd. London

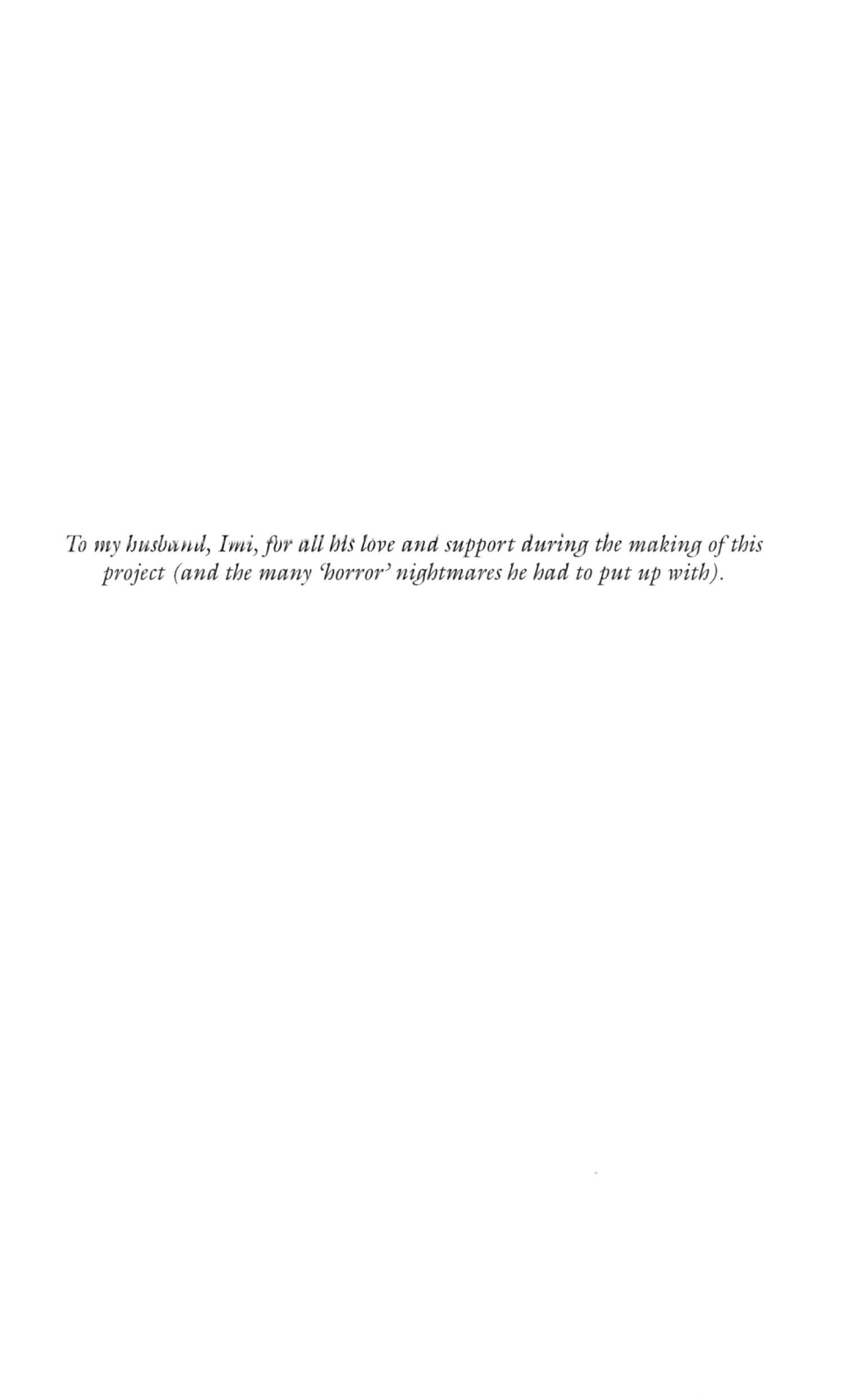

To my husband, Imi, for all his love and support during the making of this project (and the many 'horror' nightmares he had to put up with).

PREFACE

SANTA SANGRE AND THE POLITICS OF GENDER AND SEXUALITY IN LATIN AMERICAN HORROR CINEMA

I had my first taste of Latin American horror cinema at the age of 16 when I, inadvertently, attended a screening of Alejandro Jodorowsky's *Santa Sangre* (1989) at the university's film club. I found the film both shocking and, at the same time, revelatory. Not only did it provide the sufficient gore fest expected from a horror film of this nature, it also challenged and questioned many of the ideas that I considered to be paramount in the construction of gender and sexual identity circulating in the Latin American popular cultural imaginary. Sexual practices, gender performativity, templates of socio-sexual behaviour, regional and national politics, religion, idiosyncratic aspects of society—Jodorowsky does not leave a stone unturned in this Oedipal and surreal nightmare. Unsurprisingly, Bill Gibron (2011) has commented for *PopMatters* that the film is 'like a diabolical combination of Dario Argento, José Mojica Marins, and Federico Fellini (with just a smidgen of David Lynch tossed in for fever dream measure), he [Jodorowsky] transports hot button issues like religion and regional politics into a potent optical stew of suggestion and symbolism'. Over the years, and while thinking about and planning the inception of this project, I could not get this film out of my head, as it seemed to encapsulate perfectly most of the issues surrounding sexual and gender identities, gendered bodies and socio-sexual paradigms that preoccupy my research and this book in general.

At a time when most cinematic horror texts had traditionally been regarded as vehicles to explore the cultural anxieties of patriarchal control, *Santa Sangre* challenged traditional ways of watching (and reading) the horror genre. As will be clear in the following pages, this book engages with the horror genre in ways that invite the reader, as well as the imaginary film audience, to question the fixity of gender identity and of traditional male and female socio-sexual roles. Of Jodorowsky's film, in much the same way as the rest of the films analysed in this book, it could be said, as Christian Metz has famously theorised in relation to film and psychoanalysis, that

> the imaginary, opposed to the symbolic but constantly imbricated with it, designates the basic lure of the ego, the definite imprint of a stage *before* the Oedipus complex (which also continues after it), the durable mark of the mirror which alienates man in his own reflection and makes him the double of his double, the subterranean persistence of the exclusive relation to the mother, desire as a pure effect of lack and endless pursuit, the initial core of the unconscious (primal repression). (1982: 4, italics in original)

Thus the film shows the fissures existing within the system of gender identity and sexual orientation that circulates in the Latin American popular imaginary. These fissures were traditionally reinforced by popular cinema, as well as by those cinematic texts that came out of the New Latin American Cinema wave, whereby gender and sexuality had been regarded as fixed and immutable elements within the patriarchal system prevalent in such societies.

What *Santa Sangre* and most of the films analysed in this book demonstrate is that the horror genre becomes an excellent vehicle to channel alternative readings of gender and sexuality through the figure of the monster. The monster operates as the ultimate culturally and sexually ambiguous figure whose presence in the narrative may offer scenarios of female or queer empowerment. Through multiple scenarios in which the threat of castration is played out within the narrative (in ways that defy machismo within the patriarchal system), the process of acting out sexual anxieties is achieved through the victim's sympathetic look at the monster or identification with the monster itself. However, the main goal of this book is to move away from the masochistic/empathetic or sadistic/voyeuristic identification on the part of spectators (regarded by many theorists as an abstract group) and to engage more with the way in which horror cinema in Latin America provides new avenues to map out the changes in the politics of gender and sexuality as experienced in popular culture. Therefore, my application of the psychoanalytical model, as an effective strategy to read these texts, seeks to challenge the representation of gender and sexuality whereby, as Richard Nowell suggests, these 'were formulaic, excessively violent exploitation films that were fashioned to satisfy the misogynist fantasies of male visitors to grind-houses and fleapits' (2010: 4). Thus I have chosen to be slightly unorthodox and in lieu of an introduction, I will provide an overview of key terminology and issues that will be explored in this book through a close analysis of the main themes and notions of gender and sexuality that can be found in *Santa Sangre* as a seminal film of the Latin American horror canon.

Santa Sangre tells the story of Fenix (Axel Jodorowsky), a young man confined in a mental institution who escapes in order to begin a life of murderous crime acting under his mother's influence. Through a flashback sequence the audience learns how he was left heavily traumatised as a child (at a time when he and his family were circus performers), when he witnessed his father, in a fit of mad rage, severing Fenix's mother's arms and then killing himself. In the present time of the narrative, after escaping from the asylum, Fenix is reunited with his mother and then forced against his will to function, literally, as her own arms. And so the two begin a rampaging campaign of murder and revenge.

The film criticises many aspects of the deculturation of Mexican culture, as well as the problems emerging in the US–Mexican border culture. Yet its clearest message (and plot device) is the revisiting and challenging of assumed socio-cultural templates of sexuality and gender as they operate in the Latin American milieu. Furthermore, for the impressionable 16-year-old teenager I was, it was the queering of the main male protagonist and the queering of culture at large that became particularly poignant throughout the film. *Santa Sangre* turned on its head notions of sex, sexual identity and gender (especially ideas of machismo, marianismo[1] and to a large extent queer desire) as they circulate in the mainstream of

---

[1] According to Evelyn Stevens (1973), marianismo constitutes the organising tenet of female identity within the Latin American milieu. It is an ideology that regulates and drives all female behaviour in the Latin American social imaginary. It has its origin in the legacies of the Catholic Church whereby women are regarded as subservient and docile based on the assumption that their behaviour should emulate that of the Virgin Mary (see also Collier 1986). However, marianismo does not constitute an opposing force to machismo and instead runs parallel to it as a complementary element of macho ideology that helps sustain

Latin American culture. It is a film that, as Anton Bitel (2012) suggests in his review of the film for *Little White Lies*,

> grabs viewers by their metaphorical balls with its sheer creative excess. Part circus carnival, part Oedipal nightmare, part gnostic allegory of self-discovery, part Buñuelian pantomime, part psychothriller, part satire on church hypocrisy and colonial predation, Santa Sangre is a magical realist poem written in blood and set to a Latin beat, full of bold colours and grand gestures.

In contrast to typical, classic horror narratives of the 1980s and 1990s (mainly those originating from the United States), in which the emphasis is on random serial killings of teenagers and young adults (in various states of undress or at different stages of the sex act), gruesome and graphic depictions of bodies being slashed open with phallic weaponry and a fixation with psychotic male killers, *Santa Sangre* breaks away from the motives and tropes of such slasher-and-splatter films by offering a story in which all the monstrous characters and the horrific situations emerge from a world of sexual abjection. In the classic horror narrative, abjection interferes with normativity. The abject monstrous subject (be it a monster or a living corpse) disrupts normative binaries and operates in an interstitial space between the living and the dead. Abjection embraces ambiguity at its core and, as Julia Kristeva has famously theorised,

> we may call it a border; abjection is above all ambiguity. Because, while releasing a hold, it does not radically cut off the subject from what threatens it—on the contrary, abjection acknowledges it to be in perpetual danger. But also because abjection itself is a composite of judgment and affect, of condemnation and yearning, of signs and drives. Abjection preserves what existed in the archaism of pre-objectal relationship. (1982: 9–10)

However, it could be argued that Jodorowsky does away with this division between the normative and the abject and creates a world in which all characters and situations operate at a seemingly border-free symbolic level. In other words, the film reifies the erasure of the border between those symbolic orders that separate the monstrous and the human, the natural and the supernatural, normal from deviant sexual desire, as well as nor-

---

the patriarchal values rooted in Latin American culture (a more in-depth analysis of marianismo will be provided in Chap. 1).

mal and abnormal gender roles. Classic horror narratives are built on the marked difference between normativity and abjection. By the same token, many a storyline centres on some sort of monster disrupting normativity by murdering or annihilating 'normal' people, and thus breaking the status quo of heteronormative society. However, *Santa Sangre* disrupts this narrative continuum, and the director achieves this by fetishising and othering all the characters in the film and eliminating any vestiges of normativity from the main story. Jodorowsky's *Santa Sangre* presents a dystopian world in which social and sexual norms have been eroded as the regulatory forces that control and shape socio-sexual relations among individuals. Thus the film's resolution will not ultimately involve a return to normativity because such regulatory forces, this version of reality, have never existed in the film.

Furthermore, those areas of society regulating normativity—that is, law and religion—are also presented as abject territories within the narrative. The monstrous abject body is represented as a body without a soul and, as such, it represents the antithesis of the spiritual, while it contravenes the religious symbolic. The body of Fenix's mother Concha (Blanca Guerra) hyperbolically epitomises abjection not only due to the character's monstrous feminine condition, but also by the fact that it is othered through her limbless state. The flashback sequence clearly points to the way in which 'becoming abject' is at the core of the narrative, as it will be the root of Fenix's Oedipal complex and the root of his own queer male identity. After parading across town to promote the arrival of the circus, the action moves to life inside the tent and how the Tattooed Woman (Thelma Tixou) is forcing her daughter Alma (Faviola Elenka Tapia) to walk across a flaming rope. The daughter's mime-painted face is framed in a close-up showing fear and anguish. This image operates in stark contrast to the mother, framed in long and medium long shots of her exuberantly gowned body, as she screams and yells at her daughter; meanwhile, a young Fenix watches this unfold from a hideaway. The scene is interrupted by the appearance of Fenix's father, Orgo (Guy Stockwell). The moment the Tattooed Woman sees him, she proceeds to disrobe; a long shot of her body shows her wearing nothing but a very suggestive bikini, her scintillating and curvaceous body covered entirely in tattoos. The two begin to flirt rather obscenely and then Orgo asks her to stand against a wall, as he starts to throw knives at her. Every time a knife lands near her body she takes the opportunity to caress or lick the blade seductively, highlighted by close-ups and extreme close-ups, in what is obviously part of their process of courtship.

Fenix watches in a mixture of dismay and envy at the macho power emanating from his father and the way he manages to seduce a woman whose identity clearly falls outside prescribed marianismo. The Tattooed Woman's anti-mariana identity is hyperbolically depicted on her own body, as her tattoos of snakes and other exotic animals make a clear reference to the Garden of Eden. Her brightly coloured green tattoos depict wild plants and flowers and wild animals, and the snake and apple clearly represent her as a sexual temptress. Her tattooed body operates as a visually economic sign of abjection since, as Kristeva has already theorised, 'abjection, on the other hand, is immoral, sinister, scheming, and shady: a terror that dissembles, a hatred that smiles, a passion that uses the body for barter instead of inflaming it' (1982: 4). The tattoos operate at the level of the symbolic, as markers of a type of femininity that is transgressive and that operates outside prescribed normativity. Her voluptuous body, her voluminous red and curly hair, are explicit signs of a subversive ownership of desire that departs from any mariana identity.

The Tattooed Woman's body breaches and undermines cultural constructions of femininity by externalising the sexualisation of her own identity in ways that oppose the ideals of virginity and purity that are promoted through mariana identity. Via her tattoos the film essentially commodifies her body (and identity) as she breaks the symbolic challenge by an overt and direct form of domination. Furthermore, her tattooed body is inscribed in phallic dominance because she becomes objectified by the mere act of being inked. The penetration and permanence of the ink in her body carry an allegorical and material immediacy that is unachievable in other forms of identity manifestations. Arguably, her tattoos posit her as a degraded, criminal and marginal subject when compared to the normative femininity embodied through Concha's body. This is achieved in the film by the contrasting and challenging of opposing versions of femininity as understood in popular culture.

While the flirting continues between Orgo and his mistress, the narrative cuts to Concha, who is trying to impede the local authorities from pulling down the building in which her church congregates. After she fails to stop the destruction of the church, she returns to the circus to find the Tattooed Woman practising fellatio on one of Orgo's knives. In an attack of rage and jealousy, Concha quickly takes a knife out of Orgo's hand and threatens the woman with it. The contrast between the two female characters, and the types of femininities they purport, could not be more startling: Concha is dressed in what appears to be a red, long-sleeved religious gown that covers her entire body, while the other woman is practically semi-naked. Concha comes to represent an exaggerated version of marianismo characterised by, as Evelyn Stevens notes, a 'cult of feminine spiritual superiority, which teaches that women are semi-divine, morally superior to and spiritually stronger than men' (1973: 91). However, such characteristics must be played down in order to appease men and to guarantee peace and harmony within the household and society at large.

This is clearly evident in this sequence of the film when, after threatening the Tattooed Woman, Concha points the knife at Orgo. Despite the imminent danger, he looks at her defiantly, framed by a low-angle close-up, as he knows that she will not carry out her threat. The film then switches to an over-the-shoulder take, with the camera placed behind Orgo, in which only Concha's eyes can be seen as she then submits to Orgo's embrace and power of seduction. A medium shot then shows her temporarily submitting to him and, as he walks away from her while slowly and seductively undressing, she cannot resist his macho magnetism and ends up jumping on him and allowing him to carry her on his back. Concha's submission to her husband's macho attitude and his machismo reinforces the findings of Miguel A. de la Torre, who argues that 'marianismo encourages domination, aggressiveness, and a "cult of virility" that reinforces a machista culture detrimental to all women' (2009: 348). Thus this sequence suggests that regardless of the type of femininity that female subjects embrace, they have no control over their own socio-sexual persona as they submit to the hypermasculine whims and desires of the macho.

Despite the beginning of the flashback sequence operating as part of a pro-machista discourse by depicting Orgo as a hypermacho figure within the narrative, Jodorowsky wastes no time in also disavowing the notion of machismo by highlighting the failures of macho identity and the social and cultural shortcomings encountered by those who embrace this type of masculinity. Orgo clearly regards machismo as the driving force for his male anxieties and the way to externalise his own male identity; or, as David Sequeira suggests, 'the concept of "machismo" encompasses this ideal, in which men are viewed as virile, aggressive, and authoritarian' (2009: 7). The character is clearly depicted as a caricature of hypermasculinity, as he wanders around the circus dressed in his expanded tamer outfit, which barely contains his fat belly and shows a deep V-neck that reifies his status as an 'hombre de pelo en pecho'. It is no coincidence that the director depicts this embodiment of machismo through a rather grotesque body in order to highlight the incongruences and contradictions of this retrograde template of masculinity. Orgo clearly objectifies women around him and regards them as disposable items whose jobs are the provision of nurture and/or sexual favours. He is the type of macho subject who, as Stevens points out, shows 'exaggerated aggressiveness and intransigence in male-to-male interpersonal relationships and arrogance and sexual aggression in male-to-female relationships' (1973: 90).

However, the film also suggests from the very beginning of the story that the artificiality of masculinity and the constructedness of machismo are a template for male sexuality. For instance, Orgo is repeatedly shown heavily drunk in ways that suggest that his machismo, as a sexual fabrication rather than a natural manifestation of his felt sexual identity, needs to be fuelled by alcohol in order to be fully achieved or embodied. In other words, drunkenness plays an important role in the assumption and manifestation of macho behaviour and corroborates the idea that, as John M. Ingham suggests, it 'may also promote reproduction to the degree that it lowers sexual inhibitions and emboldens husbands to make sexual demands of their wives, despite the customary restrictions on sexual behaviour' (1986: 68). Perhaps it is the rather melancholic depiction of machismo that Orgo's character portrays that leads audiences to believe that machismo is the configuration of generic practices that adhere to the principles of patriarchy, guaranteeing the power of men and the subordination of women.

The film rapidly dispels the seemingly unproblematic nature of machismo as an intrinsic manifestation of Latin American masculinity. This is evidenced within the story when, later in the film and as Concha performs her own circus act (doing acrobatics while hanging from her hair), she sees Orgo flirting once again with the Tattooed Woman. Through a point-of-view shot from a very high angle—taking Concha's viewpoint from the top of the circus tent—she witnesses the two lovers as they dance, kiss and make their way out of the main tent. Realising what is happening, Concha screams to be brought down. This scene becomes all the more poignant as it is framed through an extreme long shot with a very low angle of Concha hanging from the top of the tent. The camera work conveys in the character a sense of female hysteria, while it also reduces her to a caricature of womanliness. Once Concha has been brought back to the floor, she grabs Fenix by the arms, drags him all the way to their caravan and locks him in. She then goes after the lovers, to the place where the two are about to have sex.

Once she gets there, she grabs a bottle of acid from a cabinet outside the room and sneaks in as Orgo is about to penetrate his lover. Orgo's macho masculinity is stressed by the camera work through a crane-up, behind-the-head shot of him that comes to a stop above his head (although the very top of his head is still in view) and then switches to a long shot and tilted high angle of the Tattooed Woman with her legs wide open, both pulled all the way to her sides, as she offers herself for the taking. The camera moves to a medium shot from behind her and shows Orgo ripping off her bikini and about to penetrate her. However, in a rather Samsonian turn of events, Concha approaches from behind him and tries to hit him, yet in the process she ends up ripping off his wig, stressed through a medium close shot that takes her point of narrative view. Concha then throws acid all over her husband's genitals before lurching herself against her female rival. As the two women begin to fight, Orgo forcibly grabs Concha, shown in a tracking long shot, and takes her all the way to his Wheel of Death while she laughs hysterically. He places her against it, puts her arms on the sides, stressed at this point by medium close-ups, grabs a knife in each hand and severs her arms.

Orgo's actions clearly support the notion that 'machismo or masculinity is also said to be displayed not only by the man's sexuality, especially extramarital, and other activities that indicate phallic preoccupation, but by his control over the affairs of his family, especially his wife' (Sequeira 2009: 8). He is presented as a man who embodies all the negative aspects of machismo and who has no regard for anyone but himself. He seduces, dominates and coerces to the same degree and also feels sufficiently empowered to exercise physical violence over those who attempt to rebel against him. Concha's ultimate punishment is to have her arms cut off; in this manner, she becomes the ultimate castrated figure because she now embodies the lack (a point that will be discussed later).

Jodorowsky's version of machismo underscores a rather problematic correlation between the penis and the phallus at the hand of the macho subject. This is evidenced by the fact that Orgo's fate becomes a testament that in the popular imaginary, macho phallic investment can only be achieved through the handling and possession of the penis. Orgo's character could be said to operate as the 'representation of the power that seems to be available to men in social and political terms in a male-dominated culture' (Halberstam 1998: 355). However, this power will be short-lived, since the burning of his penis with acid will function as the mechanism whereby his phallic investment is disavowed within the narrative. Although he ultimately punishes Concha for attempting to rebel against his machista domination, he quickly realises that his deformed and burnt penis can no longer generate social power and thus feels that he has lost phallic empowerment. As he stumbles from the place where he dismembered his wife, the camera shows him in a long shot while he walks past the young Alma, in clear pain and covering his bleeding penis with his hand. As he continues to walk the camera pans right and zooms into a medium shot while the song *La barca de Oro* can be heard in the background. The camera then swivels about 90° to end in a low-angle close-up of Orgo as he uses the knife to slit his own throat. The young Fenix witnesses the whole episode and screams from inside the caravan. At the level of the symbolic, Orgo's death could be said to operate as an explicit strategy for the visual dismantling of macho identity. Thus having the penis—that is, performing heterosexual masculinity in the form of extra-marital sex, as well as exercising excesses of power and oppression (in the microcosm of the circus) through violence—can no longer be regarded as the ultimate form of phallic empowerment.

The film disavows phallic power as an attribute of machismo that can and must be passed down through generations and that, although seemingly innate, must be activated while its loss is also vehemently feared. This can be noticed in the sequence after the death of the circus's elephant, when, following the funerary procession to get rid of the body, the young Fenix cries inconsolably by his father's side and is quickly told to 'Stop crying like a little girl. I'll give you something that'll make you a man.' The scene moves to Orgo taking the boy to a house, where he proceeds to undress the boy, sit him down and tie him to a chair. The camera switches to a medium close-up of Fenix's bare chest as his father stencils an eagle on it and then uses his own knife, accentuated by an extreme close-up of the blade coming out of an ink jar, to tattoo the boy's chest. The camera moves to a close-up of Fenix's face as he contorts and cries in pain. Once the tattoo is complete, Orgo takes the boy to a standing mirror and tells him 'There, now you're a man. Just like me', pointing to the very same tattoo on his own chest.

By tattooing the young Fenix, Orgo tries to perpetuate macho ideology in a historical continuum that will see this rite of passage as the entrance to both manhood and adulthood. The tattoo becomes a symbol that indicates power and dominance: a power signified by the eagle, an image that operates in the cultural imaginary as a signifier and embodiment of phallic power. Orgo utilises the tattoo as an instrument through which he can simultaneously express, recreate and pass on an aspect of his own self, in other words his machismo, through a body technology. This idea chimes with the thinking of Karin Beeler, who argues that 'the tattoo symbolizes a rite of passage, a way of marking a particular event in the narrative of life, an expression of defiance or resistance to authority' (2005: 1). However, this notion is quickly disavowed as the director sets out to challenge patriarchal structures of male domination and, especially, machismo as an ideal and fixed template of male behaviour. Despite Orgo's desire to encrypt Fenix with phallic symbolism so as to guarantee his alliance to macho ideology, the narrative very quickly portrays the adult Fenix in ways that would only fit within a queer macho identity. In fact, the adult Fenix will show an ironic sensibility that contradicts and challenges the hypermasculinist imagery that was inherited from his father as part of his own queer macho identity, and by doing so negates the oppressive masculinist nature of such signs. Or, as Richard Mohr argues in relation to gay art,

> the masculine is eroticized, but not in a way that affirms the oppressive features of traditional masculine roles. The various roles' iconographies undermine each other. In pinning these uniformly gendered but clashing images of himself, the fellow [gay macho] cannot plausibly be taken to assume the privileges of any—not even one—of the roles to which his adopted postures allude. (1992: 197)

Fenix's queering occurs not only at the symbolic level, it also becomes part of the narrative itself, since the post-flashback storyline will revolve around the murders and monstrous acts he will commit when acting and operating as if he were Concha's replacement limbs. In this light, the film clearly portrays Fenix in a very similar fashion to the monsters popularised by the type of horror cinema made on the fringes of Hollywood in the mid-twentieth century, such as George Waggner's *The Wolf Man* (1941), Phil Tucker's *Robot Monster* (1953), Terence Fisher's *The Curse of Frankenstein* (1957), Joseph Green's *The Brain That Wouldn't Die* (1962) and, most famously, Alfred Hitchcock's *Psycho* (1960), among others. Similarly to those monsters, Fenix's horrific impulses seem to be driven—and diegetically justified—by sexual traumas and sexually deviant desires in ways that suggest that the uncontrollable and sexually dissatisfied id operates as the root of monstrosity. Fenix's monstrous id emerges from his inability to break with his own mirror stage as he is torn, as a child, between the hypermacho father and the ultra-mariana mother, who both see and treat him as an extension of their own psychosexual personas. Therefore, Fenix does not experience his body as a unified totality but as fragmented, with parts that are disjointed and operate at the vestiges of seemingly contradictory sexual cultural practices. The film makes it clear that Fenix never abandons the first phase of the mirror stage and, therefore, can only create meaning from the world around him through the way in which his own parents have experienced it. The conflated ideologies behind the cultural symbolism of the tattoo on his chest in stark contrast with the feminisation of his arms (as he uses them to, quite literally, 'mobilise' his mother's identity) form the basis for the confusion between self and Other that characterises him throughout the narrative.

Fenix is, arguably, presented as a masquerading monstrous feminine, following Barbara Creed (1993a), because his monstrosity is defined and emphasised by the importance of his mother's sexual identity in the construction of his monstrosity. As Creed rightly asserts,

> the presence of the monstrous-feminine in the popular horror film speaks to us more about male fears than about female desire or feminine subjectivity. However, this presence does challenge the view that the male spectator is almost always situated in an active, sadistic position and the female spectator in a passive, masochistic one. (1993a: 7)

First, it is possible to suggest that Fenix embodies a type of meta-transvestism—which ultimately turns into a meta-transsexualism by the end of the film—because he does not, diegetically, cross-dress as a result of a gender dysphoria or some form of sexual exploration, but because he feels that he is being forced to do so by his domineering mother. Thus the film advances the notion that cross-dressing and transvestism problematically reinscribe traditional gender roles. At the same time, it hyperbolically questions the character's heterosexuality through his fixation with either hyper-masculine-looking (muscled) or queer female subjects. Fenix as a queer monster shows the fluidity of sexual and gender systems in contemporary culture, whereby cultural templates of gender and sexuality are no longer regarded as rigid and infallible in the popular imaginary. Jodowrosky speaks to the audience about machismo and marianismo as forms of cultural castration because they both polarise gender and sexual systems. These sexual templates force sexual subjects to abide by a set of behaviours that are culturally regarded as supposedly natural, while they castigate any deviation from the fixity of sexual and gender parameters. Thus the horror movie becomes the best vehicle for the director to address, as Harry M. Benshoff argues, 'any and all sexuality—not just queer sexuality—[…] as some sort of secret and monstrous thing that lurks in the night, having been forced there in the first place by a repressive social heritage' (1997: 165).

The monstrously symbiotic relationship between Fenix and Concha also permits the audience to venture into a terrain in which a new type of monstrous feminine operates: one in which the monstrous feminine both represents the lack (by means of figuring as a castrated subject in Freudian terms) and is also depicted as the castrator. As a result, it could be suggested that Concha represents a 'castrated femme castratrice', because her monstrosity, depicted through her missing limbs, reflects her adherence to the dominant symbolic order even when she tries to subvert such an order by killing those people she regards as deviant or a threat to her own self-perceived natural order. However, by becoming an armless monster, Concha—and Fenix by default—becomes entrapped within a castration complex: her body never leaves the psychosexual arena in which the child's body morphs from being symbolically castrated to the moment of sexual reconciliation through the abandonment of the Oedipus complex. In other words, Concha's body forces Fenix to remain trapped in a psychosexual childhood stage, whereby his conscious mind never fully corrects the fact that the female body is not the residual leftover of castration. By having to act through Concha's mutilated body, Fenix remains within the castration anxiety, as he loses masculine power and autonomy and is symbolically emasculated by his mother. By depicting the characters within a narrative continuum of symbiosis and rejection within the socio-sexual spectrum, Jodorowsky cleverly criticises both machismo and marianismo as cultural templates for socio-sexual behaviour through a protagonist trapped in a culturally undetermined, socio-sexual limbo. Fenix is unable to overcome his Oedipal identity as a result of his inability to reconcile himself to the acquisition of a super-ego, strongly influenced by his cultural heritage, that is destined to the reproduction of the patriarchal order. Instead, he has not only accepted symbolic castration, he has also become the instrument through which female castration is disavowed, and by doing so he obliterates the meaning of machismo as a cultural template within the social and popular imaginary.

Arguably, the horrific nature of the film derives not only from the murders committed by the mother–son monstrous figure, but also from the fact that it evidences the fissures and contradictions of gender and sexuality in Latin America. The film is very radical in its treatment of machismo and marianismo as obsolete templates of gender and sexuality, evidencing the notion that abjection in the horror text derives not necessarily only from the impossibility of the child breaking away from the archaic maternal figure, but also from the socially prescribed impositions on socio-sexual subjects that circulate in the popular imaginary. *Santa Sangre* thus follows a narrative in which the maternal figure is constructed as a monstrous feminine, since

> by refusing to relinquish her hold on her child, she prevents it from taking up its proper place in relation to the Symbolic. Partly consumed by her desire to remain locked in a blissful relationship with the mother and partly terrified of separation, the child finds it easy to succumb to the comforting pleasure of the dyadic relationship. (Creed 2002: 72)

The film also makes it clear (while trying both to reassert the position of women in contemporary Latin American society, and to a greater extent to denounce the mistreatment and abuses to which they are subjected under machista ideology) that it is women themselves who in many instances also help perpetuate machista ideology. This can be perceived mainly through one of the subtexts of the film, in which Concha acts as the leader of a cult that worships a female saint who experienced martyrdom when her arms were severed by rapists. The sequence evidences how machismo operates as an identity that is supported by and maintained through male-centred social as well as religious institutions that aim to deride female-ness and the role of women in society. Arguably, the entire sequence in the church becomes a clear allegory of the bloody nature of femaleness through menstruation, birth and other biological processes. For instance, all the members of the cult wear red gowns, while the ornaments that adorn the church itself are red crown of flowers, red candles and red ribbons. Furthermore, at the centre of the church itself, which can be clearly seen in the internal long shot as Concha opens the doors for Monsignor (Sergio Bustamante) to look around, there is a small pool filled with a red liquid that seems to symbolise blood.

In a direct allegory and criticism of the 14 stages of the crucifixion, Concha retells to Monsignor the story of the saint girl Lirio who was abused and raped by 'macho' men and whose arms were cut off as a punishment for her resistance. Within the film, the girl's story forms the basis of the beliefs on which this church is sustained. Every time Concha shows a different tableau to the priest, the camera from a slight high angle zooms into the two characters in a close-up to show both Concha's blind devotion and the man's look of disbelief. After all the tableaus have been explained to him, Concha moves towards the centre pool, shown in another long shot, and kneels down to show the man the 'miracle' that has occurred in the pool, which she believes is filled with the blood of the saint girl. When Monsignor kneels down, he claims that the pool is filled with paint; the camera cuts from a medium shot to a medium close-up of the two characters and they argue about the sanctity of the place. This immediately moves to a low-angle medium shot that zooms in as the two begin to fight. Monsignor's reaction of indignation and his use of physical force to constrain Concha—for what he considers heresy—is clearly symptomatic of a macho society that vilifies and objectifies the female form while justifying female oppression. In the present of the narrative, Concha's limbless body, in much the same way as the saint she venerated, makes it clear that the horror narrative is an excellent vehicle to provide a language for the reimagination of a self in constant transformation: a self that is regendered, ungendered and regenerated through the multiple possibilities of the monstrous body as a space that both disrupts and challenges social assumptions of the gendered body.

Ultimately, *Santa Sangre* recontextualises into a horror narrative the everyday of the socio-sexual negotiations that occur between men and women in the Latin American milieu, while at the same time challenging traditional paradigms of gender and sexuality. The dystopian reality in which the characters operate, as well as the horrors committed by the mother–son dyadic monster, conflates 'an instinctive hatred between characters representing lust and chastity, which are both seen as perversions in a world without a sane middle way' (Ebert 2003). Jodorowsky seems aware that both machismo and marianismo are obsolete socio-sexual categories that, nowadays, simply operate as unrealistic idealisations of gender and sexual systems in multiple popular, national imaginaries in Latin America. Furthermore, despite machismo and marianismo being disavowed by the narrative, it is the queerness of this film that becomes most prevalent in the story, since all the characters live outside acceptable socio-sexual categories within heteronormativity. Beyond the obvious psychoanalytical tone of the film—played out through the relationship between Concha and Fenix—it is also concerned with other aspects of the sexual cultures of the Mexican and, by extension, Latin American society in which it is set.

For instance, there is a moment in the film when Fenix, in what appears to be an unsuccessful quest to find a woman who can break the oppression exercised by his mother, ends up watching a wrestling match in which a female wrestler called La Santa (in a clear homage to the iconic figure of El Santo) fights and wins against three male wrestlers. Once again, the director sees fit to challenge cultural paradigms in relation to the role of men and women in society. This character is unashamedly queer, not only in feminising a practice that has been traditionally regarded as a macho domain[2]—and whose biggest exponent was a real-life wrestler turned film icon called El Santo—but also in being depicted unequivocally as a very muscular crossdresser. The director clearly sets out to queer the film through narrative spaces of in-betweenism, as theorised by Richard Dyer (2013), as the character is conceptualised through biological androgyny. Fenix's attraction to such a hypermuscular and masculinised woman invites the audience to wonder whether his Oedipal issues emerge more from some form of unresolved vaginal envy towards his mother, in which he did not see her as the object of desire but as the opponent to his obtaining the affection of his father. This is also enunciated through the mother figure, since her name—that is, Concha—is a slang word for vagina in the vernacular Spanish of Mexico and other Latin American countries.

Whether or not one argues that Fenix is, in fact, a character whose same-sex attraction is manifested through transvestitic practices and who uses the projection of his mother's desires as part of his own feminine psyche, the film is irreverent in its depiction of queer sexuality and its criticism of the sexual paradigms that govern male and female subjects in Latin America. It also takes the conflict between parental figures and children to a paradigmatic imagination of modernity in Latin America through the border conflict between the United States and Mexico. As Josetxo Cerdán and Miguel Fernández Labayen rightly assert, 'the problematic relationship of Jodorowsky with Mexican culture and its national symbols is again a point of discussion between critics […] *Santa sangre* posits a binary relation between a father-U.S. (represented in the role of the castrated Orgo) and mother-Mexico (Concha)' (2009: 108). The issues of the 'castrated female castratice' as discussed earlier can also be projected onto the current project of the Mexican nation through horror metaphors that see the problematic relationship between border cultures enacted through cultural and sexual anxieties. It could even be argued that the film reflects the cultural legacies of post-colonial ideology, whereby Mexican socio-sexual

---

[2] Although by the turn of the twenty-first century wrestling had become more widely practised among women in Mexico too (see Grobet 2006).

paradigms are regulated and shaped by the oppressive north. In short, providing an analysis—albeit a brief one—of the film evidences that Kent L. Brintnall is right to assert that

> cinematic horror narratives may be the best place to start in thinking about the connections between religious and popular discourses on the moral order. Through their representation of the monster and the monstrous, horror narratives identify, describe and produce not only the abnormal and terrifying, but also the normal […]. More importantly, because of the fantastic context in which horror stories unfold, these narratives contemplate social issues and concerns that may not be discussed openly and explicitly in the 'real world'. (2007: 146)

Like the film discussed in this Preface, *Gender and Sexuality in Latin American Horror Cinema: Embodiments of Evil* is concerned with the way in which issues of gender and sexuality are dealt with, revisited and challenged in a number of cinematic horror narratives from Latin America. Although this book is far from exhaustive in its analysis of seminal horror texts, it offers consideration of a number of films that are of particular importance in the way they address the socio-sexual paradigms that circulate in the continental popular imaginary and that have come to symbolise sexual and gender relations in this region. In doing so, the book traces a historisation of the horror film from the 1930s to date through analysis of issues such as machismo, marianismo, the maternal figure and mothering, homosociality and bromance, among others, and how they are re-evaluated in the context of the sexual politics that circulate in popular culture.

A quick glance at Latin American filmic production since the turn of the twenty-first century clearly evidences a resurgence of horror films that indicates both a departure from the socially committed filmic agendas that had characterised cinema since the advent of the New Latin American Cinema movement, and a desire to embrace more commercial filmic genres as valid vehicles to explore notions of national, sexual and cultural identity. By the same token, academics have also realised the importance of the horror genre to exploring issues related to identity formation and to conveying or challenging the status quo of culture in a specific milieu. However, very little has been theorised about Latin American horror cinema in terms of gender relations or sexual identity, or how horror narratives may reinforce or contest the socio-sexual paradigms that govern bodies in Latin America. Thus this book explores the different mechanisms and strategies through which horror films attempt to reinforce or contest gender relations and issues of sexual identity in the continent.

The book opens with 'Challenging Patriarchy in the Gothic Horror Mexican Cinema'. This chapter explores the role that the counter-heroine female gothic has played in terms of sexuality and gender relations in a number of gothic horror movies from the 1930s up to the late 1960s in Mexico. Although traditional in the way they address issues of gender politics and female sexuality in the country, and by extension in many parts of the continent, these movies also show an interesting shift in attitude towards the depiction of women, as well as some queer female subjects, in terms of their gendered relations and expressions of sexuality. The gothic villainess in films such as *La Llorona* (Ramón Peón, 1933) and the later version by Cardona (1960), *La Bruja* (Chano Urueta 1954) and *El Espejo de la Bruja* (Urueta, 1962), among other influential gothic films, is projected as a metaphor for the sexual anxieties of an imagined audience who see in this figure the externalisation and contestation of issues of femininity and marianismo as they circulate in the popular imaginary. By paying special attention to the gothic villainess and the female monster, Chap. 1 aims to establish whether the Mexican female gothic continues the tradition of other classic female gothic narratives found elsewhere, or whether it departs from this figure and provides new readings of femininity and femaleness in the Mexican context.

The following chapter, 'Zé do Caixão and the Queering of Monstrosity in Brazil', focuses on Zé do Caixão (Coffin Joe in the anglicised translation), who is arguably the most notorious and horrific, monstrous and anti-normative fictional character to emerge from the Brazilian horror film canon.[3] The character, the creation of Brazilian director José Mojica Marins, inhabits an interstitial space between overt machismo and clear queerness. He moves and operates between both territories without calling into question his own masculinity, or rather, without anyone daring to call into question his masculinity for fear of perishing at his hands. The character evidences the constructedness of masculinity in Latin America and, more specifically, the performativity of machismo, whereby this

[3] It is worth noticing that the 'traditional' Brazilian film canon that has gained notoriety among film scholars since the 1960s seems primarily concerned with the notions predicated by both *cinema novo* and Glober Rocha's *aesthetics of poverty*. Thus Brazilian horror cinema (as has happened with horror cinema elsewhere) has been overlooked by Latin American film criticism, which has often tended to celebrate a politicised type of cinema over other cinemas (see Tierney 2009; Bueno 2012).

template of male behaviour and sexuality is rendered a learnt behaviour—that is, a practice—more than an innate quality of all men in the continent. Chapter 2 focuses on Mojica Marins's films *A Meia-Noite Levarei Sua Alma* (1964), *O Ritual dos Sádicos* (1970), *Esta Noite Encarnarei no Teu Cadaver* (1976) and *Encarnação do Demônio* (2008), in which the character is the direct protagonist of the narrative or plays a major role within the film's diegesis (rather than other films in the director's filmography in which the character made cameo appearances or was simply inferred or referenced within the narrative). The chapter analyses the character's queer masculinity and how he undoes the fixity of male identity and machismo for the Latin American male subject, while purporting a sexual fluidity that evidences his socio-sexual otherness. This otherness is characterised by a camp aesthetics and sensibility that also disavow the seemingly inseparable relationship between camp and homosexuality. As a result, the chapter proposes a comparison between queer machismo and queer masculinity, as well as studying notions of carnival and the grotesque in the construction of a queer male monster.

Chapter 3, 'Monstrous Machos: Horror and the Crisis of Latin American Masculinity', is concerned with the different ways in which the figure of the monster, and the notion of the monstrous, operate as a metaphor of a crisis of masculinity as experienced in many regions throughout the continent. It argues that machismo can no longer separate itself from the notion of same-sex desire—either homosocial or homosexual—and that instead, this crisis of masculinity can only be overcome, in its monstrosity, by the assumption and/or externalisation of that desire. In Jorge Michel Grau's *Somos lo que Hay* (2010), the crisis of masculinity is played out through the crisis emerging from the absence of a paterfamilias figure in the household, and the struggle between two brothers to decide who should rightfully occupy this position. The film disavows the hetero-masculine symbolic order by suggesting that the main protagonist's assumption of his queer sexuality and his eventual 'coming out' are the mechanisms whereby he can become authentically macho. Similarly, Jaime Osorio Marquez's *El Páramo* (2010) shows the dissolution of machismo prompted by the impossibility of homosexual desires as a result of external, and feminised, forces. The film supports the notion that the military constitutes an outlet of institutionalised homophobia, while asserting homo-sociality, and explores how such paradigms are easily disavowed through the interruption of the macho symbolic order.

Chapter 4, 'Bloody Femininities: The Horrors of Marianismo and Maternity in Recent Latin American Cinema', departs from the idea that mothering has long constituted a topos of horror cinema, whereby the fecund female subject is directly associated with monstrosity through her ability to carry a life within and through the bodily changes that occur during pregnancy. In many a horror narrative, the pregnant woman operates as the locus of pre-Oedipal anxieties—usually manifested in unresolved conflicts between the monster and his desire or repulsion for the mother and his inability to kill her—as well as the embodiment of evilness caused by the 'trauma' of being pregnant and the biological and hormonal changes that a woman's pregnant body suffers. This chapter analyses the ways in which mothering and the maternal are problematised as part of an ongoing rhetoric of female subjectivity in the Southern Cone. To this end, the analysis focuses on Pablo Illanes's *Baby Shower* (2011) and Adrián García Bogliano's *Habitaciones para Turistas* (2004) and the way in which these two film directors posit their maternal protagonists as subjects whose pregnancies are a source of and a justification for evil. The chapter argues that the anxieties of machista ideology are projected onto the maternal body because it provides a negative reading of fertility that sees the site of reproduction as the site of counter-sexuality: the site of sin. The female protagonists in these films defy mariana codes of female sexuality by engaging in sex outside wedlock or by rejecting the support of their male partners during pregnancy. Their pregnant bodies become token sites of their ownership of desire and, by so doing, render the mariana figure morally corrupt. This chapter argues that, behind the gory deaths encountered by the female protagonists in these films, there is a more latent issue shaped by a misogynist understanding of female subjectivity in which women are punished for their attempt to break free from patriarchal domination.

The book closes with 'Bromance, Homosociality and the Crisis of Masculinity in the Latin American Zombie Movie', focusing on the zombie narrative as a metaphor to reflect on and externalise social anxieties in relation to the loss of masculine individuality—a trope that has figured prominently in popular fiction since the terrorist attack on the United States known as 9/11—and that constitutes the ultimate Other monster figure. The rom-zom-com (romantic zombie comedy) emerges as a highly hybrid genre that combines the absurd and ridiculous with the horrific. However, the films analysed in Chap. 5 depart from traditional rom-zom-com narratives because they do not centre on heterosexual couples whose love affairs are disrupted by the appearance of zombies threatening to separate them or becoming an obstacle to fulfilling their happiness. In these films, men tend to play a more pivotal role and women are usually relegated to secondary roles or are fetishised as the object of the male gaze audience. In Pablo Parés and Hernán Sáez's trilogy *Plaga Zombie* (1997, 2001, 2011), the main preoccupation of the films is not so much how to survive the zombie plague that has stricken a fictional town in Argentina, but the survival of the friendship between the three male main characters without falling within the orbit of same-sex desire. Similarly, in Alejandro Brugués's *Juan de los Muertos*, although the two main characters must fight the zombie plague that has recently attacked La Havana, the film seems to be more concerned with a friendship that has an overtly homosocial nature and explores clear moments of homoeroticism. In all these films, the affective relationship between the main male characters is shielded under the guise of a very strong friendship. These friendships are put to the test once one of the characters has potentially contracted the zombie 'virus' and risks becoming a zombie himself. At this point, the potential break in the male-to-male heterosexual friendship has the force to destabilise the pillars that sustain machismo as a rigid sexual template, thus forcing the characters to lose their innate masculinity and enter the terrain of the homoerotic by and through overt displays of male affection. The chapter explores how the zombie constitutes a queer monster with the potential to destroy the basis of hetero-machismo, while contagion seems directly associated with the loss of macho identity. This, in turn, offers evidence that the sense of masculinity of the male protagonists in these films is continuously in peril and that becoming a zombie equates to the reaffirmation of the constructedness of masculinity.

In short, *Gender and Sexuality in Latin American Horror Cinema: Embodiments of Evil* seeks to respond to a series of theoretical enquiries about the different trajectories that sexual subjects and gendered bodies have undergone in the history of horror narratives in Latin American cinema from the 1930s to the present. It also studies how the figure of the monster and the notion of monstrosity are associated with the paradigms that govern socio-sexual subjects in the Latin American context. In so doing, it traces the evolution of the monster as a socio-sexual subject in the context of Latin American horror cinema. More importantly, one of the book's primary intentions is to posit horror cinema as a valid instrument to challenge and/or comment on issues of gender and sexual identity in the region. It aims to devote serious academic analysis to a form of commercial cinema that Latin American film purists have frowned on and not considered worth the poignant criticism of social and economic conditions that was characteristic of the militant New Latin American Cinema movement. Ultimately, this project studies how effective horror narratives can be utilised to contest the socio-sexual paradigms that circulate in Latin American popular culture and are culturally regarded as fixed templates of gender and sexuality.

Contents

1 Challenging Patriarchy in the Gothic Horror
  Mexican Cinema   1

2 Zé do Caixão and the Queering of Monstrosity
  in Brazil   39

3 Monstrous Machos: Horror and the Crisis of
  Latin American Masculinity   73

4 Bloody Femininities: The Horrors of Marianismo and
  Maternity in Recent Latin American Cinema   111

5 Bromance, Homosociality and the Crisis of Masculinity
  in the Latin American Zombie Movie   147

Filmography   179

Bibliography   183

Index   197

List of Figures

Fig. 3.1	Monstrous siblings: Alfredo (Francisco Barreiro), Julián (Alan Chávez) and Sabina (Paulina Gaitan).	81
Fig. 3.2	Machismo emasculated: Sabina (Paulina Gaitan) scolds Julián (Alan Chavez) after the failed kidnap.	83
Fig. 3.3	Confronted masculinities: Alfredo (Francisco Barreiro) and Julián (Alan Chavez) discussing their failures as paterfamilia.	87
Fig. 3.4	Fighting off machismo: Alfredo (Francisco Barreiro) cries at the metro station after realising he may be gay.	95
Fig. 4.1	The protagonists arrive at their final destination: Silvia (Mariela Mujica), Lidia (Victoria Witemburg), Elena (Jimena Kruoco), Ruth (Brenda Vera) and Theda (Elena Siritto).	134
Fig. 4.2	Girls as object of the murderous gaze: Silvia (Mariela Mujica) discovers a camera watching over Ruth (Brenda Vera) in the brothers' room.	136
Fig. 4.3	Escaping machismo: Theda (Elena Siritto) helps a wounded Silvia (Mariela Mujica) find a safe hideout.	142
Fig. 4.4	Victims of machismo: Lidia (Victoria Witemburg) and Theda (Elena Siritto) run into one of the crazy church-goers while escaping from the killers.	144
Fig. 5.1	Bromanctic interactions: Juan (Alexis Díaz de Villegas) and Lázaro (Jorge Molina) walk among the zombie devastation.	166

Fig. 5.2 A bromosocial moment interrupted by zombies: Lázaro (Jorge Molina) harpoons a zombie about to attack Juan (Alexis Díaz de Villegas). 169

Fig. 5.3 Versions of Caribbean masculinities: Juan (Alexis Díaz de Villegas), Lázaro (Jorge Molina), Vladi (Andros Perugorría), La China (Jazz Vilá) and El Primo (Eliecer Ramírez) are stopped by the police. 171

CHAPTER 1

Challenging Patriarchy in the Gothic Horror Mexican Cinema

Gothic cinema, in much the same way as many other gothic narratives, provided from its inception a cinematic form that was intended to portray subversive and destabilising subjects in a given society. Such subversive stories, usually embodied in the figure of the monster, presented a deviant Other whose behaviour and actions were regarded as the epitome of moral and social ills and corruption in society. The figure of the monster in gothic cinema, as well as in the entire horror genre, has the ultimate function of confronting the notion of normality (embodied by the patriarchal and heteronormative system), the figure of the Other (the monster) and the relationship between the two. As Noel Carroll argues, the monster 'as a figure of repressed psychic material' (1990: 174) has to be understood beyond the paradigm of the return of the repressed. The monster, therefore, operates as an entity that re-enacts the suppression of moral codes while at the same time lifting moral repression on the part of the viewer. In this light, monstrosity can be seen as a process of transformation whereby a human being, in most cases a protagonist of the gothic horror narrative, accepts the dyadic relationship between the good and evil that coexist within the self. This being comes to incarnate a monstrous host, a type of anti-subject that exists within, and projects this onto the audience of such narratives. As Harry M. Benshoff asserts, 'monsters can often be understood as racial, ethnic, and/or political/ideological Others, while more frequently they are constructed primarily as sexual Others (women, bisexuals, and homosexuals)' (1997: 4). More importantly, these

© The Editor(s) (if applicable) and The Author(s) 2016
G. Subero, *Gender and Sexuality in Latin American Horror Cinema*, DOI 10.1057/978-1-137-56495-5_1

monsters usually embody and reflect the existing anxieties in a specific society in relation to social, political and/or religious affairs, while they are also strongly linked to the politics of gender and sexuality that prevails at a specific historical moment. Arguably, gothic monsters, unlike other more traditional monsters, tend to be constructed as monstrous by their murderous actions rather than by their physical appearance. The gothic monsters' appeal resides in their physical attractiveness and the fact that they may use their appearance as an intrinsic element in the process of seduction of their victims. As a result, the inclusion of the monster figure within these narratives evidences a tension between libidinous desire and (a)morality whereby the monster becomes a synonym for a type of deviant, and yet alluring, sexuality.

In Mexico, gothic narratives have been present almost from the very inception of the cinematic industry. For instance, before what could be regarded as the 'Mexican Golden Age of Horror' (broadly between the late 1940s and the late 1960s, and to which most of the films analysed in this chapter belong), Ramón Peón had already made, by 1933, one of the earliest film versions of *La Llorona*, while within a few months Juan Bustillo Oro's *Dos monjes* (1934) was also released in the country. The same year would also see the release of Fernando de Fuentes's *El Fantasma del Convento* (1934) and, in 1935, another Bustillo Oro feature called *El Misterio del Rostro Pálido*. As already suggested, although some of these films date as far back as the early 1930s, it is undeniable that the most prolific decades in the production of gothic horror films in Mexico were the 1950s and 1960s. By this point, a proper horror industry had really emerged in the country and production companies such as Tele Talia Films, Producciones Bueno, Producciones Delta and Diana Films all dedicated a great part of their production to making horror movies.

Many of these films either borrowed or extrapolated well-known gothic stories/storylines and (re)adapted them to the Mexican context. This process of (re)adaptation is what will be known as the 'tropicalisation' of the gothic narrative and will give birth to the 'tropical gothic'. This process of tropicalisation refers to a mechanism whereby the appropriation and recycling of narrative elements (or in the case of the cinema, elements of mise-en-scène) are undertaken with the express intention of making visible a sense of Latin Americanness (or in this case a strong sense of Mexicanness) within gothic narratives in ways that clearly demarcate a difference between these national productions and similar narratives found and produced elsewhere. Thus the Mexican tropical gothic[1] takes as its point of departure the centrality of the vampire figure (and narrative) and his constant transformations and transgressions. This is achieved by means of a slight modification in the presence of a Count Dracula who migrates to Mexico and becomes 'Mexicanised' despite still looking highly European, or through a radical transformation of the vampire figure, including his powers and the way he materialises himself. Most of these productions are characterised by making the Otherness of the monster character a pivotal element of the narrative. However, despite the Otherness of the characters, the narrative stresses cultural and folk elements that attest to the national specificity of the text. In the words of Gabriel Eljaiek, these narratives are characterised by

> temas, personajes y aproximaciones narrativas y visuales [...] acto de reciclar como 'tropicalización' por el interés explícito de los directores de exotizar sus filmes, de posicionarse críticamente frente a lo extraño pero también frente a lo autóctono, dando como resultado un equilibrio entre el homenaje al precursor, la crítica del género y la crítica a lo propio. (2012: 164)
>
> [themes, characters and narrative and visual approximations [...] it is the act of recycling as 'tropicalisation' for the explicit interest of directors in exoticising their own films, and to critically position themselves against that which is strange and also that which is autochthonous, so as to offer an equilibrium between a heraldic homage, a criticism of the genre and a criticism of authorship]

In the context of Mexican gothic cinema, there is a clear divide between the Other—who clearly tries to challenge and destabilise the status quo of the patriarchal order—and the native Mexican, whose ancestral and indigenous background will in most cases help him or her to emerge victorious from the evil monster's grasp.

Traditional gothic narratives (especially those found in literature in the works of writers like Justo Sierra, Vicente Riva Palacio, José Joaquín Pesado and more recently Carlos Fuentes) tend to focus on the failed

---

[1] The notion of the tropical gothic does not operate as a homogenous construct across the continent. Tropical gothic narratives elsewhere in Latin America clearly adapt in different ways to the geographical settings in which the actions develop. As Gabriel Eljaiek sugguests, 'este mecanismo implica una apropiación política de los temas así como una transformación y una transposición' (2012: 164) [this mechanism implicates a political appropriation of themes, as well as a transformation and transposition of such themes].

attempt of the monster-Other to destabilise the correct functioning of society by corrupting the values and decent morals of the protagonists. Gender roles tend to be quite prescriptive in terms of the way in which masculinity, femininity or queerness is played out by the different characters in such narratives. Thus this chapter has a threefold function. First, it will offer a brief account of a selected body of gothic films made from the 1930s to the 1960s to highlight those themes and tropes that made these Mexican films different from other gothic narratives elsewhere and demonstrate the tropicalisation of the gothic narratives. Secondly, it will look at the way in which the gothic villain not only comes to represent the battle against an Other that threatens to destabilise society, but also narrates stories of Mexican identity that put in evidence the struggle between Mexico's aboriginal ancestry and its post-colonial past. Finally, this chapter will undertake a study of the role of the antiheroine female figure within gothic narratives and will demonstrate that such characters and the sociocultural roles embedded in their actions challenge, to a greater extent, traditional gothic narratives in which female protagonists adhere to mariana identity. This is achieved by offering female characters who present a different gender-based sexual and social behaviour; one that may not necessarily correspond to that perpetuated by traditional gothic films. The Mexican gothic filmography under analysis, as could be argued about gothic narratives from other countries in Latin America, is not merely constituted by remakes or copies of the original narratives that were created in Europe or Hollywood. Instead, it constitutes a body of films characterised by the recycling, revaluation and recontextualisation—in short, the tropicalisation as previously explained—of traditional themes, characters and tropes.

This chapter will deal with those films in which the storyline can be clearly regarded as a 'purer' gothic narrative, without the use or amalgamation of other genres or tropes that would create more hybrid films. Thus it will avoid exploitation cinema and, more specifically, Mexploitation films as part of the analysis.[2] Instead, the films considered are those that enjoyed a prominent position within the country's film industry and were not regarded as products of subcultural or marginal forms of filmic

---

[2] Eric Schaefer understands exploitation movies as characterised by 'low budgets, lurid subject matter, affiliation with the most debased genres, and a subsistence at the margin of industry and culture' (: xi). Thus in this chapter those movies that amalgamate a number of genres, be it horror and science fiction, horror and wrestling cinema, horror and sexploitation, to name a few, will not be addressed.

culture. Historically, Mexican horror cinema flourished under the auspices of directors such as Chano Urueta, Juan Bustillo Oro and Fernando Mendez, among others, whose combined work made it possible that by the mid-1950s the horror genre in Mexico had become more popular than melodramas and the *Cine ranchero*.[3] Several film studios also turned to horror cinema in order to quench the thirst for horror movies that had spread across the country. As previously suggested, many of these films took as their point of departure well-known gothic horror narratives such as Dracula, Frankestein, and Dr. Jekyll and Mr. Hyde, among others, but with a Mexican twist or flavour incorporated into the story. From the simple translocation of the story to Mexican lands to the incorporation of certain aspects of Mexican folklore and tradition, these films became embedded in the national imaginary as tales of horror and terror that reflected contemporary Mexico.

By narrowing the parameters of the body of analysis, it is expected that it will be easier to understand how female sexuality and female gender relations are depicted and manifested in a number of gothic horror movies up to the late 1960s. Although rather traditional in the way they address issues of female gender politics and sexuality in the country and, by extension, in many parts of the continent, these movies also show an radical shift in attitude towards women, as well as some female queer subjects, in terms of their gendered relations and expressions of their sexuality. Thus in many such films the role of women and other subaltern individuals is both revisited and contested. Horror cinema becomes an ideal medium to channel existing and imagined anxieties about the way women conduct their relationships and they way they experience, embody or use their femininity.

As previously suggested, the monster figure in many films operates as a metaphor for the sexual anxieties of an imagined audience, who see the monster as the anti-normative embodiment of issues of gender and sexuality as they circulate in the popular imaginary. As Barbara Creed has famously argued,

> the identity of the monster, male and female, is inseparable from questions of sex, gender, power and politics. In order to better understand the dark side of our culture and the reasons why the symbolic order creates monsters, consciously or otherwise, we need to ask questions about the monster's origin, nature and function. (1993a: viii)

---

[3] The Mexican equivalent of the Western.

The horror monster or the villain, especially when compared and contrasted with the hero or heroine of horror fiction, allows audiences to explore society's darkest taboos and fears and to channel people's repressed fantasies. It could be argued that the horror narrative provides the perfect medium to break free from the constraints of society and tackle those issues that are not addressed by other popular texts for fear of alienating or shocking audiences. Thus the main purpose of this chapter will be to offer an analysis of the anti-normative female gothic—the villainess and the female monster—and to establish whether the Mexican female gothic figure continues the tradition of other classical female gothics elsewhere, or whether it departs from this tradition and provides new readings on issues of Mexican femininity and femaleness.

MALINCHISM, MARIANISM AND THE FEMALE GOTHIC

In the Mexican social imaginary the two images of femaleness (and female identity) that circulate widely among the population and shape the way women are constructed both socially and culturally are those of La Malinche and the Virgen de Guadalupe (a regional incarnation of the Virgin Mary). It could be argued that both figures operate as the opposite poles of a national, female, gendered consciousness. However, the Lady of Guadalupe, as she is known by most Mexicans, has been recognised by some theorists and writers, such as Octavio Paz, as a symbol of passivity that operates as an illustration of the feminine condition. Following on the predicates of the Virgin, mariana identity rests on the foundation that women must embody attributes such as 'virginity, piety, helpfulness, forgiveness, goodness, and devoted and selfless motherhood' (Lozano-Díaz 2002: 90). Marianismo should not be regarded as the antithesis of machismo, but instead as an intrinsic element of a female gendered identity that, in the words of Evelyn Stevens, focuses on 'the cult of the feminine spiritual superiority, which teaches that women are semidivine, morally superior to and spiritually stronger than men' (1973: 90).

Nonetheless, out of these two images of femaleness, La Malinche is the more controversial figure, because she has operated in the popular imaginary as a traitor to the Mexican nation due to her role as both the lover of conquistador Hernán Cortés and her alleged involvement in the eventual conquest of Technotitlan. La Malinche's role in history is twofold: on the one hand, her decision to betray her own people can be seen as the product of resentment at being or becoming a slave (she sees in the conquistadors the possibility of freedom and some form of social climbing); on the other, her actions are justified in the context of 'unrequited' love towards her conquistador lover. Ignacio Ramirez (2000) also asserts that La Malinche is guilty of a double treason in the eyes of both her own people and also herself, because she does not respect the role that a patriarchal society had assigned to women. By the nineteenth century and during the process of national consolidation, the body of La Malinche became a political body, a body of pleasure and a body of reproductive capacity. The image of La Malinche was to become a libidinal entity that constitutes a space of contention, because she was regarded as both the mother of all Mexicans and the whore who sold her own people in order to give herself to her Spanish lover. As Jitka Crhová and Alfredo Escandón explain, La Malinche 'eerily evoke[s] her own life: a woman not fully belonging to a specific group, the otherness kept setting her apart […] Cortés and Malinche are symbols of an unresolved secret conflict' (2011: 1–2). This unresolved conflict is carried forward in the national formation of gendered identity in which mestizaje is regarded as the direct product of the illicit relationship between the aboriginal woman and the Mexican conqueror (the former being regarded as the victim of the latter). In the popular imaginary this conflict is reflected by a desire both to recover (and embrace) the values and traditions of Mexico's aboriginal past and, at the same time, to assume the values and traditions of the foreign Other (Spanish or American) as an ideal form of identity.

La Llorona

The aforementioned conflict is best exemplified in the film versions of *La Llorona*, in which the retelling of the well-known Latin American legend has clear resonances with La Malinche's story. The first film of this legend was directed by Ramón Peón in 1933 and, although the film lacks the rhythm and pace of other contemporary horror films, it shows a preoccupation with Mexico's historical past within the actual horror narrative. It intertwines three different stories that span the whole of the post-conquest history of Mexico. The first two are played by the same main actors and are set in the 1930s and the time of the Inquisition, respectively. While in the first story Ana Maria de Acuna (Virginia Zurí) is portrayed as the perfect and abnegated wife of the well-renowned surgeon Dr. Ricardo de Acuna (Ramón Pereda), in the second she is presented as the gullible lover of an important commander of the viceroy of Mexico who falls blindly in love with a man who betrays her honour. On discovering her lover's betrayal, Doña Inés stabs her 4-year old son to death and then proceeds to take her own life, while her spirit curses the de Acuna family and pledges revenge on all future generations. This action will then, within the narrative, give birth to the legend that will drive the main story. The curse will continue to haunt the family up to the present time, when it seems imminent that on the 4th birthday of the couple's son, the curse will be fulfilled and the son will die in unforeseen circumstances. The flashback sequence to the first story and the subsequent flashback sequence to La Malinche's story will be presented as cautionary tales to warn Dr. de Acuna of the fatality that may besiege his family. As part of the retelling of the origin of the curse, towards the end of the film the narrative takes the audience back to the time of the conquest and narrates the story of La Malinche/Doña María (María Luisa Zea) and how she was betrayed by her conqueror lover Don Fernando de Moncada (Paco Martínez) due to her ethnic origin. Once again, the wounded mother takes her life and that of her son in an act of defiance towards the man who has made her abject as both a woman and a mother.

René Cardona's (1960) version of the film follows nearly the same storyline, but jettisons the Malinche storyline altogether. Nevertheless, the similarities between the legend of La Llorona and the story of La Malinche are striking. What is interesting about the two versions of *La Llorona*, and other films that may have taken a looser approach to this legend, is that monstrosity emerges as the direct result of a position of abjection in which those elements that constitute womanhood in the popular imaginary are reimagined as negative aspects of the character's psyche. The La Llorona/Malinche dichotomy reaffirms Creed's well-known theorisation that 'all human societies have a conception of the monstrous-feminine, of what it is about woman that is shocking, terrifying, horrific, abject' (1993a: 1). The different Lloronas all have in common a sense of hysteria that derives from their condition as women and, more importantly, as mothers. As Bacil Kirtley asserts, La Llorona 'is the principal figure of a floating legend, one which depicts her as the pathetic and almost blameless victim of a lover's betrayal and of her own subsequent insane grief' (1960: 155). However, unlike what is recounted by the popular legend, in which her spirit wanders aimlessly in search of men on whom to exercise her revenge, in the two film versions she targets directly the descendants of the man who originally betrayed her. In both films La Llorona comes back from the dead to claim her revenge by killing the primogenital son in a direct line from her betrayer. At a symbolic level, this killing shows the tensions between Mexico's desire to distance itself from its aboriginal past and, at the same time, a desire to recuperate it. La Llorona, in much the same way as La Malinche,

> se convertirá en un símbolo para todo el pueblo indio, seducido primero y abandonado después. El término malinchismo, acuñado como descriptivo del tipo de comportamiento que recuerda al de la Malinche, define una entrega, demasiado incondicional a veces, a lo que viene de fuera, y la incapacidad que esta actitud conlleva para valorar las raíces y lo propio de cada uno. Desde esta perspectiva, se ha considerado la Malinche como una traidora de su pueblo, una aspirante a ser algo que nunca conseguiría en plenitud, una española no-española, que dejó de ser indígena, sin dejar de serlo nunca. (Melchor Iñiguez 2007: 161)
> [will become a symbol for the whole of the indigenous population; seduced at first and abandoned later. The term 'malinchismo' was coined as a descriptor of those behaviours that are reminiscent of La Malinche and defines a dedication, at times too unconditional, to that which is foreign, as well as the inability to value individual and national roots. From this perspective La Malinche is considered a traitor to her own people, a candidate for something never fully achieved, a non-Spanish Spanish woman, one who stopped being aboriginal without abandoning her aboriginal roots]

However, there is an essential difference between the film versions: in the 1933 version the life of Juanito (Manuel Dondé)—Dr. Ricardo and Ana Maria's son—seems to be threatened not by La Llorona herself (either a reincarnation or her actual ghost), but by a group of indigenous people in cloaks reminiscent of dark priests, who lurk around the house through secret passages in order to avenge the woman's spirit. Strangely, the only direct reference to La Llorona at this point in the narrative is the female howling and wailing that are heard throughout the mansion. This vagueness about addressing the alleged main subject of the narrative is also evidenced through the camera work, in which long and medium long shots abound without paying particular attention to detail (through close-ups or medium close-ups). For instance, the first attempt at kidnapping the boy fails when the kidnapper is intercepted, shown in static low-angle long shots, while taking the boy down a secret passage. Ricardo is quick to stop the kidnapper and overpower him. When the police arrive at the mansion to investigate what is happening and arrest the kidnapper, they find a small book on the floor. Here the film adds a new narrative layer that seems to do very little for the development of the actual story beyond establishing a direct link between La Llorona and La Malinche as two prototypes of femininity within Mexican culture.

This is perhaps the most hybrid of all the films, as it tries to bind together the folk legend with the historical episode of La Malinche. The film seems more preoccupied with providing visual cues to the relationship between La Llorona and the country's pre-Hispanic past through the use of overt references to the goddesses Coatlicue[4] and Yolotlicue,[5] which can be seen in the ring worn by the kidnapper that was previously seen on the hand of La Malinche and Doña Inés, respectively, in one of the few instances where close-ups and extreme close-ups are utilised. The narration of La Malinche's story cuts back to the present time when another kidnapper succeeds in taking Juanito through the secret passage to a place that evokes a pre-Hispanic sacrificial stone. However, just before the kidnapper stabs the boy dead, the police turn up and shoot him. It is only at this point, as the kidnapper's corpse lies on the floor, that the spirit of La Llorona emerges from the body (seen through a rather rudimentary long shot montage), wails once again and then flies away. Nevertheless, despite the two versions of the La Llorona legend offered through its narrative, which serve to reaffirm the national roots of the story, the film does very little to disavow the notion of evil and abject motherhood in the narrative.

This film version prefers to avoid any references to a monstrous feminine (following Creed) and supports the rather antiquated view that Gerard Lenne proposes in relation to women in horror films when he asserts that 'is it not reasonable that woman, who, in life, is both mother and lover, should be represented by characters that convey the feeling of sheltering peace?' (1979: 35). However, historically, this representation of La Llorona as purely a victim resonates with the resurgence of nationalism that Mexico was experiencing during the first decades of the twentieth century.[6] Unsurprisingly, the only type of motherhood that is represented by the end of the narrative is that of the stereotypical female gothic, whose

---

[4] The primordial earth goddess, mother of the gods, the sun, the moon and the stars.
[5] The 'heart-her-skirt' goddess.
[6] The political and social role that women played during the Mexican Revolution must be noted and, more importantly, the importance of the figure of the *soldadera* (female soldier) within the national socio-sexual imaginary after the return to democracy. La Llorona as victim in this film, therefore, vindicates the role of indigenous and mestizo women in Mexico. This vindication as national identity can be seen in the works of Mexican muralists, as well as that of Frida Kahlo, which aimed at exalting the indigenous and pre-colonial past.

abnegation and love for her family come before her own interests. The absence of La Llorona, or any manifestation of this female spirit, in the present-day narrative of the film evidences a desire to sterilise the role of the aboriginal woman (represented by the La Llorona/Malinche dyad), whereby

> la Llorona es presentada como mujer inde desvela el gran trauma del subconciente mexicano. Iverse un alma en pena que llora la irremediable tragedia. aqui cal gothic ígena, los hijos son mestizos, son símbolo de la nueva nación. Matar a esos hijos implica la reacción interior que rechaza la mezcla de sangres y la negación violenta del mestizaje. Sin embargo ya no hay marcha atrás. Negar el mestizaje es negar la propia identidad, es como volverse un alma en pena que llora la irremediable tragedia. Aquí se desvela el gran trauma del subconsciente mexicano. (Rodríguez Tapia and Verduzco Argüelles 2008: 313)
> [la Llorona is shown as an indigenous woman, her children are mestizos, they are the symbol of a new nation. Killing those children implies an internal reaction that rejects the mixing of blood and the violent negation of the mestizaje process. Nonetheless, there is no turning back. To negate mestizaje is to negate one's own identity, it is like becoming a penitent soul that cries over an irreparable tragedy. It is here that one witnesses the major trauma of the Mexican subconscious]

Conversely, in René Cardona's 1960 version of the film, the character of Luisa del Carmen/La Llorona/Carmen Asiul (María Elena Marques) follows a transparently evil path that takes her from being a woman who endures rejection and humiliation at the hands of her lover, to one who seeks revenge against that man (and all his progeny). The narrative makes it clearer here how Luisa del Carmen becomes La Llorona after killing her own son as an act of grief on discovering that Don Nuño de Montes Claros (Eduardo Fajardo) had betrayed her love after fathering a child with her under false pretences of marriage. Once the narrative moves to the present time, La Llorona, now in the disguise of Carmen Asiul (a private nanny), turns up at the mansion of Don Nuño's direct descendants. She is hired to look after Jorgito (Marina Banquells), the only son of Margarita Montes (Luz María Aguilar) and Felipe Arnaiz (Mauricio Garcés) on whom falls the family's curse. This curse pushed Don Gerardo Montes (Carlos Lopez Moctezuma) to try to impede the marriage of his own daughter, Margarita, with Felipe, in order to avoid the woman enduring the family curse herself. The contrast between La Llorona/Carmen and Margarita makes a distinct form of femininity that reaffirms the Mexicanness of the film, since it comes to represent a marked contrast between the devotion to La Virgen de Guadalupe (the mother of all Mexicans and direct emblem of the notion of Marianismo) and the love–hate relationship with La Malinche (the cultural and historical whore).

Interestingly, the film evidences a tension with the notion of motherhood in which Carmen is unable to kill Jorgito with her bare hands and, instead, must set up the type of situation that would make the boy meet his own death. Carmen is clearly an archaic mother, following Creed, because 'the desires and fears invoked by her image [...] as a force that threatens to reincorporate what it once gave birth to, are always there in the horror text—all pervasive, all encompassing—because of the constant presence of death' (1993a, 28). Carmen's presence permeates all aspects of the construction of the feminine condition for both the heroine and, obviously, herself. It is this omnipresent condition that is used to control the heroine's identity, and this is best exemplified when Margarita's father tells her that 'te haré fuerte para que resistas o te haré débil para que obedezcas' [I'll make you a strong woman so you can put up a fight or I'll make you a weak one so you can obey]. Carmen's subversive identity operates as an allegory of the constant threat to marianismo within the socio-sexual imaginary of the Mexican nation—as its potential death.

What is interesting about La Llorona as a female monster is that, despite her evil plans and her failed attempts at killing the children of her lover's descendants, she is not constructed as a pre-Oedipal mother whose power of address originates from her lack in the order of the symbolic. It is proposed here that, although her revenge is exerted on the future generations of her original conquistador ex-lover, it is the other mothers who become the real victims of her revenge. In this and other similar films, the female monster is not signified in relation to the phallus (the figure of the father), but in relation to her desire to dispossess other women of their maternal identity. Thus La Llorona defines herself not by what she is, but by what she tries to rid other women of. This figure conflates the contradictions of modern Mexican femininity, because she is regarded as a martyr of both womanhood (her phantasmagoric penitence over the centuries to lament the loss of her children) and, at the same time, of evil as a result of her desire to kill children. In consequence, La Llorona is the perfect encapsulation of malinchismo, since despite her 'misguided' sense of maternity, her figure comes to represent 'the preference or tendency to favor what comes from abroad over what is from the country (it may include people, products, customs, values, traditions) with disdain for the domestic' (Crhová and Escandón 2011: 3). It is clearly implied, therefore, that her filicidal instincts were the product of her dealings with the foreign and treacherous conquistador who manipulated her and drove her to despair. Maternity continues to be linked to the notion of nation formation in ways that allow her to be seen, despite her evilness, as a somewhat justifiable victim. As a result, her image will be incorporated into the canon of female 'deities' who are regarded as paramount in the configuration of an imagined socio-cultural femininity within the national imaginary.

This relationship between La Llorona/Malinche and the ideas of nation formation are best shown in the sequence when Luisa del Carmen discovers that Nuño has betrayed her and is about to marry a different woman. There is a clear sense of historical revenge in her words when she tells them both that 'Os juro que mi venganza será más cruel que vuestra traición. Y que se prolongará hasta más allá de vuestros hijos y de los hijos de vuestros hijos' [I swear to you both that my revenge will be even more cruel than your betrayal. This will prolong itself beyond your children and your children's children]. As she runs away from the ball where she confronted both, the camera, in a long shot, shows how she is encircled on the street by a group of Indians who start dancing around her. The camera switches to a medium shot that shows her confused, as she tries to break free from the circle of dancing Indians. Then it moves to a close shot of some of the Indians, and finally back to her desperate face. Although she is dressed in European clothes, it is implied that her reconnection with her Indian ancestry is what drives her to go crazy and kill her children. The tensions between Mexico's post-colonial past and its indigenous legacy are expressed during the dream sequence in which Luisa remembers Nuño's deceitful words:

> *Luisa*: Lo sabías estúpido. La mitad de mi sangre es igual a la vuestra. [You knew it, stupid man. Half my blood is exactly the same as yours]
> *Nuño*: Es inútil, no pertenecéis a mi mundo, Luisa. [It's pointless, you don't belong to my world, Luisa]
> *Luisa*: Entonces, vuestros hijos son un accidente en vuestra aventura. [Then your children are an accident in this adventure of yours]

The drama of Mexican post-modern identity is clearly encapsulated in these words, as Luisa comes to represent the Mexican aboriginal nation claiming a space of vindication in the national imaginary. The message is clear: mestizaje should not be considered an accident and mestizo identity should be celebrated. However, within the narrative, it is the rejection of the aboriginal side of Mexico's (Luisa's) mestizaje that pushes her to be represented and constructed as a negative figure who associates motherhood with degeneration and a desire to reabsorb who (and what) she has given birth to. The end of the sequence clearly evidences this as the camera moves to an extreme close-up of Luisa's eyes looking angry and demented. The way the camera lingers on her mestizo facial features helps manifest an overt rejection of the character's aboriginality by linking her indigenous ancestry with her desire to procure evil.

It would be pertinent to suggest, then, that La Llorona is a type of malinchista archaic mother because she not only provides, as could be suggested by reappropriating Creed's words in her theorisation of the monstrous feminine, 'her total dedication to the generative, procreative principle. She is the mother who conceives all by herself, the original parent, the godhead of all fertility and the origin of procreation. She is outside morality and the law' (1993a: 27), she is also the connection to the female dyad that operates symbolically within the national gender imaginary. La Llorona/Carmen is an evil gothic figure who is not only depicted as purely evil, but also retains some aspects of the female gothic heroine of traditional gothic narratives such as Daphne du Maurier's *Rebecca* (1938). It is Carmen who is presented as 'purely' evil, but even then she remains confined to the order of the domestic. First, domesticity is structured around the job she carries out within the domestic space, since her plot to enact her revenge is to pass as a nanny for the family's child. Secondly, she is never fully driven by a demonic or evil instinct, since, more than trying to kill the boy herself, she simply procures situations in which the child would die 'accidentally'. It is clear that the female gothic imagination continues to regard women (whether evil or not) as 'coded expressions of women's fears of entrapment within the domestic and within the female body, most terrifyingly experienced in childbirth' (Smith and Wallace 2004: 1). Both Carmen and Margarita find themselves entrapped in the realm of the domestic: the former by disguising her killing desires through a pretended caring role, and the latter by experiencing motherhood as her own entrapment from a 'healthy' relationship (since the reason for hiring the nanny in the first place was the mounting tension between the couple because Margarita was obsessed with looking after her child and protecting him from La Llorona's curse).

The contrast between the two female leads could not be poignant within the narrative, which resorts to a number of tropes in order to emphasise the differences between the simply abject motherhood of the female gothic heroine and the phantasmatic abject motherhood of the monstrous feminine. La Llorona's motherhood is phantasmatic because it is not her capacity to bear children or her own pregnant state that transforms her into a monster; instead, it is the absence of a child and her longing to rob other women of their own children and, by doing so, to strip them of their own maternal identity that provides her with her source of evil. For instance, when Carmen first arrives at the Montes house, the camera work switches in a series of medium close-ups of her face on arrival, the 'invisible' black cat that jumps from a mantelpiece and Jorgito crying and asking for his mother. Carmen can be seen in a long shot dressed all in black and wearing a black veil over her head (as if in mourning), while Margarita runs to Jorgito's side, also shown in a long shot, wearing a white nightdress while putting on a see-through white morning gown. The fight between good and evil is colour coded for the benefit of the audience, while other elements of the mise-en-scène are also placed strategically to highlight the contrast between the different types of motherhood that the two characters embody. A medium shot of Carmen, once she has come into the house, shows her forming a perfect triangle with two replicas of white, ancient Greek–style statues. Her evilness is accentuated by her dress, her self-assured pose and her very made-up and angled eyebrows that confer on her an aura of malevolence. Carmen, and by direct association La Llorona as a female symbolic figure in the national imaginary, could be described in the words of Creed as she continues to theorise the monstrous feminine as 'reconstructed and re-presented as a negative figure, one associated with the dread of the generative mother seen only as the abyss, the all-incorporating black hole which threatens to reabsorb what it once birthed' (1993a: 27). Thus Carmen comes to symbolise the original mother, the Eve who is temptress and temptation—the mother of all mothers and at the same time the castrating mother, since her goal for centuries has been to deprive women of their own maternity by killing their offspring.

However, it is not only maternity that constructs her as monstrous. The film also builds on the notion of female beauty as a monstrous trope, one that will become recurrent in many gothic horror narratives and that could be seen to originate in fairy tales.[7] The contrast between older and younger women within the narrative carries with it a social commentary on issues of female identity. In the aforementioned scene, once Carmen is inside the house, she is drawn to her former lover's portrait. The camera cuts from a medium shot of her, to an over-the-shoulder, high-angled shot of her looking at the portrait. Then it switches to an extreme close-up of her eyes and back to the first medium shot to show now her transformation from beautiful mestiza to an old and ugly, or rather monstrous, figure. It is this transformation that signals her as a 'real' monster, since the narrative exclusion of older women implies to the audience that women can only uphold a valid place in society when they are young and sexually available. Once their reproductive phase is over, they are expected to fade out of society or risk being regarded as evil if they try to maintain an image that provides the illusion that they continue to be young and available. Thus when La Llorona shows her real self, she no longer possesses beauty as a quality intrinsic to that self, but becomes instead the prototypical old witch: wrinkled, with messy hair, and even her dress changes to a black ragged tunic.

This transformation within the film chimes with the ideas of Li-Vollmar and LaPointe, who claim in relation to female villain figures in Disney films that 'villainesses are typically drawn as caricature femme fatales. They are treacherous, sexually potent, and powerful personifications of the terrifying nature of unchecked femininity' (2003: 95). Arguably, Luisa del Carmen's transformation into a monster occurs the moment she rebels against patriarchy and thereby destabilises the prevailing gender system already operating in Mexican and, by extension, Latin American culture. She rebels against the grain of marianismo when she decides to take direct action against the abuse and betrayal of her lover. It could be argued that, rather obliquely, La Llorona takes ownership of her own desire when she uses her femininity as a tool to avenge the death of her children and that of her own love. However, her femininity, like that of many female monsters, is fluid and to a large extent reduced to an aesthetics of horror in which monstrosity and ageing (and by default ugliness) are mutually inclusive.

[7] This correlation between beauty and evil can be evidenced in novels such as du Maurier's *Rebecca* (1938), where the lead, and yet absent, character's extraordinary beauty is one of the pivotal themes of the novel and can only be compared to her abilities of compulsive lying and promiscuity. By the same token, the desire of evil characters to attain beauty as a commodity can be found in many fairy tales, such as the Evil Queen in the Brothers Grimm's *Snow White* (1854).

El Vampiro

The idea of female monsters who use their monstrous powers to preserve their beauty becomes a leitmotif in many gothic horror narratives, especially when contrasted with the 'natural' and 'well-deserved' beauty of the female heroine. For instance, in Fernando Méndez's *El Vampiro* (1957), the unchanged beauty of Eloisa (Carmen Montejo) is at the centre of the narrative, since her niece Marta (Ariadna Welter) picks on this from the moment the two meet again. Here resides one of the main differences in gender relations between the sexes in gothic horror films. Villains are usually more interested in large-scale plans (devastation or conquest of the human race or at least a large community) or gaining immortality, and—although they always manage to spare the time to pursue a beautiful damsel with whom to share eternity—they are more preoccupied with self-centred enterprises. Conversely, the female monstrous in these films tend to be depicted as vain, jealous and irrational monsters whose main consideration is to maintain their status quo as objects of the male gaze and, despite their villainous affairs, continue to be confined to the domestic sphere as nurturer and support for the male monster. The beginning of the film already brings to the forefront the notion of ageing and beauty as reflections and characteristics of female evilness and monstrous identity. Towards the end of the burial procession of one of the three siblings who own the 'Sierra Negra' hacienda, Anselmo (José Chávez) asks to see the corpse of his sister one last time. As the men who are carrying the coffin open it, the camera cuts from a long shot of the burial procession to a medium shot of his sister María Teresa (Alicia Montoya) dressed in black inside the coffin. She wears no make-up, although the area surrounding her eyes appears in marked black shadow. Her hair is long and unkempt and falls to her sides. She seems very old and already has a ghostly appearance. In contrast, her sister, who was at the back of the burial party but is seen walking in the opposite direction, looks very young and dresses as a sort of mourning bride with a low-necked, black, tight dress and black veil running from the back of her hair.

This notion of evil beauty is further articulated by Rebecca Sullivan in her analysis of Disney's villainesses when she argues that 'the older woman in a position of power [must be regarded] as evil or as other [...] older women have no place in society. This is what is implied and reaffirmed by their absence in all forms or positions of societally-recognized power' (2010: 5). It is clear that the power of address of such characters derives from their ill-attained beauty, and this is all the more evident by the end of the film when, after María Teresa has killed Count Lavud (Germán Robles), the scene instantaneously moves to a close medium shot of Eloisa from her bust up as she lies on the floor and ages instantly to death. Unsurprisingly, the camera lingers a few seconds on every phase of her transformation and eventual disintegration to highlight even further her rapid ageing, to the point that becoming bones and ashes, as she ultimately does, is the worst punishment a villainess can receive. And, although María Teresa is depicted as an old woman, her advanced age is not a punishment, but operates instead as a narrative device that reaffirms her mariana identity and allows her to be included in the story without having to polarise her into the other two categories of gothic femaleness: naïve and naturally beautiful heroine or evil and ill-attained beautiful villainess. Her presence in the narrative does not threaten normative gender roles because she is never regarded as a sexual object or a predator—as embodied by Ariadna and Eloisa, respectively—since she is stripped of any external signs of sexual allure by her flowing and unkempt hair and the loose black dress, as well as the Christ she carries with her at all times. Eloisa's beauty, on the other hand, is evil and must be exterminated. The portrayal of her sexual beauty as a monstrous characteristic emphasises that 'within patriarchal culture there is a long-standing tendency to restrict the multidimensionality of female identity [...] Polarizing morality by gender always results in oversimplifications about what women are really like' (Korolczuk 2004: 36). Such oversimplifications are essential in gothic narratives because they provide a clear-cut distinction between good and evil, socially acceptable and unacceptable or, simply put, heroine and villainess.

La Bruja

A more ambivalent reading of female beauty can be found in Chano Urueta's *La Bruja* (1954), in which the central character's beauty becomes a 'blessing and a curse' and operates as a signifier of the moral compass of its bearer. The film revolves around Doctor Boerner's (Julio Villarreal) plot for revenge on the three men who, he believes, have caused the death of his daughter. In order to exercise his revenge he enlists the help of a woman known as La Bruja (Lilia del Valle) due to her disfigured face, who lives in a Mexican underworld. Doctor Boerner creates a scientific formula that allows La Bruja to become extremely beautiful; however, he plans to use her beauty to seduce the three men responsible for his daughter's death and kill them. Although Condesa Nora (La Bruja's beautiful incarnation in disguise) does not physically kill anyone herself, she knows that she is being used as bait to seduce the men and eventually to kill them. In a way, the film becomes a warning to those women who depart from the roles socially assigned to them by mariana society as nurturers and carers, or abnegated mothers and daughters. La Bruja could be said to operate as a female grotesque whose presence serves to remind the audience that

> the female body as grotesque spectacle is a mark of excess: too much make-up, [physical deformity], outrageous clothes, loud laughter, and behaviour which flaunts the limits of physicality, sobriety and sexuality. By transgressing the norms of femininity, the female grotesque refuses the limits imposed on her body and embraces the ambivalent possibilities such transgressions offer. (Mallan 2000: 26)

La Bruja is obviously grotesque when she appears physically deformed but, arguably, she is even more grotesque in her beautiful impersonation because she embodies a lack that sees her as socially unfit. That is to say, by embodying such an extremely beautiful woman, she becomes the lack, she cannot be disassociated from what she is not. Although she is not monstrous or evil by direct action, her desire to attain physical beauty through easy and non-natural means makes her actions transgressive, and she breaks the moral codes that govern mariana identity in society. Her longing to become beautiful echoes the narratives of fairy tales, further stressed in modern society by film companies such as Disney, in which beauty becomes a currency within the notion of femininity. The more beautiful women are, the more powerful they become. However, an unnatural beauty—one that is attained through sorcery, diabolical pacts or other unnatural means—can only bring horror. Thus this kind of woman cannot escape her fate of becoming monstrous.

The La Bruja/Nora character clearly borrows narrative elements proper to the Dr. Jekyll and Mr. Hyde gothic novella, but it reverts them in ways that associate physical beauty with monstrosity. In this film the deformed character does not possess evil characteristics, but it is her transformation into a beautiful woman that procures evilness in her. What this film does is to disavow the seemingly intrinsic relation between ugliness and evilness characteristic of many gothic stories, as well as fairy-tale and folk narratives, in which witches are portrayed as deformed and ugly beings who inspire fear and horror through both their physicality and their actions.[8] La Bruja is the Other whose personal figuration does not become part of the project of the Mexican nation. In fact, within the film she is not an isolated case of otherness, she is part of a network of otherness that operates as an underground and subaltern society. The film sees the Others as both victims and aggressors. They are victims because they have obviously been rejected from the mainstream of society, and they all seem to share certain traits that make them different to the accepted ethnic and social types that enjoy a higher degree of citizenship in contemporary Mexico. From the fleeting images of the members of this underworld and El Tribunal de la Noche (a tribunal made up of key members of the underworld in charge of judging and imparting justice to people from mainstream society who break the law, but whose actions are not judged or questioned by the authorities), one can observe that they all share certain ethnic (aboriginal and Indo-mestizo) and socio-economic (abject poverty) traits that operate as visual markers of their otherness. Arguably, the film suggests that femaleness is another manifestation of a cultural and social Other, and as such this otherness operates regardless of whether this femaleness is found in a deformed woman or a beautiful one. As a result, Nora is portrayed more as an instrument of evil than an evil monstrous herself, unlike the monstrous characters who have been previously analysed. Thus La Bruja/Nora represents a form of the female grotesque that remains both socially and sexually repressed and underdeveloped.

At all times, the femininity of La Bruja/Nora subscribes to a form of marianismo whereby men are in possession of and control her socio-sexual persona. Nevertheless, halfway through the story, she seems to transform into a female gothic type of character. She returns to her 'natural' monstrous state when, towards the end of the film, she comes back to Dr Boerner's laboratory and pleads with him to spare the life of Fedor (Ramon Gay), since she has fallen in love with him. As they start to argue, Nora produces a gun and points it at Dr Boerner; however, he does not seem scared of her and instead retrieves a bottle of nitric acid, which he

---

[8] Once again, du Maurier's *Rebecca* also offers in Mrs. Danvers (the cold-hearted, stern and overbearing housekeeper) a character whose less attractive physical appearance is always contrasted to the extreme beauty of the late Rebecca or the second Mrs. de Winter. By the same token, ugliness and old age are equated with evilness in the Brothers Grimm's *Snow White* when the Evil Queen transforms herself into the old woman in order to trick the young protagonist into eating the poisoned apple.

obviously intends to throw at her with the objective of disfiguring her face once again. It is here that the film tries to construct Nora, albeit only momentarily, as a monster, and it could be argued that her monstrosity is derived from a direct threat to her physical beauty. This monstrous transformation is stressed by the camera work in which, after a close-up of the doctor's hands as he takes the bottle of acid, the camera switches to a close-up of Nora's face, looking panic stricken. The image then cuts back to the doctor, who approaches Nora with the bottle of acid and holds it above his head, ready to throw it at her. At this point the camera switches to a low angle, medium shot of Nora pointing straight at the camera as she shoots the doctor. By making her kill 'her creator' and be depicted as a villainess, one that perhaps seems more akin to the traditional femme fatale than a female monster, the film brings back to the forefront of the narrative the fact that beauty, in many such narratives, masquerades as monstrosity.

In the end, *La Bruja* evidences that, as Roger Sale has rightly pointed out in relation to fairy tales, 'the fear here is not of the wish for beauty, but of the power of that wish when separated and isolated from love, from handsome princes; the wish is that beauty will not be thus isolated' (1979: 42). That La Bruja/Nora is exterminated by the end of the narrative is no surprise; what is interesting, though, is the way in which the very end of the film continues to focus on her beauty as the one element that sustains her female identity. This last scene in the film, after Nora has been fatally stabbed as she tried to protect Fedor from certain death, shows her face distorting back to the original and malformed La Bruja (in ways that are very similar to the previous film). The close-up of her face shows the transition from the beautiful and seductive Nora to the ugly and deformed La Bruja, making it clear that Judith Halberstam is right to suggest that

> the grotesque effect of Gothic is achieved through a kind of transvestism, a dressing up [or making up] that reveals itself as costume. Gothic is a cross-dressing, drag, performance of textuality, an infinite readability and, indeed, these are themes that are readily accessible within Gothic fiction itself where the tropes of doubling and disguise tend to dominate the narrative. (1995: 60)

The film illustrates the dynamics of disguise within the gothic narrative as La Bruja's change of appearance operates at the level of the symbolic through not only the changing of her physiognomy in order to become beautiful, but also the utilising of her beauty as an instrument of power for her evil deeds. La Bruja's grotesque appearance could be said to reveal itself as a costume that masquerades as the ambivalences found within mariana identity. As such, the final transformation into the ugly Bruja reveals how the trope of doubling and disguise had been paramount in the construction of a female gothic identity (clearly entwined with mariana identity).

El Espejo de la Bruja

Unlike La Bruja/Nora, a gothic heroine who truly turns into a monstrous feminine is Elena (Dina de Marco) in Chano Urueta's *El Espejo de la Bruja* (1962). The film seems to be partly inspired by Du Maurier's novel *Rebecca* (1938), as well as Alfred Hitchcock's film adaption (1940), but with a clearer supernatural and horror element added to the storyline. However, differently from the heroine in *Rebecca*, in *El Espejo de la Bruja* Elena makes the conscious decision to become a spectral figure by allowing her husband Eduardo (Armando Calvo) to poison her, thus turning into the ghost who will haunt him and his new wife. In this film, Elena as a ghost is not narrated as an absence but, instead, very much as a presence within the narrative.

For instance, the mirror alluded to in the title of the film becomes the passage to connect the world of the living with the world of the dead, while it also permits Elena to keep a watchful eye over the people in the house. This mirror is also the passport to provide Elena with agency from the beginning of the story, since she manages to uncover her husband's ploy with the help of her Tía Sara (Isabel Corona), the housekeeper, who uses her knowledge of witchcraft to discover Eduardo's ploy to kill Elena in order to marry his lover. Unlike the previous monster, Elena is conscious and seems happily to embrace her new trajectory as a monster, as she sacrifices her earthly life to become a horrific yet beautiful ghost who will demand revenge from those who have wronged her. This transformation is marked by some physical changes in Elena, who ceases to look like the stereotypical female gothic (sweet face, harmless looking, innocent beauty) and becomes stoic, serious and with a macabre appearance to her persona. She becomes a spectre who will relentlessly haunt Debora (Rosa Arenas). This haunting at first operates at a psychological level, when she meddles with her nemesis's mental sanity by making her own favourite flowers appear in her old bedroom, making the piano play her favourite tune, or making her own private diary disappear after Debora starts reading it. In short, she torments Debora in the hope that she will make her lose her mind, even before she does any physical monstrous damage to her. Thus audiences are confronted with a monster who is conscious of her monstrosity and desires to be monstrous, a monstrous who manifests in her persona the multiple dynamics of the horror narrative where horror operates as a pre-existent condition to the human condition. This notion is supported by Dana B. Polan when she argues that 'part of the significance of recent horror films lies in the way they reject or problematize this simple moral binary opposition to suggest that horror is not something from out there, something strange, marginal, ex-centric, the mark of a force from elsewhere, the in-human' (2004: 143). In other words, monstrosity (as the ultimate manifestation of horror) can be procured and bestowed on the female protagonist when harm and treachery come her way and make her depart from the role she would have been culturally assigned as a traditional female gothic.

This film is one of the very few in which the narrative centres primarily on female relations while men take a secondary role. The relationship between the three main female figures could be said to provide an approximation to new readings of femininity and marianismo in Mexican culture. First, the opening of the film already depicts a form of female kinship between Elena and Tía Sara: although the film does very little to suggest that the two are blood related, there is a bond between them that goes beyond the lady of the house and servant relationship. Unlike in *Rebecca*, the relationship between Elena and Tía Sara is not tinged with a lesbian subtext; instead, it focuses on the repression of the maternal and the maternal as monstrous. In the opening sequence, Tía Sara has taken it on herself to teach Elena the dark arts and uses this knowledge to offer protection against Elena's husband. Arguably, Tía Sara operates as the symbolic projection of a monstrous psyche that seems to be too evil, destructive and ugly to belong to the beautiful Elena. Unsurprisingly, Tía Sara seems to adhere more to the notion of the witch as represented in fairy-tale narratives: she dresses very conservatively and in black, is clearly a much older woman, her face shows a degree of harshness, and she possesses a calculating vengeance that is absent from Elena. She operates as a projection of the dark side of the protagonist while becoming the helping (and physical) hand that aids to torment and haunt Debora. Within the context of the Mexican national imaginary, Tía Sara comes to represent a form of malinchismo that seeks to disavow the type of marianismo that has been imposed on women as a template for female behaviour and identity. Tía Sara is an archetypal monster because she disavows the notion of marianismo, whereby 'marianismo refers to a concept that incorporates female gender roles. The term is derived from the Virgin Mary. Embodied in this term are the concepts of virginity, chastity, honor and shame, the ability to suffer and willingness to serve' (Salyers 1998: 3). In other words, Tía Sara siphons off the negative aspects associated with malinchismo and, within the narrative, comes to represent the type of monstrosity that opposes the values of the traditional female gothic. In this way, her role within the story is to be regarded as the original monstrous feminine whose evil femininity influences and corrupts the pure and abnegated Elena.

The confrontation between Elena and Debora demonstrates that, as Creed argues in relation to the film *The Exorcist* (William Friedkin, 1973), 'woman is constructed as possessed when she attacks the symbolic order, highlights its weaknesses, plays on its vulnerabilities; specifically, she demonstrates that the symbolic order is a sham built on sexual repression and the sacrifice of the mother' (Creed 1993a: 41). In this light, Elena's actions seem to be simply the logical continuation of Tía Sara's evil and monstrous teachings, as she shows that embracing suffering can turn women into evil beings capable of exercising revenge on a patriarchal system that has historically repressed them. Elena becomes 'possessed' the moment she decides that she has the right to haunt and torment those she deems responsible for her death. However, her possession should not be regarded as a symptom of female hysteria, since she is very much conscious and aware that she has to become monstrous in order to exercise her revenge. She is a monster, in all senses of the word, as she fully complies with what Halberstam theorises as the gothic monster, one that 'traditionally or conventionally represents multiple modalities of fear and desire and otherness [...] [monsters] represent a doubleness that is more than double, a threat that produces monstrosity precisely at the site of human identity' (1995: 110). Elena is clearly more than a double owing to her being possessed and the different expressions of identity that coexist within her socio-cultural persona (as she reveals herself to be torn between marianismo and malinchismo through her actions). Her monstrosity makes her multifaceted in ways that evidence the fissures of polarised female identities that govern femininity within the socio-sexual popular imagination. Thus her evilness should not suggest a slippage into a hysterical id where she loses control of her conscious self; instead, it shows that she makes the conscious decision to be and act evil because she feels that it will avenge her 'unfair' death.

Once again, the mirror is used as the instrument that allows evil to enter the realm of the living. After Elena's ghost has been haunting the newly-weds for a while, Debora finds herself in Elena's old bedroom. Once there, she looks into the mirror, shown in a medium long shot, and sees Elena's ghost as if walking towards her and reflected in the mirror; Debora immediately screams and faints. Eduardo runs into the room and is given a lamp by Tía Sara, who was conveniently positioned outside Elena's bedroom to do just this. The action is shown in a long shot that permits a full view of the body-sized mirror the moment Eduardo enters the room, as he kneels down to check on Debora lying unconscious on the floor. As he turns towards the mirror, he sees Elena's ghost getting closer as she appears to be gliding towards him. The camera then switches between a low-angle, medium shot of him startled in panic, still holding the lamp, and another low-angle, medium shot of Elena walking towards the camera that ends in a close medium shot of her. Her image is shown in high contrast and low-key lighting that focuses on her face, which is looking sternly straight ahead. The camera then switches once more to both characters on the floor, and focuses on Eduardo as he throws the lamp at the mirror. However, when the mirror breaks into pieces, Debora catches fire and runs out of the room, screaming and in flames. At this point the camera moves to Tía Sara, who enters the room and in a very low-angle, medium shot, framed by the arches that adorn the ceiling, tells Elena 'ya puedes descansar, tu venganza está cumplida' [you can rest now, your revenge has been fulfilled].

After this episode, the next part of the film will reference, once again and as previously discussed, the notion of beauty as a form of female agency that is utilised within horror narratives to justify and provide agency to women's evil. Beauty becomes an asset, and patriarchy both fears and rejects its loss. However, it could be suggested that by burning Debora alive, the film punishes the scopophilic pleasures of patriarchal culture in which women are objectified and valued mainly by their personal appearance. Elena also breaks with the seeming relationship between sin and abjection as something that is inherent to female identity, and proves that women are not innately and deceptively treacherous. In this light, the audience are asked to regard Elena's actions not as the result of disobedience or rebellion (towards the patriarchal ideological system that has coerced her female identity), but as motivated by alienation and estrangement. Elena's 'evil' actions, as a ghostly and demonic entity, are not driven by a wilful desire to sin, but by her frustration at discovering that her mariana identity forces on her social expectations that allow her husband to abuse her both physically and psychologically. Within the film's narrative it is possible to suggest that the actions that may be considered sinful on the part of Elena are what enable her to break the cycle of abuse at the hands of her abuser. Elena's conscious, yet demonic, decision to haunt and torment her estranged husband and his new wife is evidence that sin becomes, as Mary Potter Engels rightly observes, 'a distortion of the dynamic tension between freedom and dependence' (1990: 163). Elena's condition of abjection is overcome by two specific actions: her willingness to sacrifice herself as an abnegated mariana and her eventual desire for revenge on those who have wronged her. This idea chimes with the thinking of Carol L. Schnabl Schweitzer, who points out in her work on abjection and sin that 'abjection is overcome by learning to overcome fear and falsehood (false selves) in a process of object-relating which raises desire' (2010: 48). As a result, it is possible to argue that the horror within the film emerges from the fact that Elena has departed from her 'proper' feminine role and has made a decision to claim a space of power within patriarchal and machista society.

El Vampiro Sangriento

Of all the villainesses in gothic Mexican cinema of the time, the character that best embraces monstrosity while breaking away from patriarchal society is one that has only a supporting role within the narrative in the film *El Vampiro Sangriento* (Miguel Morayta, 1962). Frau Hildegarda (Bertha Moss) is the evil housekeeper of Conde Siegfried von Frankenhausen (Carlos Agosti), yet she is depicted in many instances as more monstrous and evil than the vampire she serves. Frau Hildegarda differs from the Tía Sara character in *El Espejo de la Bruja*, in that she is not only a helping hand for El Conde, she enjoys the freedom to exercise evil without having to justify it as carrying out someone else's orders. What makes Frau Hildegarda a very exciting character among all the female monstrous villainesses already studied (and those that will be analysed later) is that she disavows the two main characteristics of the female gothic: the 'natural' physical beauty of such creatures (Kilgour 1998a) and being a blameless victim of patriarchal oppression (Long Hoeveler 1998). She is a queer monstrous feminine because she does not necessarily abide by the rules of a prescriptive heterosexuality or homosexuality and, instead, opens up a space of female ambivalence whereby she effectively manages to shift from male to female agency without much trouble. She is queer inasmuch as she could be said to go beyond 'the concepts of normative heterosexuality and traditional gender roles to encompass a more inclusive, amorphous, and ambiguous contra-heterosexuality' (Benshoff 1997: 93). She depicts what could be labelled a butch femme gothic: a type of gothic villainess that effectively manages to blur dichotomist divisions of gender roles and sexual pleasure, without necessarily becoming trapped in the sort of gendered stereotypes commonly found in gothic narratives.[9]

This butch femme gothic character must not simply be regarded as some form of closeted lesbian, since such an assertion would be rather reductionist. Although a subtle degree of masculinisation is to be found in her pose and demeanour, as well as her clothing, she still operates as a female castrator. However, she manages to avoid the sort of narratives of revenge against the excess of patriarchal abuse found elsewhere for such characters. Creed (1993a) sees the castrating woman as a rather sympathetic figure whose actions are almost never punished and whose monstrosity is justified within the narrative.[10] These female figures are either psychotic women—whose monstrosity derives from unresolved traumas—or women who actively seek revenge after being mistreated, raped or abused. In either case, this type of female monstrous is regarded as somewhat of a victim (either of a mental illness or the excesses of the patriarchal order). Conversely, Frau Hildegarda is not depicted as a victim and seems very conscious of her own actions throughout the film. Unlike Creed's female psychopath, who 'represents a more conventional view of female monstrosity in that woman transforms into a monster when she is sexually and emotionally unfulfilled' (1993a: 122), Frau Hildegarda depicts a form of sadistic pleasure whereby her pleasure derives from creating and inflicting pain; in other words, she is allowed autonomous horror agency.

For instance, in one of the first sequences in the film, El Conde and Frau Hildegarda arrive at the castle only to find that Doctor Riccardo (Raul Farell) was about to leave the place escorted by La Condesa's faithful servant, Lázaro, (Enrique Lucero). After a brief exchange, Frau

---

[9] Such gender stereotypes are accurately pointed out by Donna Heiland when she argues that the plot of the classic gothic novel can be regarded as the 'melodramatic story of an innocent young woman trapped by one man and rescued by another' (2008: 1). To which it can be also added that other female figures within gothic narratives tend to be regarded as villainesses who try to oppress the heroine.

[10] Creed focuses her analysis of the castrating woman on films such as *I Spit on Your Grave* (Meir Zarchi 1978), *Sisters* (Brian De Palma 1973) and *Psycho* (Alfred Hitchcock, 1960).

Hildegarda accompanies the Doctor out and ensures that he has left. Meanwhile, El Conde takes a whip, shown in a distant long shot, and strikes Lázaro with it. Frau Hildegarda, who can be seen far in the background, seems to practically glide across the floor towards where Lázaro lies with a big grin on her face, stressed by the camera focusing on her face through a medium close-up. She has obviously enjoyed witnessing pain being caused to another human being, and does not need to justify such pleasure in ways that are somehow smokescreened by the 'injustices' of machista society.

In a later sequence, Lázaro is seen tied to a post while being whipped by a muscled servant, once again through the use of long shots. This occurs after Lázaro has been interrogated and it is discovered that he had betrayed El Conde by bringing the daughter of his archenemy to work in the castle disguised as a female servant for La Condesa. After discovering his servant's treason, El Conde orders that his tongue to be cut out. Frau Hildegarda then nods to the man and he proceeds to sever Lázaro's tongue; yet while this is happening, the camera shows Frau Hildegarda who, in a medium, slight low-angle shot, watches the scene lustfully and then bursts out in a stereotypically evil laugh. By procuring some form of enjoyment from witnessing evil and horrific acts, she manifests an ownership of desire that seemed somewhat absent in most previous villainesses, as they never achieved any form of gratification within the diegesis of the film. Such obvious gratification constructs her as a phallic woman because she wields power that is constructed as phallic; she is feared by both male and female characters, as she is regarded as the embodiment of pure evil.

This can be seen in the scene in which she enters the town's tavern, where Lázaro and Justus (Pancho Córdova) are exchanging information and plotting against El Conde and his servant. As Frau Hildegarda enters the tavern, the camera cuts to a slight high-angle, medium shot of her stern face as she looks at them with contempt, rightly believing that they are conspiring against her master. From her face the camera cuts to the two men, who are framed in a low-angle close-up of their panic-stricken faces as they find themselves discovered by the evil woman. This image of men experiencing such fear at being discovered, in conjunction with the tense incidental music, helps construct Frau Hildegarda as a phallic woman whose power derives from a 'transgressive "confession" conditioned and confronted by both feminist and misogynist forms of repudiation' (Butler 1993: 86). She is phallic because she blurs and problematises the boundaries of femininity and masculinity by showing signs of female and male behaviour (assuming behaviour as a gendered construct), while being slightly androgynous in her presentation of the self.

In order to stress her phallic investment visually, Frau Hildegarda is heavily troped in ways that offer an alternative reading of existing gender systems and prescribed gendered roles. Such elements can be said to constitute a butch femme gothic aesthetic that offers a visually economic means of constructing the butch femme gothic in ways that would not confuse it with female gothics or other female characters found in such narratives. However, despite the use of the word 'butch', the term does not imply a move to territories of same-sex desire; instead, it simply functions as a way to set apart those bodies that are regarded as quintessentially feminine and those that break such stereotypical representations of femininity or use butchness to suggest same-sex desire. Frau Hildegarda does not use her body to try to reinforce gender systems (whether gay or straight) through a performance of gender, but evidences that the fixity of the body is pure effect. Thus she combines elements attributed to purported masculinity and femininity in ways that are neither genderfuck nor androgynous. Instead, she belongs to that space of in-betweenism theorised by Richard Dyer (2013), which through a paradoxical inversion embodies a rejection of rigid gender role differentiation. This, in itself, makes her all the more monstrous because she cannot be easily categorised or deconstructed. The film stresses her otherness in many ways: for instance, although all the characters are given foreign, and rather Eastern European, names in an attempt to keep some faithfulness with the Romanian vampire legend, it is only Frau Hildegarda who speaks with a strong foreign accent, while the rest of the characters have a very distinctive Mexican one. Her rather foreign accent already sets her apart from the other characters and provides her with an even more perverse sense of self, arguably even more perverse than El Conde himself.

Costume and make-up also help stress the evilness of the character, as she wears a plain, long-sleeved, tight-fitted (from the waist up) black dress and her blonde hair (another Eastern European trope) is done in a bun, with the sides folded towards her face. She is depicted as somewhat stern and stoic, and somewhat masculinised in a still feminine way. Thus by amalgamating such an array of 'looks', she breaks with pre-established codes of gender depiction in classic cinema. However, despite suggesting that Frau Hildegarda's look and poise emerge from that place of in-betweenism, the narrative never implies that she is a lesbian or that she has feelings of same-sex desire. On the contrary, the story makes it clear that she has feelings for El Conde that go beyond mere servitude, fear or adulation, as she is obviously attracted both physically and emotionally to him. Frau Hildegarda's phallic power of address within that space of in-betweenism reifies the notion that the phallus operates as a veil to an ambivalent site of normative sexuality whereby it raises 'questions of imitation, subversion, and the articulation of phantasmatic privilege' (Butler 1993: 85) within (Mexican) machista culture. In other words, her purported femaleness may follow social and cultural normative values as prescribed within the realm of heteronormativity, yet her rather 'masculinised' behaviour—regarded as masculine only by its opposition to traditional mariana identity and behaviour—does not make the character slip into the orbit of same-sex desire. The slippage between traditional male and female gendered behaviour that can be noticed in her persona at different points of the narrative evidences that the materiality of the body extends beyond simple gay/straight, butch/femme dichotomies. The butch femme gothic illustrates a point of crisis for feminine sexuality: it is a body that cannot be recuperated into the realm of patriarchal order, nor will it belong to the realm of lesbian desire, and by being such it shows that female sexuality, and sexuality at large, is multiple and fluid. However, despite how radical this character and her characterisation of gender are, the butch femme gothic will not be allowed the fulfilment of her desires, partly because the fate of the villainess in most gothic narratives is punishment and annihilation, and partly because her presentation of the self is constructed as monstrous in relation to male, machista fantasies.

La Maldición de la Llorona

The last part of this chapter will address the female vampire subjectivity in Rafael Baledón's *La Maldición de la Llorona* (1963). Although Selma (Rita Macedo) is not a vampire in the blood-sucking sense of the word, the narrative constructs her as such with a series of tropes that are most commonly associated with vampirism. This film is unapologetic in its amalgamation of horror tropes, national and gothic themes, and the depiction of a villainess who shifts in terms of her own subjectivity. Despite the title making a direct reference to the legend of La Llorona—and this is very briefly touched on at one point in the narrative—the female protagonists in the film are not motivated by the sense of abject maternity that was previously discussed in relation to other film versions based on the Latin American folk legend. In contrast to the narrative in the previous

La Llorona films, the villainess protagonist in *La Maldición de la Llorona* actively seeks to exercise her revenge by killing all the men who cross her path. She sees men as enemies, while her obvious hatred for patriarchy, and thus men, has been passed on for generations. This hatred originates within the storyline in both the decimation of the real La Llorona—who was regarded as a witch after killing her children according to the original folklore tale—and her desire to create a world in which powerful women claim a space of superiority to macho men. Arguably, this film could be regarded as the most feminist of all the ones analysed here, as it explores themes of gender (in)equality, female solidarity, the attempt to gain and obtain female empowerment, women's rights and the rebellion against patriarchal sexism.

La Maldición de La Llorona could be viewed as a real attempt to take the female villainess's subjectivity outside the 'safe' confines of the domestic sphere and to present a female 'monster' whose desire to annihilate, murder and conquer extends beyond offering unconditional help to a masterful male figure—for instance, a more powerful vampire—or fulfilling a male, heterosexual fantasy of lesbianism (as seen in many other vampire narratives, especially those more closely linked to Mexploitation cinema[11]). Instead, Selma represents the willingness to rebel against Mexican machismo and the patriarchal sexism that it sustains. Interestingly, Baledón does not resort to eroticisation of the female monster in order to make her more appealing to other males in the narrative or the imaginary male audience who see the film. Her power of address does not derive from her capacity to use her beauty and physique as instruments to lure others to a painful end, but from her capacity to resist patriarchal control and to claim the ownership of her own desire. The central character, then, conforms to Jacinda Raed's theorisation of the female vampire and begins to show how the character can be conceived as vampiric in some sense, as she

> represents the liberation of female sexuality, a liberation that is threatening because it is no longer confined to providing sexual pleasure for the male. Rather, female sexuality becomes either a lure to trap and destroy the unsuspecting male or, because it has been liberated from its association with marriage and heterosexual romance, exclusive or self-sufficient. (2000: 181)

The narrative makes it clear that Selma has used her powers to control and dominate the men in her life. For instance, her husband, now a kind

---

[11] A clear example would be the many female vampire characters in El Santo's films.

of werewolf, remains incarcerated in a cell in her mansion. She also shows her phallic power by having a deformed male servant always at her mercy, while her niece's husband Jaime (Abel Salazar) falls victim to her witchcraft and demonic powers. Moreover, a great deal of the narrative is devoted to Selma's attempts to kill Jaime in order to guarantee that Amelia (Rosita Arenas) breaks all ties with the patriarchal order and becomes her unconditional ally, which in turn will help her to reawaken the corpse of the original La Llorona.

Although Selma never attempts to bite anyone's neck or suck anyone's blood, she is repeatedly troped as a vampire. For instance, her lack of a reflection in mirrors is thematically repeated throughout the film, first when early on Amelia realises that there are no mirrors to be found anywhere in the mansion, and second when Amelia becomes aware that, as the curse of La Llorona begins to manifest in her, she can no longer see her own image reflected in a mirror. Arguably, this lack of a reflection could also be regarded as a visually economic means to represent female detachment from patriarchy. The female gothic—that is, the heroine—is most usually associated with the domestic ambit and her plight is one whereby the narrative revolves around antagonistic forces trying to derail her from her role as abnegated mother and/or companion. By depicting Selma through the vampiristic trope of lacking a reflection, the character disavows the notion that the heroine is, as suggested by Claire Kahane with reference to the gothic mirror, 'imprisoned not in a house but in the female body, which is itself the maternal legacy. The problematics of femininity is thus reduced to the problematics of the female body, perceived as antagonistic to the sense of self, as therefore freakish' (1985: 343). When Amelia screams at her own reflection in the mirror, or the lack thereof, she is really screaming as a reaction to the sheer panic of abandoning her sense of mariana identity and thus losing her mariana subjectivity. Although the narrative makes it clear that there is a genealogical affiliation between the three main female characters, both maternity and the mother continue to be regarded as spectral figures that are in direct opposition to the gothic villainess. Taking the Lacanian mirror stage as a point of departure, the psychoanalytical valences in the film could not be more poignant. For the child—in this case female—the precursor of the mirror is the mother in which she first sees herself reflected. Since for the most part in gothic narratives the female gothic tries to comply with her role (as socially ascribed within a patriarchal system) as mother and companion, the villainess in this film obliterates marianismo as an intrinsic aspect of female subjectivity.

By doing so she demonstrates that, in Creed's words, she is 'in conflict with the family, the couple and the institutions of patriarchal capitalism' (1993a: 61, b).

What distinguishes Selma from other female vampires is the fact that she breaks with many gothic vampire stereotypes, like those found in films such as *Santo Contra las Mujeres Vampiro* (Alfonso Corona Blake, 1962) or *Alucarda, la Hija de las Tinieblas* (Juan López Moctezuma, 1978). This character, instead, is neither masculinised nor highly sexualised, and there are no suggestions that she may be a lesbian or bisexual in a way that brings to the forefront an ambivalent sexuality as part of her subject identity. She, however, offers an alternative reading of her maternal subjectivity, as she regards herself as a matriarch and devotes the greater part of the narrative to trying to awaken the deceased La Llorona in order to create a new world order in which women take charge of the fate of humanity. As a result, Selma effectively disrupts 'the formal and highly symbolic relations of men and women essential to the continuation of patriarchal society' (Creed 1993: 61, b). Although she is ultimately unsuccessful in her quest—unsurprisingly, she will be killed by the end of the film—the character's subjectivity evidences the constructedness of mariana identity by showing that her maternal instincts are not related to a desire to fulfil gender expectations, to use children as visual tokens to reify her own femaleness/womanliness or to keep a man by her side (a common leitmotif in melodrama that tends to spill over into other Mexican film genres). The film also makes a clear distinction from the maternal, such that the relation between the three main female characters, albeit the third is a corpse, is never depicted as a mother–daughter relationship despite the genealogical links that are clearly established (Amelia addresses Selma as 'Tía', although the exact nature of their family ties is never really unravelled). Thus Selma's interest in rekindling her relationship with her niece and her desire to protect her and make her 'one of her own' make it clear that, as Anna Chromik-Krykawska asserts, 'the vampire, as an epitome of the abject feminine, can be treated as an expression of the anxiety of dissolving the clean and proper identity of the self [...] they represent the anxiety of the threat "unruly" femininity poses to patriarchy' (2010: 485).

This decidedly unruly femininity of the female vampire is externalised not only through Selma's physical appearance, but also by the space she inhabits. Kathryn Robson argues that 'the female vampire tradition is rooted in an intimacy and identification between women that is often associated with the relationship between mother and daughter; the female vampire is often portrayed as a melancholic mother figure' (2002: 56). This melancholy is reflected throughout the mansion and is highlighted from the beginning of the film, when Amelia and Jaime arrive and he comments on the clear decay of the property. The visible state of deterioration clearly reaffirms that Selma has lost touch with her mariana identity, since she no longer regards the appearance of the house as an intrinsic element (and more importantly a reflection) of her own subjectivity. There is a clear tension between the appearance of the household—which is closely related to mariana subjectivity—and female empowerment—which is regarded as monstrous. Thus it is possible to argue that the dilapidated state of the haunted mansion in this film, as well as in many other gothic narratives, operates as an externalisation of the monstrous feminine. By the same token, the dungeons or torture chambers underneath the house could be regarded as an externalisation of the monstrous id of the villainess. Subterranean and labyrinth-like passages, as well as secret corridors, all converge in the same space of torture and evil, a space that could be seen as the womb of the melancholic mother whose abject maternity makes her all the more terrifying. In this light, it is possible to see that, as Leslie Fiedler points out,

> beneath the haunted castle lies the dungeon keep: the womb from whose darkness the ego first emerged, the tomb to which it knows it must return at last. Beneath the crumbling shell of paternal authority, lies the maternal blackness, imagined by the gothic writer as a prison, a torture chamber. (1960: 132)

It is this anti-mariana womb that must be destroyed in order to restore the patriarchal system, a space of horror and oppression that symbolises the temporary failure of female emancipation, as well as a failed attempt to break from the patriarchal system.

Selma's haunted mansion is, thus a space in which the heroine must be entrapped in the eternal womb of the spectral maternal body, which comes to enforce the point of entry and departure of the ego. This is a space that overtly seeks to rid itself of men—whether by transforming, killing or simply expelling them—and to entrap the female gothic until Amelia has fully transformed[12] into a monstrous feminine. The spectral womb becomes an imaginary space for male castration; it is here that Selma's husband—now

---

[12] A transformation that is also visually evidenced by her physical change, as her face transfigures into a monstrous and deformed one with hollow eyes, whose symbolism has been already suggested in the analysis of *La Bruja*.

transformed into a werewolf-like monster—remains incarcerated; it is also the space where Jaime will be brought to be tortured so as to break any links between him and Amelia. It is no coincidence that Selma's demise will also constitute the demise of the family's mansion and that as Selma is killed, the house will burn in flames through a fire that originated from its evil womb; that is, the dungeon. In this sense, the gothic narrative continues to reaffirm that, as Kate Fergusson Ellis points out, 'the home has lost its prelapsarian purity and is in need of rectification' (1989: ix), even when that rectification comes in the form of a razed house. In much the same way that the coffin is connected to the vitality of the vampire, the haunted house is connected to the life of the female villainess in the film. The dungeon seems to be the space from where evil forces emanate and the place designated for the resurrection of La Llorona. Following other traditional vampire narratives, it will also be the space where both Selma and La Llorona will be, once and for all, annihilated. By utilising the ultimate vampire trope, the use of a stake through the heart to prevent the resurrection of La Llorona's corpse, Amelia will finally re-restore patriarchy and annihilate any possibility of a matriarchal order being established.

Conclusion

The gothic horror narrative has traditionally been regarded as one that ultimately encapsulates a cautionary tale whereby the reader (or the audience) is warned against the perils of subverting patriarchal order. The gothic horror narrative shows the tensions between sex, gender and sexuality and evidences the uneasy relations between male and female subjectivity. As in most traditionally patriarchal texts, the antihero in the gothic tradition embodies all the negative aspects of patriarchal culture. Kahane is right to assert that 'the terror that the Gothic by definition arouses [is] the motif of incest within an oedipal plot. From this perspective, the latent configuration of the Gothic paradigm seems to be that of a helpless daughter confronting the erotic power of a father or brother, with the mother noticeably absent' (1985: 335). Very little work has been devoted to studying villainesses and their twofold disruption of the patriarchal order. On the one hand, they demonstrate that femininity and maternity are neither fixed nor intrinsic to female subjectivity. On the other, they prove that the gothic may also convey 'the spectral presence of a dead-undead mother, archaic and all-encompassing, a ghost signifying the problematics of femininity which the heroine must confront' (Kahane 1985: 336).

The gothic villainess represents a rupture with regulatory norms of gender and sexuality and is presented as deviant and perverse. However, as Lynda Hart has suggested, these villainesses were portrayed as occasional offenders whose uncontrolled sexuality and behaviour met an unparalleled punishment that serve to remind female audiences of the 'shaky foundation upon which their own claim to respectability had been erected, but also to blur the distinction between "bad" and "good" women' (2005: 29).

In the Mexican context, the archetypal villainess has been traditionally associated with La Malinche, who in turn, and in the context of gothic narratives, has morphed into the figure of La Llorona. As has been discussed, in the film versions of this legend, La Llorona represents aspects of abject maternity in which the woman uses her offspring as a tool to seek revenge against her lover's betrayal. In an act of pure hysteria, she kills her children in order to assert revenge and defy the patriarchal order. Although in none of the film versions here analysed does she become victorious after attempting to claim revenge, she demonstrates that mariana identity is not necessarily and blindly subjugated by patriarchal sexism, and that the macho figure must also be made accountable for her actions. Thus the different film versions of La Llorona's story question the patriarchal ideology that has traditionally kept an anti-patriarchal vision of her femininity. However, as Alma Zamorano points out, in *La Llorona* films 'el personaje toma un cariz diabólico y vengativo para hacerlo mucho más amenazante, se podría decir que el mito popular mexicano se adaptaría al cine como sustento argumental, desnaturalizado hasta convertirlo en mero pretexto' [the character takes on a diabolical and vengeful appearance to make her more menacing, it could be said that the popular Mexican myth would be adapted in cinema as the basis of the storyline, unnatural until it became a mere pretext] (2011: 1273). In this light it is clear that these films show a preoccupation with the gothic genre at the expense of the accuracy of the national legend. They also portray a feminine archetype in which the villainess becomes a female monster, a powerful monster-anima, dangerous and melancholic, that reappears in different reincarnations in order to seek revenge on the man, and the lineage, who first betrayed her. However, her failure to assert her revenge only serves to maintain the status quo of machismo within such a society.

Another aspect of the gothic villainess presented in these films refers to female beauty deployed as a stratagem to exercise evil and subvert patriarchy. Most gothic narratives will insist on a distinction between natural, 'good' beauty and unbridled, 'evil' beauty. The gothic villainess will be depicted as sexually alluring and maleficently beautiful, in contrast to the sort of natural beauty that her mariana counterparts will purport. Whereas the female gothic is characterised by the innocent beauty found in female protagonists in fairy tales, the gothic villainess usually attains her sexually alluring beauty by diabolical or artificial means. This desire to remain beautiful and youthful will operate as a constant motive to separate the female gothic from her evil counterparts, while sudden or involuntary ageing will be regarded as the ultimate punishment for her evil doings. Consequently, these films continue to be 'indicative of a continuous trend within society to marginalize older women and put them in the place of other by depicting them as isolated hags or sexually predatory "cougars"' (Sullivan 2010: 3). By the same token, the female grotesque evidenced by images of witches and aided by some degree of physical deformity in the villainess will help highlight the mark of her transgressive excess. She obliterates the limits of her own body and 'by transgressing the norms of femininity, the female grotesque refuses the limits imposed on her body and embraces the ambivalent possibilities such transgressions offer' (Mallan 2000: 143). In this way, the female spectator can enjoy the scopophilic pleasure of engaging in the enactment of those transgressive behaviours that are socially frowned on by mariana identity.

Grotesqueness, however, does not require bodily transformation or deformation and, instead, can also be found in an exaggerated sense of otherness that is imposed on the character to make her clearly discernable from other female gothic figures. Whereas in many of the gothic narratives under study in this chapter villainesses become evil as a direct result of a desire for revenge on the males who have either hurt or wronged them, there are a few others who are depicted as 'naturally' evil, thus both their physical appearance and their actions will be portrayed through a series of tropes that encode the notion of evilness: physical deformity and ugliness. To Mallan, such characters have 'the physical attractiveness of screen characters, but their parodying and embodying of femininity through gestures, voice, dress, hairstyle, make-up, sensuousness, and their rebellious and transgressive acts […] offer a source of subversive viewing pleasure and illicit desire' (2000: 146). The monstrous feminine does not need to be diegetically justified in the narrative through clear acts of male abuse or betrayal; it can be considered, at times, an innate quality of the female subject. However, it is important to point out that in contrast to other gothic narratives from elsewhere, in these Mexican films there are no suggestions that such villainesses are queer or that their evilness is not a mark of the boundaries of their own femininity. By remaining 'essentially' heterosexual but still committing evil acts, these women disavow marianismo as a controlling force against female sexuality and behaviour. Ultimately, this desire to challenge the status quo of patriarchal society will also empower such women to seek to extend their monstrous control beyond the physical boundaries of the domestic sphere.

Among the films analysed, the one monster who most overtly seems to have a desire to escape the confines of the domestic gothic sphere is the female vampire. She could be regarded as the monster who best subverts marianismo, since her actions are

> particularly disturbing because of the way the act of bloodsucking reverses the 'natural' female role as nurturer and provider of life, rather than taker of the same. By definition, then, the female vampire rebels against the natural laws that are supposed to govern her existence and her overt eroticism further distances her from the conventional role of passive woman she is intended to play. (Williams 2008: 23)

Nevertheless, it is important to bear in mind that Selma does not need to become a bloodsucking monster to achieve this level of monstrous subjectivity. Clearly, the female vampire analysed here differs from other such narratives in that her transgression is not regarded as a slippage into queer territories; the female vampire is not constructed as a lesbian evocation of desire. Instead, she rebels against patriarchy in a clear attempt to disrupt the macho order and install a matriarchal system that, at the level of the symbolic, intends to undo centuries of gender oppression. In short, the vampire may be, as Creed has theorised, abject, but this does not necessarily code her as passive. Instead, spectators are offered a female vampire who is empowered by her own desire to conquer and create a world where the symbolic order represented by patriarchy has been disavowed, even though all these narratives ultimately end with a female monster who is punished or annihilated from the story. Unsurprisingly, none of the feminine monstrous figures analysed in this chapter enjoys a 'victorious ending' or any sort of ending that would imply the demise of machismo, yet it is possible to ascertain that at least these women make a real attempt at rebelling against the macho institutions that have traditionally repressed them, while also offering an, albeit evil, alternative to mariana identity as the sole form of female subjectivity accepted within Mexican culture.

CHAPTER 2

Zé do Caixão and the Queering of Monstrosity in Brazil

José Mojica Marins's films *A Meia-Noite Levarei Sua Alma* (At Midnight I Will Take Your Soul, 1964), *Esta Noite Encarnarei no Teu Cadaver* (Tonight I'll Possess Your Corpse, 1976), and *O Ritual dos Sádicos* (1970) among others constitute a Brazilian horror cult series of films that has as its main evil protagonist Zé do Caixão. Zé do Caixão (Coffin Joe in the anglicised translation) is, arguably, the most horrific, monstrous and anti-normative character ever to emerge from the Brazilian horror film canon, as well as the only recurrent monstrous protagonist from a horror film series in the continent. It is well documented that Mojica Marins had no other option but to play the part of Zé himself, because none of the actors he approached would agree to do so because they considered the role too subversive and depraved (Barcinski and Finotti 1998). Through Mojica Marins playing the part himself, Zé do Caixão would become not only his archetypal horror figure, but also the director's own alter ego. Although Mojica Marins's films entered Brazilian—and soon enough Latin American—culture at a crucial moment when filmmaking was being theorised as a tool of dissent across the continent, the films (and the protagonist) gained notoriety and fame among transcontinental audiences.[1] The director created a character that is, in itself, a pastiche of tropes and

[1] According to Barcinski and Fanotti (1998), Mojica Marins's films did not really enjoy a great deal of popularity in his native Brazil on release. While visiting the United States Barcinski showed a number of the films to Mike Vraney (who owned the independent film

motifs in horror cinema and other well-known horror narratives. Zé combines gothic elements of the vampire (such as the black morning suit and black cape), as well as a top hat worn by gravediggers (his trade in the films). By the same token, his extremely long nails remind the viewer of the iconic Count Orlok from F. W. Murnau's *Nosferatu* (1922). The main storyline in the trilogy focuses on Zé's quest to find the perfect woman to bear his offspring and continue his blood line. In order to do so, he will annihilate anyone who interferes with his plans, while also killing for the pure sadistic pleasure of watching torture and pain.

Despite his 'obvious' machista intentions, Zé is a character that inhabits an interstitial space between overt machismo and clear queerness. He seems able to trespass into both territories without calling into question his own masculinity; or, rather, there being anyone who would dare to call into question his masculinity for fear of perishing at his hands. The character also evidences the constructedness of masculinity in Latin America and, more specifically, the performativity of machismo, whereby this template of male behaviour and sexuality is rendered a learnt behaviour more than an innate quality of all men of the continent. Marvin Leiner suggests that machismo 'requires individual men to make a display of physical power and social domination, and to disdain any feminine, or supposedly feminine traits' (1994: 79). While it is clear that Zé uses his physical power and his horrific antics as a medium for exercising social domination over those around him, it is impossible not to notice that his own version of his masculinity is tinged with a camp 'sensibility' that would, for other individuals in such a milieu of Latin American socialization, be conceived as antinormative. His own masculinity does not necessarily follow the behavioural patterns established by machista culture; yet he does not escape machismo altogether, since he also evidences, as Evelyn Stevens suggests in her analysis of machismo in Latin America, an 'exaggerated aggressiveness and intransigence in male-to-male interpersonal relationships and arrogance and sexual aggression in male-to-female relationships' (1973: 90). However, Zé's queer performance of the self disavows the notion that hypermasculinity is an intrinsic trait of Latino masculinity. In the Brazilian context he would not be considered a *viado* (homosexual) or worse a *bicha* (queer), as effeminate men are referred to in the Brazilian popular jargon, whose masculinity is questionable or considered non-existent.

company Something Weird Video), who decided to release the films in the American market, which led to Mojica Marins's work beginning to be recognized elsewhere.

It is possible to argue that Zé depicts a queer masculinity that, as theorised by Robert Heasley, is 'defined here as ways of being masculine outside hetero-normative constructions of masculinity that disrupt, or have the potential to disrupt, traditional images of the hegemonic heterosexual masculine' (2005: 310). However, unlike those queer masculine men to whom Heasley's work refers, Zé does not lack legitimacy as a form of masculinity, and his masculinity is not problematised by the narrative or the films themselves. His attraction to and desire for women remains a narrative constant throughout the series. He is regarded as a destabilising force to heteronormativity and, more specifically, to patriarchy, since the women who are attracted to him are also constructed as somewhat deviant (which diegetically justifies their attraction towards him). Therefore, for the purpose of this analysis it will be of prime importance to understand queer beyond its same-sex connotations and assume it as a force that has the power to destabilise heteronormativity without necessarily being associated with same-sex desire. Zé's queer masculinity undoes the fixity of male identity and machismo for the Latin American male subject, and evidences a fluidity that manifests a type of otherness. This otherness is characterised by a camp aesthetics and a camp sensibility that also disavow the seemingly inseparable relationship between camp and homosexuality, as theorised by Susan Sontag (1966) when she argued that camp is a manifestation of a gay form of sensibility. Instead, Zé's campness should be regarded as the external manifestation of a heteronormative destabilising force that seeks to challenge patriarchal culture through elements linked to trash culture and horror rhetoric. Thus Mojica Marins's films permit the audience to break with the monolithic perception of heterosexual masculinity by experiencing and even valuing other desirable ways of 'being straight' that may not subscribe to the typical macho figure that circulates in Latin American popular culture.

Towards a Conceptualisation of Queer Machismo in Latin America

The conceptualisation of a notion of 'queer masculinity' in Latin America should be regarded as a very necessary enterprise, as it would help shed light on 'new' forms of masculinities that are (re)surfacing in many societies across the continent. As the caricaturised figure of the Latin American macho continues to fade away—one that has been popularised in the cultural imaginary through film, media, literature and other cultural texts[2]—new forms of cultural dialogues begin to emerge that take into account less machista forms of male sexuality. The notion of queer masculinity in Latin America would sit, rather uneasily for some, at the intersection of machismo and mariconería. This is a space where both identities conflate, repel and even depend on one another for their own survival. As has been widely argued (Mendès-Leite 1993; Murray 1995; Gutmann 1997, 2006; Kulick 1998, 2000, 2002; Chant and Craske 2003), Latin American sexual identity is socially formulated, and therefore enacted, not on the basis of a sexual desire or identification, but on the externalisation of a specific sexual behaviour, which most people would associate with a very specific sexual identity that is deemed 'intrinsically natural'. Simply put, as long as the male individual projects an image of himself that does not contravene the sexual parameters that regulate sexuality in a specific locus of socialisation, his sexual identity will not be at stake or questioned. Murray (1995), Arboleda (1995), Lumsden (1996) and Gutmann (2006), among others, argue that Latin American masculinity, and more specifically its vernacular manifestation under the umbrella of machismo, depends heavily on the exaggerated and overt display of a hypermasculine behaviour. Thus those individuals whose behaviour breaks this culturally established mold are regarded as subversive socio-sexual entities. Kimmel (2006) argues that Latin American masculinity is defined in terms of a 'man in power', or a 'man who possesses power' (manifested through force, success, authority and control), and that men are considered men as long as they exercise some form of control over the people around them.

Traditionally, both gender and sexual systems in the continent are believed to be shaped by a hypermasculinist model based on a rigid male/female, active/passive, dominant/submissive, hetero/homosexual dichotomy. More recent research into Latin American (homo)sexuality (Parker 1985, 1991, 2003; Mendès-Leite 1993; Cantú 2000; Carrillo 2002; Subero 2014) has departed from this dichotomist view of sexuality and acknowledges a series of slippages in socio-sexual behaviour and sexual attraction that blur this sexual rigidity. Many men break the binaries on which a supposedly normative sexuality is based and demonstrate that contemporary masculinity is multiple and fluid in the way in which it is

---

[2] For instance, the television series *Sólo para machos* (Bolivia 2015), novels such as Jaime Bayly's *No se lo digas a nadie* (1994), and the films by Julián Hernandez in Mexico are a few examples of anti-machista texts that have become popular across the Latin American continent.

internalized and manifested. For instance, some 'straight-acting' homosexual men may rightly oppose a machista ideology; yet there are still some for whom machismo is at the forefront of their sexual behaviour and who treat their male partners in the same misogynistic way that many 'traditional' (heterosexual) machos would their female partners (Cruz 2000).

Despite the mounting research that seeks to disavow machismo as an inherent form of male identity in the continent, it is clear that the figure of the macho continues to circulate in the popular imaginary as the prevalent form of heterosexual male typology. As Peter M. Beattie suggests, following Matthew Gutmann (1997), 'the *pelado* stereotype of the uncouth Mexican plebeian who drinks hard, beats his wife, and commits unpredictable acts of violence served as a symbol of rugged Mexican independence and as a justification for the urban poor's marginalization by their political and economic superiors' (2002: 304–305). Arguably, this misogynistic image has also circulated across the rest of the continent and was further perpetuated in the continental popular imaginary through caricaturesque depictions of machismo in film, media and other cultural products such as the iconic *O Cangaceiro* (Barreto 1953) and *Pixote* (Babenco 1981). In the Brazilian context, the *chanchada* played a pivotal role in perpetuating such stereotypes, with the subgenre of *pornochanchada* (the equivalent of sex comedies elsewhere) operating as the main vehicle for transmitting and embedding machista ideology.[3] In trying to create a sense of continental masculinity, Latin American men's self-perception has been torn between discordant and vague ideas of authority and tradition. For such men, the real task is to construct an image of the self that responds to their felt reality instead of what is socially expected of them. Thus machismo appears to be the product of a cultural anxiety that makes men symbolically abject because it separates them from culturally constructed ideas of the self.

Machismo can be a rather contentious term that seems to be challenged by the very people who also embrace it. It is a category that evidences a crisis of masculinity. Its constructedness demonstrates that it operates at the level of the symbolic through a performance of gender that is in constant contestation, since a persistent trait of this identity is the need to out-macho other men in order to claim some form of male supremacy. There are four different types of machismo, as theorised by Rolando Andrade

---

[3] Among the most notable films of this subgenre are Sílvio de Abreu's *A Árvores do Sexos* (1977) and *Mulher Objeto* (1981), and Oswaldo de Oliveira's *Histórias que Nossas Babás não Contavam* (1979).

(1992), which he recognises as encompassing an array of prescribed masculinities in Latin America. He asserts that there is a conqueror macho whose sense of identity derives from his role as a conquering man in all aspects of battle and engagement, such as championship, virility and courage; a playboy macho who sees women as objects and trophies and uses them as visually economic tokens for his maleness; a masked macho who uses his own machismo to compensate for his self-perceived inadequacies; and, finally, an authentic macho whose behaviour seems to represent all the positive values in society. It is clear that Andrade uses the banner machismo to refer to different degrees and perceptions of masculinity found in men, while the term itself is rendered fluid, as it breaks with the supposed fixity of such an identity. However, what Andrade effectively manages to achieve is to disavow the idea that, as Chris Girman suggests, a 'static definition of machismo—and by extension Latin American men—simplifies analyses of male sexuality into simplistic active/passive dichotomies' (2004: 45). However, one is left to ponder what happens when a man whose behaviour clearly responds to all the parameters that a purported machismo entails still does not conform to normative sexism and disrupts the seemingly correct functioning of patriarchal heteronormativity.

On the other side of the socio-sexual spectrum, queer seems to emerge as an alternative to the dichotomist division of gender and sexuality that has culturally typified heteronormative societies. Queer has operated in Anglo-academic jargon as an umbrella that makes it permissible to theorise beyond the limitations of sexological reductionism that operate via the hetero/homosexuality divide. It also opens up new paths to reimagining the relationship between sexuality/ies and individuals in a given society. Queer theory emerged in what could be deemed the 'traditional' West, as a site of signification for lesbian, gay, bisexual, transgender (LGBT), intersex and other people whose sexual orientation or gender identity challenges heterosexist notions of gender and sexuality. The term embraces the coexistence of multidimensional and sometimes contradictory identities, yet it seems to be most commonly used to designate an apparent subsection of the LGBT community. Although the term was used to denigrate gays and lesbians and other individuals who were seen as operating outside heterosexual gender norms, it was reappropriated in the 1980s to legitimise those very individuals and to reclaim a space of visibility in the realm of culture. Besides the emergence of queer as an emergent area of socio-sexual enquiry and an umbrella for academic research on non-heteronormative identities, the advent of the AIDS pandemic and the creation of radical activist groups such as ACT UP in the United States also helped consolidate queer as a new arena of contestation of the patriarchal system.

However, many queer theorists have fallen into the trap of using 'queer theory' to study lesbigay experiences, and by doing so they have reduced the very term that was supposed to fight reductionism. For many theorists, queer has simply become a substitute for lesbian and gay and, as Noreen Giffney rightly points out,

> in the process, they [queer theorists] have reduced queer to an identity category alone, or the ontological and epistemological extensions of an identity category/umbrella descriptor. Those who employ queer theory for anything other than the location of non-heteronormative—yet non-gay or lesbian—identities risk charges of mis-appropriation, mis-use, and misunderstanding. (2004: 73)

However, it is this misappropriation, misuse and misunderstanding that should really interest queer theory and that should drive queer as a site of political and ideological engagement with that which is outside the norm; or, as Michael Warner claimed, that which should define 'itself against the normal rather than the heterosexual' (1993: xxvi). Queer should question and challenge both normative and non-normative identities that may not even be directly related to gender and sexuality. It should be used to deconstruct and dissect categories of desire in socio-sexual subjects, whereby some of these desires are regarded as normal while some others are seen as subversive or abnormal. By the same token, desire should not be regarded as an intrinsic manifestation of sexuality, but as a force that provides some form of investment to those individuals who embody it. Such an investment may sit well, at least on the surface, within heteronormativity, but by daring to interrogate its seeming normality, this investment allows new ways of reading society that are not prescribed through a dichotomist division of such relations. Queer, as Arlene Stein and Kenneth Plummer indicate, becomes an organising principle of the social order that offers

> 1) a conceptualization of sexuality which sees sexual power embodied in different levels of social life, expressed discursively and enforced through boundaries and binary divides; 2) the problematization of sexual and gender categories, and of identities in general. Identities are always on uncertain ground, entailing displacements of identification and knowing; 3) a rejection of civil-rights strategies in favor of a politics of carnival, transgression

and parody which leads to deconstruction, decentering, revisionist readings
and an anti-assimilationist politics; 4) a willingness to interrogate areas which
normally would not be seen as the terrain of sexuality, and to conduct 'queer'
readings of ostensibly heterosexual or non-sexualized texts. (1996: 134)

It is this willingness to question and challenge those areas of culture that
may not, at first hand, seem to be related to sexuality and/or gender that
motivates a line of enquiry into how to make sense of a queer machismo
in Latin America. It is proposed that films such as the Coffin Joe trilogy
clearly evidence a moment of category crisis, because Zé do Caixão, the
psychopath and monstrous protagonist of these films, cannot be easily
categorised within the existing gender and sexual system believed to operate in the Latin American continent. This chapter attempts to theorise a
notion of queer machismo that seeks to demonstrate that queer identity
must be separated from the figuration of the homosexual or ideas of same-sex desire and, instead, can be present within those paradigms of male
behaviour that rely on a hypermasculine presentation of the self and even
borderline a caricature of masculinity. The use of the word 'machismo' as
part of the theorisation is both intentional and essential to the understanding of such a new category, because it will demonstrate that these extreme
versions of masculinity and chauvinism posit themselves outside the realm
of normative gender and sexuality. The figuration of the queer macho
may not respond to the stereotypical versions of machismo that Carlos
Alberto Montaner (2001) sees narrativised in popular cinema, folk songs
and soap operas, in which the macho is depicted as a womaniser, trouble-maker and alcoholic individual whose sense of masculinity derives from
his willingness to oppress others around him. Instead, the following pages
will examine the seemingly anachronistic characteristics of Zé do Caixão as
a character whose socio-sexual behaviour seems rather incompatible with
his own externalisation of the self.

Zé do Caixão as a Queer Macho Monster

In the horror cinema genre, monstrosity has been traditionally associated
with queer desire. As was suggested in Chap. 1, most horror narratives
tend to centre on the relationship between normality (understood as the
realm of heterosexual normative desire) and the Other (people whose
desires fall outside this realm). Monstrosity, thus, marks a sign of ethnic, racial, political, ideological, cultural and sexual difference. As Harry

Benshoff rightly comments, 'many monster movies (and the source material they draw upon) might be understood as being "about" the eruption of some form of queer sexuality into the midst of a resolute heterosexual milieu' (1997: 4). The queer monster disrupts normative sexuality because it embraces sexual ambivalence, and by doing so shakes up the pillars that sustain hegemonic heterosexuality. A small number of monsters seem to present a clear, or rather economically decipherable, gender in their pursuit of a character as a victim, as an object of desire and, in many cases, as both. However, most monsters are depicted as rather androgynous figures whose behaviour may not be all that 'compatible' with the seeming externalisation of gender that they offer. These monsters tend to be characterised by inversion and androgyny, and their physiognomy usually makes it difficult to establish their real socio-sexual nature clearly through some form or manifestation of biological gender. The queer monster is figured as a deviation from the natural order, a figure that represents social and sexual illnesses in society and externalises people's innermost fears. These fears are not merely based on the disruption of the natural social order—which in the horror narrative would be equated to perishing at the hands of the monster—but also on violating people's own assumptions of normativity.

Monsters, therefore, constitute 'powerful images of ostensibly perverse desires and fantasies [that] disorient our currently prevailing assumptions—symmetrical and pluralistic—about our own and other people's sexual orientations by bringing home to us the shapes of desires and fantasies that we ordinarily disavow as our own' (Moon 1998: 16). The queer monster in film both produces fascination and repels its audiences because it becomes the manifestation of perverse desires. Such desires may subconsciously become heavily attractive to the audience who can, at least momentarily, enjoy the pleasures of non-normative desire without questioning their own normative desires. What makes the monster queer is the fact that it operates beyond—and outside—the category/ies of normative heterosexuality and traditional gender roles. Monsters break with the symbolic order by playing out on their own bodies the fluidity of gender performance, invoking Butler (1993), whereby the monster's body becomes an externalisation of the perverse id that remains under the control of the strictures of normative society. For the male monsters, this normative disruption is visually executed through an effeminisation of their own monstrous persona. As Creed has theorised, 'ambivalence underlies the male monster's uncanny alignment with death, the animal and the maternal body—uncanny because the male symbolic order designates these areas as "other", as being outside the realm of what constitutes proper phallic masculinity' (1993a: viii). The queer monster is amorphous and ambiguous, and these two aspects make him all the more terrifying because all victims, especially male victims, always run the risk of becoming objects of his perverse desires.

Zé do Caixão manifests this ambiguity in his external appearance and behaviour, yet his own masculinity is never questioned because on the one hand, his ultimate goal is to find a perfect woman who can carry his child and preserve his lineage. On the other, he manages to outman the other men who live in his neighbourhood and who will, eventually, fail in every physical confrontation with him. However, he is more than a mere monster or a monstrous embodiment of machismo, he is a dual character that blurs the lines between purported machismo and excessive campness. Diana Anselmo-Sequeira is right to describe him as 'a small-town gravedigger by day and philosophical murderer by night' (2013: 141). Arguably, part of his Otherness (depicted in the film as excessive campness) originates in his superior intellect and his derision towards those who are not as 'enlightened' as he is. Anselmo-Sequeira highlights his otherness when she continues to describe him as a person who is 'claustrophobically entrapped by his barren surroundings as by his existential doubts, Joe is spurred by a eugenic enterprise: to engineer an offspring that will mirror his superior intellect' (2013: 141). His self-perceived intellectual superiority is theatrically externalised through his clothing, since he wears a black dinner suit, top hat and a cape at all times in what can only be perceived as a desire to appear gentlemanly. His attire becomes a reflection of his intellectual and un-Brazilian refinement, in ways that invoke images of Dracula and other popular vampire narratives. Naturally, the character seems at odds with his surroundings at all times, his costume reminiscent of that of a rather gothic vampire from the romantic period, in stark contrast to the peasantry and poverty of the rest of the characters (also evident through the mise-en-scène and the other characters' costumes). Zé will waste no time in reminding people that they will never compare to him, thus 'bloodshed, nudity, and blasphemy further punctuate Joe's recurrent diatribes against a country sedated by decades of fear, superstition, and class repression' (Anselmo-Sequeira 2013: 141).

Zé evidences the constructedness of machismo through a performance of gender and sexuality by means of machista posing. Following Sylvia Molloy, posing could be regarded as a strategy that refers to the unnamed, to the *it* or the *thing* the inscription of which [...] is posing itself; thus posing *represents*, is a significant posture. But [...] the unnamed, once named and rendered visible, may be now dismissed, in a specific Latin American context, as 'just posing'; thus posing once again represents, but this time as a masquerade, as a significant *imposture*. (1998: 151)

However, unlike Molloy's notion of posing—which she understands as intrinsic to male effeminacy (through her analysis of José Ingeniero's work)—it could be possible to assert that Zé's queer monstrosity comes from the ambiguity of his own intertextual posing. The marked contradictions between his seeming refinement (in both attire and speech) and his murderous actions reaffirm that posing is to pretend to be something while not really being it. Zé's significant imposture is clearly an affectation rather than the externalisation of his felt sexual identity. It is here that one must separate affectation from effeminacy, where queer can more unproblematically fit into the Latin American categories of gender and sexuality. It is by avoiding socio-sexual cultural stereotypes that Zé do Caixão becomes a queer macho monster, because he can cross the border that separates queer and heterosexual maleness, and by doing so widens the space in which masculinity operates without compromising or questioning his own sexual identity. This character represents an exacerbation of repressed sexual desires and, although the film does very little to place women in a less passive role within the narrative, Zé epitomises a new form of masculinity that does not need to ascribe to the Latin American macho male stereotypes of the *malandro* (scoundrel) or the *pachuco* (flashily dressed) in order to assert his own masculine identity visually.

As previously suggested, the construction of Zé do Caixão's sociosexual persona borrows elements of well-established constructions of masculinity in Latin America, as well as more caricaturised elements deriving from both comic books and other literary and visual horror narratives. This combination of caricaturised (and rather humorous) tropes and horror tropes not only queers the nature of the character, but also places it within the confines of the grotesque. The grotesque originates from the line that separates horror and humour and, as Mikhail Bakhtin argues, 'grotesque images preserve their peculiar nature, entirely different from the ready-made, completed being. They remain ambivalent and contradictory; they are ugly, monstrous, hideous from the point of view of "classic" aesthetics' (1968: 25). As will be demonstrated, Zé operates at the interstice of regulatory and non-regulatory socio-sexual practices and gender identities that use the grotesque as the mechanism to define his own identity (as will be explored in more depth later in this chapter).

Mojica Marins clearly understands the necessity to construct the character through fairly recognisable iconography in order to ascertain his evilness and his monstrosity even before he kills anyone. In an interview with the director, Karla Karina Delgado asserts that both the black top hat and the black cape were used in order to pay homage to one of Mojica Marins's favourite cartoon characters, Mandrake the Magician (2008), while it could be added that Zé's very long nails were used purposely in order to give him an air of monstrous androgyny. However, despite his rather affected and theatrical self-presentation and florid speech, his masculinity is never questioned because of his ability to yield a knife and physically overpower other men around him. Traditionally, the use of knives has been regarded as an intrinsic element of the malandro's identity and has been associated with excessive manliness, potency, masculinity and the willingness to die for one's honour. The malandro's dual identity both transgresses social codes and, at the same time, reaffirms his affiliation to socio-sexual paradigms. Lisa Shaw is right to assert that 'despite his liminal status and aptitude for transgressing conventional social boundaries, the mythical malandro was characterized, particularly in the lyrics of samba, as an inveterate womanizer and philanderer' (2007: 95). Although Zé's masculinity is not characterised by a desire to gain as many female conquests as would be deemed necessary to reaffirm his machismo, he clearly breaks with social codes as he does not regard his crimes as a disruption to the established social order.

Zé's gender identity and socio-sexual behaviour seem both to repel (based on socio-sexual paradigms of hegemonic normativity) and to conflate the notion of queer machismo. His queer machismo demonstrates that, as suggested in this chapter, there are 'ways of being men'. In these films, the narrative never casts any doubts on the protagonist's sexual desires, his choice of sexual partners or his sexual identity, but it is the conflation of his gender identity and his externalisation of his socio-sexual self that become paradigmatic in the film and blur elements of heteronormativity that are believed to be found only on the surface of the body. Mojica Marins uses the character's clothing and external appearance as a clear and powerful sign of difference. Zé's suit, cape and hat externalise his Otherness and become a visually economic means to differentiate him from other people around him. Clearly, the director has been inspired by more stereotypical images of vampirism and other gothic monsters in order to construct this character visually; however, Zé's appearance is anachronistic when compared to the other men who are in the film and who are depicted through their clothing as either peasants or lower class, in much the same way as the *pachucos* discussed by Simon Webb are 'not simply grotesque dandies parading the city's secret underworld [...] they were the "stewards of something uncomfortable," a spectacular reminder that the social order had failed to contain their energy and difference' (1999: 264).

Zé disavows the notion of hypermasculinity as a sine qua non of macho identity and uses his physical appearance to distance himself further from social normativity. Thus he makes it clear throughout the narrative that he only regards his own version of masculinity as a pure and enlightened identity and blames society for losing control of its 'proper' and real values. Furthermore, his queer machismo is also highlighted by the fact that he openly criticises some aspects of macho culture, as in the scene from *A Meia-Noite Levarei Sua Alma* in which he beats up a man who had been physically mistreating his own son. In this scene Zé finds himself on his way to the bar when he spots a man scolding his son and about to beat him. Unlike most scenes in the film, this scene is filmed outdoors and with natural light, so Zé's actions seem more heroic than horrific when he confronts the man and beats him for trying to abuse his son. The medium shot and low angle in which the action is framed only help highlight the protagonist's 'seemingly heroic' actions. It is this type of contradiction to his persona that constructs the character as queer, because he breaks with all cultural and social expectations based on his gendered self.

Zé's queer machismo remains 'othered' because he does not subscribe completely to the caricature of the macho that circulates in the Latin American popular imaginary. He proves that any deviation from traditional depictions of masculinity become too problematic within the masculine paradigm that is socially and culturally accepted as normative. This, in turn, corroborates Robert Heasley's words:

> 'traditional males,' on the one hand, are the ones society understands; even if there are problems associated with the image, there is acceptance and legitimacy accorded to the typicalness of his presentations. The 'nontraditional' male, however, presents an unknown, unfamiliar package; even if qualities the male exhibits are desirable, his difference demands justification, explanation. (2005: 311)

As a result, the character's seeming unmanliness (in appearance and behaviour) appears to clash, on the surface, with his sexual desires.

Notwithstanding his rather campy gestures and his tropicalised dandyism, his excesses of physical aggression guarantee that his unequivocal heterosexuality is never questioned. For instance, in *A Meia-Noite Levarei Sua Alma*, Zé is shown as a macho figure from the very beginning when he defies socio-religious codes by eating meat on Good Friday and mistreating his wife. The camera is always ready to present him as a grand evil character through low-angled shots and close-ups that stress his perceived superiority to other people around him. Unsurprisingly, throughout the film he commits a series of crimes against other people who either try to question his authority or become an obstacle to his plans. The camera work in most of these scenes fluctuates between long and medium shots that are reminiscent of Italian neo-realism, and then close-ups and extreme close-ups that are more characteristic of horror cinema. Indeed, throughout this film alone Zé cuts the fingers off a man against whom he plays a game of cards, forces a bar owner to commit blasphemy by eating meat on Good Friday, tries to sexually harass the bar owner's daughter and his best friend's girlfriend Terezinha (Magda Mei), kills his best friend Antônio (Nivaldo Lima) by strangling him and drowning him in a bath, rapes and beats up his own wife Lenita (Valéria Vasquez) while sadistically licking her bleeding wounds, and finally murders her by letting a tarantula fatally bite her after he realises that she cannot bear him any children. He also kills Doctor Rodolfo (Llídio Martins Simões)—who was responsible for Lenita's autopsy—by blinding him after poking his eyes out with his long nails and then burning him alive, and even uses a crown of thorns from a Christ figure that is in the bar to stab the bar owner. Cecilia Maria B. Sardenberg (1994) is right to say that 'machismo in Brazil remains institutionalized and very much alive and kicking, or better said, and "killing"'. Ironically, by the end of the narrative, the film sanctions with violence the protagonist's own violent acts.

The ambivalence of the character demonstrates not only that sexuality, sexual identity and gender identity are fluid and multiple, but also that the refinement of his intellect and behaviour, in stark contrast with the gruesomeness of the killings, demonstrates that he is constructed through 'simulations'. His entire socio-sexual persona is posed, and these simulacra of 'the brutal but cultured undertaker embodied by Mojica' (Anselmo-Sequeira 2013: 142) become a new form of seeing and understanding male relations and machismo in Brazil. He is depicted as a perversion of reality and, as Creed suggests in relation to Dracula—a figure who shares many similarities with Zé himself—is 'a figure of perverse sexuality and a changing symbol for the sexual problems of the age' (1993a: 69). The queer monster uses his monstrous persona, whether through costumes or a bodily transformation or mutation, to disguise his real self.

Carnival and the Grotesque

Undoubtedly, the figuration of Zé's onscreen persona also borrows elements of carnival, as theorised by Bakhtin, by portraying him as an ambivalent character that challenges patriarchal structures and authority while, seemingly, making fun of them. Zé is an ambivalent carnivalesque character that is both a figure of horror authority and a symbol of parodic gender reversal. This helps, somehow, explain the rapid and sudden rise to fame that Mojica Marins's character underwent during the 1960s and 1970s. In Brazil, Zé do Caixão was not simply a monstrous figure that resided as such in the popular film canon, but one that managed to filter into the popular imaginary, aided in great part by the country's carnival tradition. The cultural importance and relevance of the carnival festivity mean that Brazilians are, to a greater extent, accustomed to the idea of parodic excess as part of everyday life.

Zé do Caixão also emerged at a key moment in Brazilian history, at the height of repression during the last military dictatorship. As a result, the character could be read at the level of the symbolic to embody a set of cultural anxieties in which the theatricality and paraphernalia of his horror persona set out to criticise other figures of authority and repression represented by the junta. What is interesting about the character is that it manages to embody many of the values of repression and coercion of the military dictatorship, but from a space of irony by invoking the carnivalesque as an intrinsic manifestation of the character's persona. In this way, the notion of the carnival becomes intertwined with the everyday. Zé's world appears to be dictated and controlled by the unspoken rules of the Brazilian carnival as theorised by Lauren Langman, who comments that 'carnival expresses an alternative experience and tradition, a social history of the poor as opposed to the official history celebrated by elites in festivals of the state [...] it applauds the historical continuity and distinctiveness of the unique montage of Brazilian society' (2003: 70). Therefore, it could be suggested that the character's queer machismo is conceived as a rejection and a criticism of the machista values promoted by and through the dictatorship.

The biggest irony in the film is the use of a machista character (albeit an anti-establishment one, inasmuch as he criticises the modus operandi of the military junta) to mock the establishment itself. Zé could be regarded as a figure that breaks with authority, that rebels against patriarchal and heterohegemonic structures and, by doing so, destabilises social and gender systems. He is the ultimate carnival figure because he lives the freedom of the carnival in his everyday life. However, as will be the fate of most monsters in horror narratives, this excess will have to be contained and controlled at some point to guarantee and restore the 'normal' functioning of society. Zé, as a carnival figure, uses his grotesque body to externalise the cultural anxieties of conflicting notions of machismo through the ultimate abject body: his own. His queer machismo is abject because it is at odds with all forms of prescribed normativity; as previously discussed, his embodiment of the self is in contrast to his social surroundings. It is a sense of difference that he continuously points out during the narrative as a way to justify his own actions. His performance of macho masculinity is in contrast to other men around him not because he is seeking to contest either hypermasculinity or misogyny, but because his slightly effeminate affectation seems to contradict his purported machismo and make him a grotesque figure.

Zé do Caixão's grotesqueness operates at two distinct levels. First, his alleged cultural refinement is grotesque to the men who live in his neighbourhood—although it obviously attracts some of the girls who willingly offer themselves to be tried out in order to carry his baby—but also he is made abjectly grotesque by physical disfigurement; in this case his trademark long nails. In this way the character embodies Kristeva's idea of horror in which 'abjection is reabsorbed in the grotesque: a way of living it from the inside' (1982: 165). The long and disfigured nails are utilised as a way to externalise the character's grotesqueness. Arguably, Zé's abjection comes from within (like his nails) and continues to augment in size and evilness (like his nails) in an organic fashion as he terrorizes others around him. Unlike other monsters such as Frankenstein or even La Bruja (as analysed in Chap. 1), Zé is a monster whose evil abjection has been incorporated into his monstrous persona and they become one and the same as the narrative progresses.

Zé's monstrous queer machismo, as manifested by his monstrous persona, evidences the conflict between the proper body (one that entwines the symbolic with the political) and the abject body (regarded as monstrous). His body remains at the interstice of the human and the non-human, while his actions in the narrative posit him at the borderline of what it means to be a queer monster. In other words, what makes him all the more monstrous is the fact that his character's positionality is never clearly defined within the narrative, and he never enjoys or achieves a subject positionality that operates outside the dichotomist structures that regulate gender and sexual identity within normative culture. This idea is best explained by George E. Haggerty, who points out in his analysis of sodomy, abjection and the gothic that

> he [the monster] is made monstrous to the degree that he is unknown and unnameable. If he represents a dread and unspeakable desire [...] a desire that places him outside the family and at odds with even himself, then he also represents culture's refusal to do anything with his intense excess but identify it, reject it, and attempt to destroy it. (2006: 57)

In other words, Zé's monstrosity increases and is exacerbated by people's inability to find a clear definition of his monstrous persona. It is the slippage in the process of identity construction (as he moves from macho to queer territories rather seamlessly) that makes him all the more monstrous. He is at odds with himself also because his affectation and mannerism seem to contradict the very notion of machismo that he purports through his actions. For instance, there is a clear and rapid evolution of the character in *A Meia-Noite Levarei Sua Alma* whereby Zé goes from being a heretic (he eats meat on Good Friday), a bully (all the men in his local bar are obviously scared by his actions) and a chauvinist (he hits his wife and tries to assault his best friend's girlfriend) to becoming a serial killer. However, the real grotesque transformation of the character can be best perceived during the 'journey through hell' sequences in both *Esta Noite Encarnarei no Teu Cadaver* and *O Ritual dos Sádicos* (Awakening of the Beast, 1970).

Interestingly, despite Zé's evilness and all his murderous actions, he is portrayed as a character whose actions haunt him to the extent that, in these two films, he is tortured in a series of psychedelic, brightly coloured, nightmarish sequences in which those he has killed, and even the devil himself, come to torment him. However, in *O Ritual dos Sádicos* spectators notice a change of tone in the way the grotesque is used to strongly characterise his onscreen persona. As previously suggested, in these films, and in particular in the two sequences mentioned, Mojica Marins clearly uses the grotesque as a key element to represent both the material side of the human being and that which is more sublime; that is, his evil soul.

The inclusion of the grotesque in these films establishes the limit between two orders: the object and the human, the real and the fantastic. The grotesque in these sequences evidences a simultaneity between comedy and tragedy, as it prevents the audience from situating themselves firmly in either. Instead there will be a fluctuation between anguish and laughter, as the scenes oscillate between the tragic and the comedic.

Mojica Marins uses the grotesque in both his depiction of the main protagonist and the actual hell scenes in ways that demonstrate that 'el grotesco representa una tercera posición frente a la realidad. Comprometido con ella, expresa un mundo desquiciado, pues cree en la posibilidad de un mundo armónico. Por ello el grotesco es una de las formas más comprometidas de comunicar el mundo y el hombre' (Discépolo and Cossa 2008: 37) [the grotesque represents a third position in relation to reality. Involved with this third position, it expresses a deranged world, as it believes in the possibility of a harmonious world. Thus the grotesque is one of the most compromised means to communicate the world and mankind]. The grotesque for the director has the liminal function of allowing his villain-turned-antihero to become a dual character that audiences both abhor, pity and laugh at. Zé do Caixão represents that third position that sits outside the binaries established within heteronormativity. The grotesque is both an intrinsic element of his persona and also an experience that he undergoes at the hands of a rather psychedelic id that is visually manifested in the form of a cinematic hell.

The grotesqueness in Mojica Marins's films is stressed through the use of close-ups of the character's face, extreme close-ups of his eyes, an intense use of the zoom, a mise-en-scène that verges on expressionism—with a small degree of realism clearly influenced by *Cinema novo* and the aesthetic of hunger[4]—and a religious syncretism, with iconography from a number of religious and spiritual practices ranging from Catholicism to Santería, as well as visual elements typical of circus and gypsy cultures. This syncretic mixture of elements within the aesthetics of the films and the characters themselves could be likened to the *grotesco criollo*. Although

---

[4] *Cinema novo* emerged in Brazil in the 1960s and was characterised by a willingness to favour the social and political agenda and stories of films over their aesthetic qualities. Film directors and theoreticians emphasised the political commitment and the necessity to intellectualise filmmaking. The aesthetics of hunger derived from the ideas of cinema novo and was theorized by Glauber Rocha. In his manifesto, Rocha argues for a cinema with a documentary quality, using hand-held cameras, shot in black and white and with simple stark scenery that emphasised the harshness of the Brazilian landscape.

the *grotesco criollo* emerged in Argentinian theatre during the 1920s, it shares many characteristics with the type of grotesque that Mojica Marins depicts. Following Armando Discépolo and Roberto Cossa's analysis of the *grotesco criollo* in Argentina, it is possible to notice the following common elements between the Argentinian experience and that of Mojica Marins. First, the main protagonist is depicted as foreign while his name is intrinsically related to his profession. Although Zé do Caixão is not foreign by nationality, his affectation and the way he is depicted show a marked national and even regional otherness when contrasted to his contemporaries. He obviously does not belong to the rural environment in which the action develops in the first two films, nor is he embracing any form of known or stereotypical 'Brazilianness'. Furthermore, the name 'Caixão' (coffin) relates to his job as undertaker and to the object that he uses to bury people in. In this way, aspects of the grotesque are made tangible through naming and are hyperbolically visible to the audience even before they see the character commit a crime or witness a grotesque act.

Secondly, the dramatic construction of the narrative centres on the final agony of the hero. Although the protagonist is not constructed or intended to be regarded as a hero per se, the way in which the narrative focuses on his plight and psychological suffering forces viewers to sympathise with him in a manner akin to the suffering of the traditional hero figure. Finally, the story is usually set in the suburbs or outskirts of a big metropolis. Interestingly, in the first two films the action takes place just outside São Paulo, but by the third film of the trilogy, this suburb has been absorbed into the city and has become a shantytown outside the main urban periphery. The shantytown itself is made grotesque by its (d)evolution into a run-down, more violent and impoverished area of the city. Alongside these elements, the grotesqueness of the protagonist's body is accentuated by his unkempt and overgrown beard and his extremely long nails. Through such tropes, the character reinforces genre expectations that have as their ultimate goal to foster the audience's identification with cruelty and repression. Spectators see the grotesque as the uncanny combination of man and monster, and the director plays with his audience's expectations as they struggle to reconcile the character as either purely evil or partly victim.

The Grotesque and the Underworld

In all these films, the director utilises aspects of the grotesque to externalise the estranged world that exists in the protagonist's psyche, one that operates as a reflection of his evil and dark id. The film visually represents the repressed (that terrain within the id that is separated from the ego by a barrier of resistance), evidenced in the breaking of the filmic conventions of expressionism and gothic genre that dominates during the black-and-white section of the narrative and, instead, moves to the terrain of the psychedelic and the plain surrealist in the Dolby-colour section of the film. In these sequences the director opts for much wider takes, and abandons the close-ups in favour of medium and long shots. Hell is now a world of cavernous and brightly coloured walls and texturised surfaces that resemble human guts made out of fabric. There are white cavern tops, shown in low angle, on which human limbs and human heads bleed to death; this is clearly a vision of hell in which bright reds and yellows predominate. In this world Zé do Caixão is no longer the only embodiment of grotesqueness, but a subject who is also made abject through his difference and his alleged suffering in this estranged underworld.

The underworld does not follow the filmic conventions that have characterised these films thus far: the use of close camera shots, low angles, a prevalence of darkness and excessive use of chiaroscuro, which have helped create an atmosphere of terror. Instead, these sequences depict a rather comic or tragicomic version of hell and suffering. At a key moment in one of the sequences, Zé stumbles into a cave in which three people are cemented up to their knees in pedestals and are being tortured by a red, muscled demon. The scene is shown in a wide shot with a slight left tilt, a bare-breasted woman depicted sideways on the foreground, while in the background the demon approaches the first of the three penitent souls and stabs him in the chest with a trident. As he does so, the man raises his hands and waves in pain while screaming loudly. The scene cuts to a low-angle, medium shot of Zé as he observes the events unfold and then walks further into the cave. As he does so, the camera is positioned to the right showing other penitents being punished, then follows Zé in a pan left as he is also stabbed by the demon he passes. It is hard to see this scene, and similar others, as terrifying or scary because the use of psychedelia breaks with the tropes of horror commonly found in gothic or horror films.

By including this type of scene, the director demonstrates that the grotesque, as formulated by Wilson Yates in his study of Wolfgang Kayser's work, entails the 'fusion of realms which we know to be separated, the abolition of the law of status, the loss of identity, the distortion of "natural" sign and shape, the suspension of the category of objects, the destruction of personality, and the fragmentation of the historical order'

(1997: 17). As such, the inclusion of these sequences within the narrative permits a contrast of different realms, one a horror-fantasy realm and the other a horror-reality realm, which may well overlap but never become one. Therefore, the narrative operates in a two-dimensional reality for the protagonist. For instance, in the first sequence Zé's status (as a murderous killer) is eroded to the extent that he is no longer in control of the narrative action, but becomes haunted and physically punished by the people he has killed; although the narrative makes it clear that this sequence is only a nightmare. Victimising Zé in these sequences makes audiences aware of a distortion of the natural sign and shape of the character's narrative scope. He becomes more vulnerable, and this mixture of evil and vulnerability makes him a more grotesque and incongruous character as the director plays with the audience's expectations on matters of identification within the horror genre. In other words, familiar and natural signs and behaviours are turned on their head to become strange and ominous. This sequence and the one in *O Ritual dos Sádicos* epitomise the grotesqueness in the films, since they both show absurdity and madness as intrinsic elements of reality. Rather than suggesting a rupture between reality and fantasy (horror fantasy, to be more precise), the films simply acknowledge a multilayered reality in which absurdity and madness can become part of the everyday. The absurd in these films evidences the impossibility of meaning in the actions and suffering of the protagonist; there is no greatness in the hero; and, instead, the absurd and the experiences of the protagonist suggest madness as a paradigm.

If, as Yates suggests, 'the final premise of the grotesque is an attempt to invoke and subdue the demonic aspects of the world' (1997: 18), then it is possible to see how the films, and especially the sequences under analysis, provide cinematic form to such demonic aspects. However, these versions of hell are not as horrific or terrifying as the other sequences in the films in which Zé actually commits his crimes. They operate as smokescreens of the gore and killings witnessed throughout the story. The vulnerability that the character shows while walking through hell seems incongruous compared to the evil shown when he has been physically violent to others around him. Once again, the purported hypermasculinity of the character is heavily contrasted with the way in which he is presented on screen. Despite his violent outbursts and his sexist demeanour, while walking through hell he portrays himself in a non-masculine way by the popular Brazilian standard. In these sequences, the queerness of the character is highlighted by the refinement of his black silk pyjamas in contrast with the semi-naked, decomposing bodies of the penitents who inhabit hell. Thus it is possible to argue that in Mojica Marins's films, audiences experience a counter form of the *criollo grotesco* in which there is a constant tension between the moral codes and social standards of the main characters. Ultimately, Zé do Caixão is constructed as a morally and socially failed character, yet he is also provided with an ambiguous physical space within the narrative in which he is no longer fully demonised. Claudia Kaiser-Lenoir claims that in the traditional *criollo grotesco* 'los personajes aquí se convierten en grotescos por el choque constante entre su interioridad sensible y la realidad externa que los dehumaniza' (1977: 62) [characters become grotesque through the constant clash between their sensitive interior self and a external reality that seeks to dehumanise them]. However, it is Zé himself who dehumanises his own immediate reality by performing murderous acts while, it could be argued, his journey-through-hell sequences actively seek to rehumanise him. This is also cinematically achieved through a grotesque version of reality created by the syncretic mixing of elements of mise-en-scène pertinent to very specific film genres other than horror.

As has already been suggested, these films borrow stylistic elements of Italian neo-realism, expressionism and surrealism to depict a multilayered reality in which fantasy, horror and the politicisation of the cinematic image appear to be, at times, intertwined. Mojica Marins does not seem to, nor does he apparently feel he ought to, adhere to any specific filmic convention, as he creates a world in which there is a metamorphosis of reality. This juxtaposition of styles and cinematic conventions makes his films all the more grotesque because such depictions defy logical explanation (within the narrative) as well as the audience's interpretation. There are three apparent narrative layers that can be identified in the Coffin Joe films. First, audiences see sequences with an abundance of long, static shots, a reliance on natural lighting, and real-life settings that provide an insight into the socio-economic conditions and harsh reality of the people living in the suburbs of Rio de Janeiro where the action takes place. Secondly, the action moves to indoor spaces in which the mise-en-scène becomes more theatrical with the presence of crucifixes, candlesticks, religious and profane iconography and camera work that relies on close medium and close shots, low angles, cast shadows and chiaroscuro to provide a rather gothic feeling to such scenes. These grotesque juxtapositions can also be found in the character himself, as has been suggested, since, as Lucio dos Reis rightly points out, o próprio Zé do Caixão e uma representação desse sincretismo, uma mistura de Exu—a quem certamente remete com a sua postura desafiadora e anárquica—com conde Drácula, com sua barba cerrada, capa preta, cartola e unhas compridas. Poderíamos até afirmar que se o Diabo existisse, no Brasil se vestiria daquele modo. (2002: 187)

[Ze do Caixão himself is a representation of [Brazilian] syncretism, a mixture of Exu—whom he certainly delivers through his anarchic and defying posture—with Count Dracula, with his tight beard, his black cape, top hat and long nails. It could be suggested that if the Devil really existed, in Brazil he would dress in this fashion]

Despite the character's numerous diatribes criticising and overtly rejecting his Brazilian origins, Zé continues to use elements of Brazilian culture to recreate his monster persona. It is this type of 'Dracula *criollo*' that arguably appeals to audiences because, on the one hand, it offers a new version of masculinity and, on the other, it dares to point out those aspects of Brazilian culture and national figures of authority (through a direct criticism of the dictatorship) that may not be regarded as progressive.

Mojica Marins's visions of hell certainly reappropriate elements of carnival while further queering the character of Zé do Caixão. Halfway through the last hell sequence there is a moment where the carnivalesque and grotesque nature of the character is brought to the forefront of the narrative, while also highlighting the queer nature of the monster character. As Zé continues to wander around hell, shown in medium shots, he comes to a point in which he is confronted by the devil himself (played also by Mojica Marins as Zé do Caixão). In a scene that could, in some ways, be regarded as a precursor to Federico Fellini's *Satiricon* (1969), Zé's devil persona is framed through a medium shot as he sits on a throne dressed in a rather luxurious Roman-style gown, his head adorned with a crown of laurels, surrounded by naked women as he eats grapes from a bunch resting in his hand. The montage of the split image between the two versions of Zé serves to contrast two aspects of the character's psyche and to demonstrate that, as Bakhtin argues, 'the grotesque body [...] is a body in the act of becoming. It is never finished, never completed; it is continually built, created, and builds and creates another body. Moreover, the body, swallows the world and is itself swallowed by the world' (1968: 317). Zé's body is in a continuous reinvention of the self and in the first two films seems to be in search of a clear identity that allows him to demonstrate his felt superiority. His version of queer masculinity defies the machismo that predominates in Brazilian society, while his body operates as a site of ambivalence without necessarily threatening his gender or sexual identity. His body becomes anti-normative because it does not adhere to the images of masculinity that circulate in the cultural imaginary. The materialisation of the grotesqueness of the character's body shows the fluidity of sexuality and gender in contemporary culture. This is achieved by demonstrating that the seemingly rigid templates of sexuality and gender that operate in machista societies can easily be disavowed by a figure like Zé who destabilises gender and sexual norms.

Zé in the Popular Consciousness

By the time of the release of *O Ritual dos Sádicos* in 1970, Zé do Caixão had become established in the Brazilian cultural imaginary as a national monster, to the extent that this one film combines a rather unapologetic meta-textual relationship between horror genre, drug culture and the cultural legacy of Mojica Marins's work in Brazilian society. *O Ritual dos Sádicos* is, perhaps, one of his most irreverent films, with a seemingly disjointed storyline that only makes sense towards the end of the narrative with the inclusion of Zé do Caixão as a narrative thread to a number of individual stories. The film is made up a number of vignettes showing drug-fuelled, sexually deviant aspects of Brazilian culture in the 1960s while, at the same time, a group of intellectuals on television debate the devastating effects of drugs in Brazilian society. Almost an hour into the film, the storyline moves to four different people who volunteer to take part in an experiment led by a psychiatrist (Ronaldo Beibe) in which the four are dosed with LSD and then examined as they trip on the drug and while having visions of Zé do Caixão. It is only at this point in the narrative that Zé becomes part of the story, as he shows every volunteer a different version of a psychedelic hell that resembles the one found in the previous film. Interestingly, this time both the penitent souls found in hell and the four volunteers are represented as grotesque bodies in ways that suggest, as Lilian Craton points out in relation to the Victorian freak show, that 'images of the grotesque body—characterized by extremes of size, contradiction, and emphasis on bodily orifices—encourage a fluid exchange between normative ideas in a culture and the varied, often non-ideal human beings who test such expectations against their own lives' (2009: 20). *O Ritual dos Sádicos* could be regarded as Mojica Marins's most grotesque film, inasmuch as he rids the film of any realist aesthetics and, instead, shows a preference for more expressionist and surrealist imagery. The film pays voyeuristic attention, through an intense use of close-ups and zoom-ins, to the characters' body crevices, their lacerated bodies, wounds and other orifices caused by substance abuse and/or sadomasochistic sexual practices.

Furthermore, the film sets out to queer the filmic gaze in ways that resonate with Haggerty's assertion that what is meant 'by "queer" is odd, strange, and uncanny, but as several critics have argued the term could also resonate with a hint of transgressive sexuality' (2006: 134–135). Despite the fact that this film does not follow Zé as the main character in the narrative, he becomes the driving force within it who has the power of queering the grotesque. Returning to a premise suggested at the beginning of this chapter, queer has to be understood beyond same-sex desire and be open to encompassing an incomprehensible force that cannot be easily identified, but operates as the objectification of the id. Queer transgresses and operates outside the norm; it is indefinable and yet easy to recognise. *O Ritual dos Sádicos* epitomises Zé do Caixão as an established element of a 'queer' Brazilian cultural imaginary by depicting him as part of a queer national id.

The moments of intertextuality in the film greatly corroborate this idea. Throughout, the vignettes are often interrupted by short sequences in which Mojica Marins (as himself) participates in a roundtable with two other men (a journalist and the psychiatrist who will eventually lead the experiment). The scenes are filmed through close medium shots, and in a very strong chiaroscuro that barely permits the viewer to discern the participants. These sequences both disrupt the different narratives and provide a glimpse into the aftermath of the film itself, as the participants discuss the implications and consequences of the experiment carried out on the four patients with LSD and the impact that the figure of Zé do Caixão had on their drug-fuelled experiences. The director is both aware of and wants to stress the important position that his fictional creation enjoys within the national cultural imaginary as a horror myth. Zé do Caixão is constructed as a key element of the national horror canon and, as Anselmo-Sequeira argues, 'Mojica had been catapulted into a controversial spotlight: From obscure director-for-hire he had become a national celebrity, the personification of Brazilian nightmares. The protagonist of *At Midnight*, Coffin Joe—the brutal but cultured undertaker embodied by Mojica—had struck a cultural nerve' (2013: 142).

The inclusion of Zé as part of the national horror imaginary queers Brazilian culture, because the character himself rejects the type of horror masculinity that is found in other characters of the national horror folklore, such as the *homen marinho* (merman), *jaracara* (vampire snake), *besta-fera* (centaur devil) or even *Boto* (an enchanted dolphin that shapeshifts into a handsome man to seduce women). Instead, his horror persona is an amalgamation of Western horror images, particularly early film versions of Dracula and Nosferatu or, as Gustavo Dahl states, 'Zé do Caixão e um personagem que veio para ficar, tanto assim que parece ter existido desde sempre. Visão interiorana do demônio, cartola, barba, longas unhas, lúbrico, perverso, estamos diante de um diabo brasileiro, circense' (cited in Ferreira 2000: 87) [Zé do Caixão is a character that came to stay, so much so that it seems like he has always existed. Face of a demon, top hat, beard, long nails, lustful, perverse, we find ourselves facing a Brazilian circus devil]. It is this circus-like quality that makes the character grotesque, because it combines elements of the fantastic within everyday reality: caricature, satire, tragicomedy, the bizarre and the macabre. However, it is not Zé's appearance that makes him more monstrous, since this circus-like appearance can easily relate to carnival festivities and to the carnival as part of the everyday in Brazilian culture. Zé becomes a means of representing those aspects of macho culture that constitute a caricature of masculinity. His external appearance simply gives a tangible aspect to the macho culture he seeks to criticise. What makes his appearance and behaviour queer is the ability to give aesthetic form to the subversion of such a retrograde template of sexuality. Zé's body constitutes the site of becoming; it is a body that points to the fluidity of sex and gender, a body that outgrows its own self and transgresses its own limits. It is a body in constant evolution and transformation that garners at its centre a social critique of what being a man constitutes in such a machista country.

Zé do Caixão is a queer macho monster because the character is constructed and routinely positioned in stark opposition to what would be considered normative. His physical presence and horrific actions transgress heteronormative gender and sexuality by offering a presentation of the self that breaks with established codes of gender performativity. Meanwhile, by committing bloody crimes he carries the marks of abjection, as he operates outside the borders of what is socially, morally and even legally acceptable. During the 1960s, and as a result of the popularity the character achieved among Brazilian audiences, he was also considered a subversive element that stood in direct opposition to the ultra-conservative values imposed by the military junta in the late 1960s. It is well documented that Mojica Marins was detained, interrogated and even incarcerated for short periods as a direct result of his portrayal of Zé do Caixão. By the same token, his cinema also opposed the aesthetic and socially militant values of *Cinema novo* in ways that validated 'him not as merely exploitative exercise in guts and gore, but as a discerning social critique of a country in crisis' (Anselmo-Sequeira 2013: 143). The work of Mojica Marins became part of the emergent *Cinema do lixo*[5] (trash cinema) in Brazil that sought to move away from the aesthetic principles that *Cinema novo* promoted.

By the early 1960s the character of Zé do Caixão had already permeated the popular consciousness through the horror magazine *O Estranho Mundo de Zé do Caixão* (The strange world of Zé do Caixão). This photo-comic was a joint effort of Rubens Francisco Luchetti and José Mojica Marins and was characterised by horror narratives set in typically Brazilian urban and rural scenarios. Thus it is not surprising that by the time Zé do Caixão made it onto the big screen, there existed a fairly well-established following for both the character and the movies among the Brazilian population. This fame was only catapulted further by the time of the cinematic releases. Mojica Marins's films became hugely successful (*A Meia-Noite Levarei Sua Alma* was shown in São Paulo for 16 months) and Zé do Caixão became an instant and core element of the Brazilian horror canon. Indeed, the character had struck a chord in a national narrative that saw normativity and repression as one and the same. The anti-normative nature of the character responded only too well to a historical moment in which the Brazilian population was eagerly awaiting someone who could stand against the normative values imposed by the military government, even if this person was himself a murderous killer. Unsurprisingly, as Dolores Tierney suggests, Mojica Marins was the most censored film director in Brazil during the years of military rule and 'his films were perceived as a radical threat to the military authoritarianism which then ensued and, potentially, that the avant-garde *cinema do lixo* and the more commercial and mainstream Cinema Novo was not' (2009: 121).

---

[5] *Cinema do lixo* was a type of cinema that emerged after the dissolution of *Cinema novo* (towards the end of the 1960s) and lasted approximately three years. It enjoyed a clandestine existence due to the desire of filmmakers, but also due to the obstacles for distribution and censorship that prevailed in Brazil at the time. Paulo Emilio Salles Gomes regards this type of cinema as proposing 'an anarchistic culture [that] tends to transform the populace into rabble, the colonized into trash. This degraded sub-world, traversed by grotesque processions, condemned to the absurd, mutilated by crime, sex, and exploitation, hopeless and fallacious, is, however, animated and redeemed by its inarticulate wrath' (1997: 269)

The misogynistic tone of Mojica Marins's films is evidenced through the exploitation of the female form for the benefit of the male gaze, the many instances of female nudity, as well as the exploitative nature of the eroticisation of the female body. However, the character of Zé do Caixão continues to be constructed as quintessentially queer because in his quest to find the perfect female partner, he does not embody more vernacular and normative versions of masculinity. Thus not finding anyone to father his son will leave him incomplete as a man. As much as the films disavow the notion of machismo by using an affected but hyperviolent figure as its ultimate critic, they also deconstruct the figure of the monster by presenting Zé do Caixão as a queer monster whose libidinal desires remain too othered to be clearly understood within the orbit of a single heterosexual and even homosexual desire. The queer macho monster's libidinous desires are relative, and it is the uncertainty of where these desires may lie that makes the monster all the more monstrous. Despite Zé's obsession with finding the perfect woman to bear his child, and the objectification to which he subjects many of the women with whom he comes into contact, he remains somewhat unambiguous about his true sexual desires. His is a sexually deviant body that confuses gender, sexuality and desire. As has been already argued, he is ambiguous in his presentation of the self, and even more ambiguous about his ability to pleasure women. Although the storylines in most of the films centre on his impossible quest to find the perfect woman to bear him offspring and begin a generation of 'superior' beings that carry his 'superior' genes, doubts are clearly cast over his ability to please these women sexually. As a result, it could be argued that his sadistic killings are also the result of his frustration to live up to a masculine ideal. In this light, Zé's queer monstrosity, as Rhona Berenstein suggests,

> propose[s] a paradigm of sexuality in which eros and danger, sensuality and destruction, human and inhuman, and male and female blur, overlap, and coalesce. In this schema sexuality and identity remain murky matters, steeped in border crossings and marked by fuzzy boundaries. Thus classic horror may invoke existing definitions of sexuality, but the genre embellishes them with perversions that defy and exceed traditional categories of human desire. (1995: 27)

The ambiguity of the character disavows the construction of machismo as a template of male sexuality in Brazil, and by extension the continent. However, the character also operates as a counter-hero, because he opposes the forces of the patriarchal order (both within and outside the diegesis) that are revealed to be the real villains. This ambiguity also becomes an asset in the construction of the character's sexual persona, as it makes him, arguably, more attractive to all those female subjects who, deep inside, may reject mariana identity.[6] His counter-masculinity is queered because it shows fluid alternatives and interpretations of masculinity that are traditionally rejected in machista societies.

CONCLUSION

Judith Halberstam has famously theorised the notion of 'technologies of monsters' (1995) as the cultural processes whereby society makes use of the figure of the monster as a site that recognizes the fallibility of, and challenges, normative assumptions about corporeality. Monsters attain and constitute meaning by being 'remarkably mobile, permeable, and infinitely interpretable' (1995: 21). As a result, the figure of the monster in popular culture, and more specifically the monster in horror cinema, has a long tradition of pointing out the possible interpretations and assumptions of gender and sexuality and the real fissures existing in such categories, as they show the impossibility of gender and sexual fixity. The monster can be regarded, as Elizabeth Stephens suggests, as 'an inherently empty cultural category into which the changing anxieties that characterise its various historical and cultural contexts can be projected' (2012: 171). The figure of the monster in horror cinema can be regarded as symptomatic of the slow transitions or changes in attitude with regard to sexuality and gender at a specific historical moment. The monster operates as the visual metaphor for cultural anxieties and as the vehicle to channel those anxieties in ways that allow audiences to deal effectively with those issues.

In the Brazilian context, José Mojica Marins's Zé do Caixão has become the quintessential monster figure by permeating the cultural imagination of the nation to transform and influence people's ideas about the relationship between sexuality and monstrosity. A hybrid monstrous figure, the cinematic onscreen construction of Zé's persona is clearly influenced by

[6] This rejection of mariana identity is best shown in the character of Laura (Tina Wohlers) in *Esta Noite Encarnarei no Teu Cadaver*, who defiantly opposes her father (an army colonel) in order to become Zé's partner. The way she rejoices at the tortures to which she is subjected in order to prove her worth, as well as the way she encourages Zé to commit evil crimes, clearly contradicts the predicates of mothering and nurturing that make up the basis of mariana identity.

other iconic horror characters from the horror cycles of Universal Studios in the 1930 and 1940s. Visually, he presents similarities with the vampire figure: a formal suit, wearing black from head to toe—including the cape—and his long nails, as well as his air of superiority in relation to the superstitions of the people in his service in the rural village below his castle. Despite the clearly Brazilian and rather humble setting of the films, the interior of Zé's house clearly borrows elements of traditional horror narratives and resembles the traditional gothic castle. The mise-en-scène is marked by strange sculptures of arms and hands emerging from the walls together with stuffed animals, as well as other horror tropes such as mysterious winds that blow curtains, ghostly voices that echo through corridors, paintings whose false eyes permit spying on other people, and rooms with secret passages that lead to a concealed room that serves as either dungeon or laboratory.

The director shows a preference for ambiguity in many aspects of his films. For instance, his creation is a pastiche of the classic horror cinema monster, political and social satire, and a direct reaction to the postulates of Brazilian cinema and militant and guerrilla cinema (these were still heavily influenced by Italian neo-realism). However, one of the merits of Mojica Marins's films is that they manage to adapt classic horror cinema clichés to the Brazilian reality (a tropicalisation of tropes), without having 'faithfully' to imitate the Hollywood or European models. For instance, this is evident in the religious syncretism that can be observed in the house of the gypsy witch (Eucaris de Morais) in the first film of the trilogy, where Catholic iconography operates in unison with elements of *candomblé* and *macumba*. The director intended a product that could be both easily recognisable by horror fans worldwide (through the insertion of elements of the mise-en-scène that were typical of the genre) and also had a clearly Brazilian tone that would greatly appeal to national audiences. The presence of fantastic elements within the narrative is also intrinsic to these films, since the character takes every opportunity to defy the dogmas of the Catholic religion, but also questions any other beliefs or superstitions. Furthermore, although the sequences in hell previously analysed would be a testimony to the contrary, the character is also presented as the ultimate apostate because he does not believe in any other superior being but himself. In a way, Zé do Caixão embodies the ultimate revolutionary figure because he questions the religious, social and sexual status quo of Brazilian society in an attempt to demonstrate that many of the paradigms that govern socio-sexual subjects in that society are simply outdated.

The character differs from most classic horror monsters because he does not originate from the world of the supernatural, but is in direct conflict with that world.

By the same token, the notions of masculinity explored in these films follow the same syncretic pattern, whereby there is a clear criticism of the macho ideology that circulates in the popular socio-sexual imaginary and the notions of masculinity found elsewhere. As Beattie suggests,

> machismo shapes how Latin societies have been perceived by outsiders and how many Latin Americans describe their own society in relation to others. The term has been widely adapted as a reference point for describing sometimes favorable but mostly offensive behaviors associated with male abuse of sanctioned social prerogatives. (2002: 303)

Machismo as an exaggerated stereotype is continually questioned, challenged and revisited in these films through a monstrous being whose onscreen persona clearly defies the type of macho masculinity that circulates in the popular imaginary. He offers an anti-normative version of masculinity that rejects all known categories of gender and sexuality as they operate in Brazilian, and by extension Latin American, culture. Although it could be argued that his behaviour towards women and the objectification to which they are subjected at his hands constitutes one of the most prevalent features of macho ideology, it cannot be denied that his mere presence also shakes the foundations of machismo itself, because he does not fit so readily into such a category. Thus an in-depth analysis of the character's own version of masculinity is necessary to understand and challenge the existing notions of machismo that operate in Latino cultures. The character's body becomes the outlet where social and personal identity are merged and through which the performance of gender roles is executed via various body parts and bodily articulations. It is through Zé's body that culturally prescribed gender norms are examined.

Throughout this chapter it has been suggested that the version of masculinity that is performed by the character of Zé do Caixão refers to what could be labelled queer macho monstrosity. His articulation of masculinity has been dissected into three specific areas: the meaning of monstrosity within notions of masculinity, the construction of macho identity in the Brazilian milieu and, finally, the effects of the queering of both identities. This idea reifies Chris Girman's idea that 'examining the macho body is the most effective manner to determine the substance, effect, and recalcitrance of machismo gendered norms' (Girman 2004: 110). This queering of the macho monster occurs by a disruption of the macho order, whereby Mojica Marins's murderous protagonist destabilises gender norms by his ability to pick and choose those aspects of prescribed masculinity that best suit his idea of the self, even when those chosen aspects are in stark contradiction to the socially accepted notions of macho identity. Thus his body becomes a site of contestation in which his elaborate and affected verbal and physical posturing, his murderous actions and his desire to be a father demonstrate that male identity is not fixed, and that the performance of gender simply constitutes a tool deployed to guarantee social acceptance in a specific context while questioning its supposedly fixity. Zé do Caixão's queer macho monstrosity resists and transgresses heteronormative sexualities and genders and through hypermasculine behaviour (externalised through physical violence and terror) and the hypersexualisation of his own persona (as he offers himself as the object of desire for women), he destabilises machismo as a masculine template. His onscreen persona breaches the archaic laws that govern the boundaries between normative and anti-normative genders, sexualities and desires.

Zé's queer macho monstrosity eroticises a set of negative stereotypes by distancing the identities from their normal social power; that is to say, his onscreen persona criticises mainstream masculinity while it also criticises traditional monster narratives as they circulate in the popular imaginary. What is interesting about these films is that the strong rejection and critique of mainstream masculinity are achieved not by opposing or criticising such behaviour, but by exaggerating it. The notion of monstrous queer machismo advanced by these films reaffirms that through the rejection of heteronormative mainstream masculinity, and yet the continued adherence to certain masculine traits of dominance and aggression, the queer macho monster reinterprets masculinity by disavowing purported masculinity itself. The films do not intend to offer an alternative form of masculinity that opposes macho attitudes, nor do they try to get the audience to feel empathetic towards the main protagonist. Zé is not presented as a hero, but his queer macho monstrosity can be read as the rejection of heterosexual mainstream masculinity through the continued adherence to and exaggerated performance of certain masculine traits of dominance and aggression. He reinterprets masculinity and establishes how machismo constitutes a performance of masculinity that is neither fixed nor inherently equal for all males.

To reinforce further the notion of fluidity that accompanies the character's identity, the director makes use of the grotesque as an inherent characteristic of his persona. Throughout the films, the world of Zé do Caixão is presented as a carnival of horrors in which, through the camera work of the tortures and murders he commits, spectators are exposed to an alternative version of reality that seeks to challenge the ruling of the 'elites'. This vision of reality combines the comic and the playful with the fearful and creates a counter-reality in which the superiority of the protagonist is reinforced through his narrative position and stressed by the camera's point of view. Zé must be understood as a monster created through a metonymy of horror. His monstrosity is built on elements of the macabre that are designed to cause repulsion: coffins, cemeteries, spiders and snakes, the disfigured helper, stuffed animals and the images of hell. This evidences feelings of repulsion that do not necessarily originate from the character himself, but from the macabre elements that surround him.

Unlike other horror narratives, Mojica Marins's films do not devote any diegetic space to the development of any other character but Zé himself, and although resolution, within the expectations of the genre, is achieved (Zé is ultimately punished in every film), spectators do not get to see the process whereby this resolution comes into being or get a sense of character development for any other figure within the story. What makes Zé do Caixão all the more interesting as a queer macho monster is that he is constructed within the narrative as a natural, rather than supernatural, character. He is a man who is an actual victim of the supernatural, a man who oozes all the evil that exists within him without the need for metaphors to confront his gender or sexuality openly. The character clearly alternates between a disrupting evilness and moments of calm rationality that give him a dual identity. Zé is a monster whose impurity does not reside in his physical appearance, but in his association with macabre elements that build a metonymy of horror. This, in turn, is cinematically conveyed in order to instil terror in the audience through repulsion.

In short, Zé do Caixão is not a Brazilian copy of the traditional monsters found in Hollywood or European horror narratives, but an authentic horror character whose originality can be demonstrated when compared to other such characters. He not only disrupts classic horror narratives, he also evidences a desire to challenge and question the fixity of male templates of sexuality and gender by offering a version of masculinity that clearly breaks with the rigidity of machismo. His queer macho monstrosity illustrates that masculinity is ambiguous, multiple and open to interpretation, and that the constructedness of masculinity within Brazilian culture has to be understood beyond such strict parameters.

CHAPTER 3

Monstrous Machos: Horror and the Crisis of Latin American Masculinity

Since the advent of cinema in Latin America the figure of the macho, in his many manifestations, has played a key role in the way in which this template of masculinity circulates in the continental imaginary, as has been previously suggested and as has been theorised elsewhere (Subero 2014). Machismo, as the expression of a monolithic notion of hypermasculinity, has been embedded in Latin American cinema through an array of cinematic male figures who have, at different historical times, both perpetuated and, in more recent decades, even contested such an image. During the Golden Age of Latin American cinema (from the 1930s to the mid-1950s) the presence of male singers-turned-actors such as Carlos Gardel in Argentina and Pedro Infantes in Mexico heavily influenced the way in which machismo was understood and perceived. These images of masculinity were not necessarily homogeneous, thus helping to fuel and circulate different versions of machismo in the continental social and popular imagination. For instance, Carlos Gardel's image

> posee un atractivo sexualmente irrealizable; tiene una marcada faceta de *gigoló*, en tanto que sabe valerse de su imagen para conseguir aquello que pretende de las damas; su excesivo cuidado físico le hace caer en el narcisismo; se muestra como el prototipo de 'macho seductor' pero desde una posición de insinuado afeminamiento. (Luengo López 2008: 23)
>
> [possesses an unachievable sexual attractiveness: he has the marked facet of a gigolo, since he can use his own image to obtain what he wants from

women. His excessive physical care makes him appear slightly narcissistic. He shows himself as the prototype of a 'male seducer', but from a position of suggested effeminacy]

On the other hand, the image that Pedro Infantes portrays in his films 'signifies a radical departure from the dominant image of the aggressive, arrogant, *criollo* (Mexican-born but of 'white' Spanish ancestry), upper-class Mexicans [...] Infantes represents a positive machismo' (de la Mora 2006: 80). However, regardless of the type of machismo that different actors present, these versions of a purported Latin American masculinity continue to project and reinforce gendered images that are already in circulation in the popular imaginary; images in which a real macho possesses, or at least claims to possess, invincibility, while he also showcases his sexual prowess and conquests. He utilises fathering as a visual token of such sexual prowes and shows an excessive valour evidenced by a willingness to engage in physical violence in order to assert his *hombría*.

Although such archaic notions of machismo (as paradigms of male sexuality in contemporary Latin American culture) are nowadays vastly contested, it is undeniable that they continue to be regarded, culturally, as the templates through which masculinity is measured and (re)assessed. The filmic images of machismo that originated during the 1940s and 1950s would later infiltrate and be perpetuated in the popular imaginary with the advent and popularisation of telenovelas in the continent, even though such images may now be regarded somewhat as caricatures of masculinity. More contemporary filmic depictions of machismo have sought to challenge such backward and vernacular notions. They have opted to provide images that reaffirm a more socially inclusive type of masculinity and do not fall into a caricature of male chauvinism. Charles Ramírez Berg rightly asserts in relation to Mexican cinema—and this is something that can easily be applied to most Latin American cinema—that '[m]en have been no less affected by the sexual revolution, and their screen image and role in society [are] in crisis as well [...] Machismo has been shattered, leaving the Mexican male scurrying desperately about for an appropriate role model to take its place' (1989: 179). This is evidenced in recent box-office hits such as *Amores Perros* (Alejandro Gonzalez Iñárritu, 2000), *Y Tu Mamá También* (Alfonso Cuarón, 2001) and *Rudo y Cursi* (Carlos Cuarón, 2008),[1] in which the types of macho famously discussed by

---

[1] Although not within the scope of this chapter, it is interesting to see how all these films have Gael Garcia Bernal playing protagonic roles and operating as the emblem of the new

Rolando Andrade (1992) are revisited and deconstructed in order to open a space of dialogue between the stereotypical images of machismo offered in mainstream culture and the changing realities of men in contemporary Latin American society. As Carlos Alberto Montaner has rightly theorised,

> el 'macho'—a juzgar por los corridos, el cine popular o los culebrones televisivos—es un tipo mujeriego, pendenciero y amante del alcohol, que lo mismo se lía a tiros que a trompadas por defender su territorio de varón dominante. Odia a los homosexuales y de ellos se burla mediante chistes procaces—muy populares en la cultura iberoamericana—que también sirven para subrayar la hombría de quien los cuenta. (2001: 107–108)
> [the macho man—according to folk songs, popular cinema or soap operas—is a womaniser, troublemaker and loves alcohol, who will easily get into a gun or fist fight to defend his territory as a dominant male. He hates homosexuals and makes fun of them through lewd jokes—very popular in the Iberoamerican culture—that also serve to stress the manliness of those who tell them]

Montaner is quick to signal that this description merits little sociological and anthropological recognition, as it merely offers a caricature of masculinity as a sexual template. However, this type of machismo continues to be used as a recurrent trope in many films dealing with Latin American masculinity since, as Rudolfo Anaya signals, '[machismo] is essentially a learned behavior; as such it is a conditioned behavior. We males learn to act in a "manly" way from other males around us; the "macho" that preceded us was learned from the cultures from which it evolved' (1996: 59).

Therefore, and as already suggested in Chap. 2, machismo could be regarded as a natural quality of the male monster figure. In many horror features, the monster embodies all the negative aspects of human civilisation and attacks against the very pillars that sustain normative society. As Barbara Creed suggests, 'the male monster is familiar yet unfamiliar, a monstrous creature that is male and phallic yet also deeply connected to the domain of the primal uncanny' (2005: viii). The male monster in Latin American horror cinema also operates as the embodiment of the primal uncanny, as he regulates and utilises machismo as a male force. In

vision of revisited machismo. This new embodiment of revisited and rather modernised macho values can be explored in some queer macho roles that he also plays in films such as Pedro Almódovar's *La Mala Educación* (2004) and even English-language features such as Michel Gondry's *The Science of Sleep* (2006) and Alejandro González Iñárritu's *Babel* (2006), to name a few.

traditional terms, the monster, like the macho, is a figure whose power derives from his ability to incite terror, to chastise and objectify women, to use excessive physical force to overpower others, and to kill indiscriminately. Thus it is possible to see how the monster in horror cinema shares many of the attributes of the stereotypical macho, inasmuch as 'by his very existence, the male monster points to the fact that masculinity, as defined by the symbolic economy, is a fragile concept, one that is rarely, if ever, fulfilled' (Creed 2005: xvi). Like the macho man, the monster becomes a subject whose 'way of being' is fluid and in constant evolution and change. There is no fixed subject positionality for the monster, as he offers different readings of his socio-sexual persona according to the situations that he faces within the narrative. In most horror narratives, it is the impossibility of a fixed identity that ultimately prompts the demise of the monster himself. Similarly, being a macho man in today's Latin American societies lacks the fixity necessary for the subject ever to fulfil the symbolic economy in which he operates. The inclusion of new categories within macho identity, for instance queer machismo as theorised by Daniel Enrique Pérez (2004) and Gustavo Subero (2014), demonstrates that contemporary machismo is in constant flux and that men find themselves torn between archaic and chauvinistic ideologies that are perpetuated by the media, as well as some ideological institutions and the advances that sexual minorities have gained in matters of civil and social rights that make such ideologies rather obsolete.

From this point of departure, this chapter is concerned with the different ways in which the figure of the male monster, and the notion of the monstrous, may operate as a metaphor for a crisis of masculinity as experienced in many regions throughout Latin America. It argues that machismo can no longer separate itself from the notion of same-sex desire—either homosocial or homosexual—and that, instead, this crisis of masculinity can only be overcome, in its own monstrosity, by the assumption and/or externalisation of those desires.

In Jorge Michel Grau's *Somos lo que Hay* (2010), the crisis of masculinity is played out through the predicament created by the absence of the paterfamilias figure in the household, and the struggle between the two protagonist brothers to decide who should rightfully occupy this patriarchal position. The film disavows the hetero-masculine symbolic order by suggesting that, towards the end of the narrative, the protagonist's assumption of his queer sexuality and his eventual 'coming out' are the mechanisms whereby he can become an authentic macho (following Andrade) as he 'seeks to carry out his responsibilities to the best of his ability, the man who loves and tries to take care of his family' (Andrade 1992: 33). Similarly, Jaime Osorio Marquez's *El Páramo* (2010) shows the eventual dissolution of machismo resulting from the impossibility of the film's protagonists acting on their homosexual desires as a result of external, and diegetically suggested, feminised forces. The film supports the notion that the military constitutes an outlet of institutionalised homophobia, while it asserts a form of institutionalised homosociality. In this way, and as Eve Kosofsky Sedgwick has famously theorised, 'the homosociality of this world seems embodied fully in its heterosexuality; and its shape is not that of brotherhood, but of extreme, compulsory, and intensely volatile mastery and subordination' (1992: 66). However, this homosocial harmony is disrupted by the soldiers' encounter with a female figure, who will be regarded as a witch and whose presence will act as a destructive force among the military squad at the centre of the narrative. In this film the female presence will operate as the catalyst for the emergence of the inner macho monster in the different members of the squad, who will no longer be able to disguise their homosexual desires as homosocial. The death of the male protagonists in both films can then be regarded as the symbolic death of machismo as a fixed template of masculinity, as it circulates in the popular imaginary throughout the continent.

MONSTER IN THE CLOSET: COMING OUT AND THE DEATH OF MACHISMO IN *SOMOS LO QUE HAY*

In the horror film, the relationship between machismo, as an expression of a purported vernacular hypermasculinity, and monstrosity must be produced through a dynamics whereby the two are simultaneously the object of seduction and repulsion. The spectator develops a fetishistic fascination with the monster figure inasmuch as he is perversely seduced by the horrific acts he commits and longs to witness the moment when he is annihilated, or at least punished, for attempting to destabilise the pre-established social order. Han-Yu Huang rightly observes that 'monsters may disrupt visual pleasures, they capture the audience's scopic drives; they both attract and repel, comfort and unsettle: they are objects of adoration and aberration, attraction and repulsion' (2007: 41). However, in Grau's *opera prima* the real monster is an absent monstrous father who leaves a vacuum of leadership that operates as a metaphor for the project of the Mexican nation.² As a result of the micro-social emptiness left by the absence of a clear father figure, the film points to a clear crisis of male representation, since the two teenage, male protagonists will spend the duration of the film trying to attain, embrace and assert—willingly or otherwise—their own macho monstrosity. The film explores the problems that a family, living in poverty, faces on the death of the father figure. The teenage boys must take responsibility for the family system and guarantee that the family unit remains intact. However, this task is all the more difficult since the family practises a cannibal ritual as their only form of nourishment, for which the father has always provided them with new victims. Faced by the vacuum left by the paterfamilias, the perpetuation of the family ritual lies at the hands of the oldest son who must, according to tradition, take his father's place and provide for his family. Nevertheless, he is reluctant to take on this role, while his younger brother is just too eager to become the new head of the family.

From the outset, the film contests the stereotypical image of machismo that has been perpetuated in popular culture and that, within the narrative, is embodied by the younger brother. Julián's (Alan Chávez) aggressiveness and uncontrollable lascivious desires—albeit towards his own sister—portray him as a macho man whose behaviour can be defined as the configuration of generic practices adhering to the ideas of patriarchy that guarantee the power of men and the subordination of women. He tries at all times to overpower his older brother Alfredo (Francisco Barreiro), as he hopes that such actions will demonstrate that he should be considered the new head of the family. His behavior reifies the notion that 'las familias y culturas tradicionales asignan a los varones el papel sociocultural y psicosexual de "machos". Aquellos que lo adoptan exhiben agresividad, dominio y extremada prepotencia en sus relaciones con las mujeres. También exageran su intransigencia y hostilidad hacia los demás hombres' (Navarro Arias 1999: 187) [traditional families and cultures assign all males the sociocultural and psychosexual role of 'macho men'. Those

---

² The dynamic of the absent father figure within Mexican politics can be observed in the hailed failure of the 'war on drugs' declared by the Mexican now ex-president Felipe Calderón. According to the *Borderland Beat*, Calderón's efforts failed during his presidency, when drug-related crimes, extortion and substance abuse dramatically increased in the country. By the same token, Enrique Peña Nieto's term as president has been characterised by one of the worst national crises in recent years, prompted by the disappearance of 43 students in September 2014, as well as mounting accusations of corruption and abuse of power.

who adopt this behaviour show aggression, dominance and extreme prepotency in their relations with women. They also exaggerate their intransigence and hostility towards other men].

Within the narrative this behaviour seems only natural, considering that the opening sequence has already painted a rather negative picture of the macho monster as embodied and portrayed by the father (Humberto Yáñez). The film opens with a disorientating high angle that frames the father going up the escalator of a shopping centre and later walking with difficulty as he contorts in obvious pain. He stops by the window of one of the stores, shown in a medium shot, in which can be seen a couple of female mannequins, wearing bikinis. Grau accentuates the character's monstrosity through a close-up of his unshaven face and toothless mouth, in ways that make him more resemble an animal than a human being. This animalistic monstrosity is further stressed by the contrast of the father's reflection in the shop window as he stares and salivates in lust at the mannequins. The way he looks at them clearly fetishises the female form and places women as the object of the macho gaze. However, this moment of fetishisation will be short lived, as seconds later the father collapses on the same spot and dies.[3] Nonetheless, although his death could not be regarded as a narrative resource to recuperate the female agency of which his sadistic and lascivious gaze had already stripped the female form, it does question the basis of phallocentric normativity from the outset. The sequence establishes a direct relationship between the macho gaze and monstrosity whereby the dying male monster operates as a metaphor for the imminent death of machismo and the cultural values that it purports.

Similarly, Julián's behaviour shows clear signs of a culturally prescribed machismo, as he uses physical force and violence to claim a space of visibility and sense of belonging within the social and cultural spaces in which he interacts. For instance, in a very early scene he is quick to react violently after one of the customers at the local market where the family has a watch kiosk calls him a 'pinche escuincle' [bloody kid]. This remark is enough of

---

[3] Many critics and commentators regard the end of this sequence (when cleaners, framed by an aerial establishing shot, appear suddenly to take the body away and quickly mop clean the spot where he died, as if nothing had ever happened) as a direct criticism of late consumerism in a 'Mexico [that] is now a middle-income country with a large moneyed class [while] announcing a new mode of horror that cites zombie and vampire pictures but places them in a setting that is all too everyday' (Smith 2010). By the same token, the scene also pays direct homage to George A. Romero's *Dawn of the Dead* (1978) and its criticism of a brainless society that simply focuses on material consumption as the only form of human interaction.

an insult for him to jump over the stall and start punching the customer, at which point the camera shifts from a long shot of the scene unfolding to a medium close shot of Alfredo, who simply rolls his eyes, signalling his brother's reaction as repetitive behaviour. Despite the overt criticism of machismo as a template of male (hetero)sexuality, the main drive of the story will be the journey of attainment of a queer (masculinity) identity that Alfredo undertakes throughout the narrative. On hearing news of the father's death, Alfredo is both reluctant to become the new paterfamilias and keen to pass this responsibility to his younger brother. He is constructed as the antithesis of the macho whose identity is 'made from a series of absolutes: they never cry, they must be the best, they must always compete, they must be strong, they must not get affectively involved, and they must never retreat' (Viveros Vigoya 2001: 240). Instead, he is shown as weak and docile, submitting to his brother's machismo, as in the scene where the three siblings are planning where to get their next victim for their cannibal ritual. As they stand outside their mother's room (trying to work out whether she is doing fine after hearing of her husband's death), the camera frames them in a medium long shot that shows Alfredo and Sabina (Paulina Gaitan) by the door while Julián waits a few steps behind them. Once Paulina decides to give up waiting for an answer, she grabs Alfredo by the arm and both get close to their brother. The camera cuts to a close-up, framing the two brothers with Alfredo in focus in the background (left), while Julián appears out of focus in the foreground (right). Immediately a series of shot reverse shots of the two brothers discussing their next course of action begins, until Alfredo tries to make a suggestion and Julián cuts him short with an aggressive 'cállate maricón' [shut up, you faggot], at which Alfredo simply looks down in submission (Fig. 3.1).

Undeniably, the film constructs machismo as a performative act that controls and shapes male relations within a national socio-sexual imaginary, something that is evident for most of the narrative. Julián personifies the type of machismo that, as Chris Girman suggests, is 'both enacted (conscious exaggeration of macho stereotypes) and socially constructed (inherited, internal subconscious reproductions)' (2004: 73). He realises that in order to bestow his machismo, he needs people on whom he can exercise this excessive form of masculinity, an idea that resonates with Sergio de la Mora, who rightly asserts that 'machismo needs the joto [homosexual] to define and affirm itself as much as it needs a clingy woman' (2006: 05) because these two figures, by being the opposite to what a macho is, validate this type of identity. However, Julián's machismo is not infallible, and it is continuously challenged within the narrative by both his sister and

Fig. 3.1 Monstrous siblings: Alfredo (Francisco Barreiro), Julián (Alan Chávez) and Sabina (Paulina Gaitan). *Somos lo que Hay* ©Centro de Capacitación Cinematográfica

Patricia (Carmen Beato), his mother, who both chastise and emasculate him. Thus the film not only challenges machismo as a paradigm of male authority and phallic investment within Mexican society, it also offers new possibilities of gender equality by delineating a set of female characters who are powerful and manage to break with patriarchal control in order to claim a space of visibility within the micro-cosmos in which they operate.

A prime example can be seen in the sequence after the brothers have failed to kidnap a homeless kid for their cannibalistic ritual. On the boys' return, Sabina takes the role of nurturer and starts by cleaning Alfredo's bruises and cuts. This sequence is characterised by a series of close-ups and medium close-ups of the two characters reflected in the bathroom mirror. The decay of the mirror adds a blurriness to the sequence that somewhat eroticises their reflections, while their semi-nakedness (Alfredo remains shirtless so that Sabina can clean his bruises, but at the same time her nightdress is opened at the front, showing part of her cleavage) suggests a level of sexual intimacy that is not usually forded to siblings. As the sequence continues, the two characters are shown through a series of close-ups that provide a more intimate atmosphere to the scene. While Sabina cleanses Alfredo, she tries to convince him that he ought to assume the role of head of the family:

Sabina: Tú eres el mayor Alfredo. Tienes que tomar el lugar de papá. [You're the oldest one. You have to take dad's place]
Alfredo: ¿Si no quiero? [What if I don't want to?]
Sabina: No se trata de querer. Eres el más capáz, el más sensible. Eres el más centrado de la familia. [This is not about wanting to or not. You're the most capable, the most sensible. You're the most centred in the family]
Alfredo: No es cierto. [That's not true.]

Despite Sabina's apparent position of mariana submission, she clearly rebels against machista patriarchy by inciting Alfredo to become the new head of the family. She proceeds to list Julián's inability to be the natural leader of the household because he is 'torpe' [clumsy] and 'violento' [violent]. This criticism against machista patriarchy is further stressed by the next scene, when Julián goes into the bathroom to receive a similar treatment to his brother. This time a close-up of Sabina arranging herself seductively and looking intensely into the mirror cuts to a medium shot of the bathroom—partly framed by the door—as Julián sits down on a stool. At this point Sabina lowers herself by leaning on Julián's knees and looks him straight in the eyes, framed by a medium shot of the bathroom, as she commands him: 'De ahora en adelante vas a obedecer a Alfredo. Ahora si él te dice de comerte una puta, te la calas como lo hacía papá' [from now on you're gonna do as Alfredo says. If he says to you to eat a slut, you do it like when dad was around]. She then proceeds to take the cloth she had been using to clean Alfredo's wounds and throws it at Julián in anger. Her actions clearly obliterate mariana identity and show that Ramírez Berg is right when he claims that the crisis of masculinity is the result of a process that (Fig. 3.2)

> weakens Mexican patriarchy by splintering *macho* solidarity; by breaking the chain of male exploitation of women, a crucial psychosexual mechanism from which much of the male's power and self-identification derives; and consequently by implicitly supporting the ascendance of women, which intimidates *machismo* all the more. (2010: 125)

Somos lo que Hay signals a moment of crisis in the national sexual imaginary—a moment when the paradigms that have traditionally governed and regulated socio-sexual relations between the sexes and among gendered identities are no longer seen as monolithic and infallible. Thus the film responds to a shift in attitudes towards gender and sexual minorities as both women and queer subjects start to occupy a place of relevance and

Fig. 3.2 Machismo emasculated: Sabina (Paulina Gaitan) scolds Julián (Alan Chavez) after the failed kidnap. *Somos lo que Hay* ©Centro de Capacitación Cinematográfica

visibility in the fabric of society.[4] Cannibalism becomes a metaphor of a crisis of sexual categories in which women and gay men are no longer at the mercy of machismo and rebel against patriarchal normativity. This socio-sexual crisis is revealed in different layers that range from the social commentary regarding subaltern groups such as homeless kids and female prostitutes (both lacking any form of sexual citizenship within the project of the nation), to the female emancipation that Sabina experiences by the end of the film. As Grau comments in an interview with Andres Jaquez (2010), there is

> la insinuación sexual en todos los personajes, (es una película tremendamente sexual pues todos los personajes, hasta el papá muerto, viven una crisis sexual, que toca fondo en el puente musical) me venía perfecta a través del canibalismo, qué hermosa metáfora la de comerse sexualmente a alguien. Disfrutar hasta el orgasmo un pedazo de piel. Emocionante.

---

[4] The rise of the queer subject(s) in the fabric of mainstream society can be evidence in films by Julián Hernández or Mario Bellatin's *Salón de belleza*, where the male protagonists offer new readings of queer subjectivity as part of a national agenda.

[sexual innuendo in all the characters (it is an extremely sexual movie, since all the characters, including the dead father, live a sexual crisis. One that is manifested through musical linkages). It all came together through cannibalism, as there is no better sexual metaphor than that of eating someone sexually. Enjoy a piece of flesh to the point of orgasm. It's very exciting]

Unsurprisingly, the turning point in the film occurs when Alfredo assumes his homosexual identity. It is only at this point that the film stops cannibalising the sexual subaltern and is prepared to stand against machismo as a valid socio-sexual template within Mexican sexual culture.

Although by the very nature of the traditional horror genre spectators are not necessarily expected to empathise with the monster figure but rather with the victim, this film, nonetheless, invites the audience to side with Alfredo's plight. *Somos lo que Hay* builds the narrative towards the point when Alfredo finally frees himself from the constraints imposed on his sexual persona by patriarchal machismo (despite the fact that by doing so he becomes a monster himself). Interestingly, Alfredo's moment of 'sexual awakening', and the climax of the film, allows him to conflate a number of identities that seemed, until that point in the narrative, to be absent from his persona. After another moment of crisis in the household—and a confrontation between Alfredo and his mother—he runs away from the house. He proceeds to get on a bus and at this point the camera cannibalises the spectatorial gaze through a series of shot reverse shots in close-ups and extreme close-ups of the exposed flesh of the other passengers: a hand resting on the back of a seat, elbows of people holding the upper handrail. As the bus comes to a stop, Alfredo notices a bunch of young guys walking down the street and one of them turns around and looks at him rather flirtatiously. A high-angle shot shows Alfredo's face framed by the bus window and then making his way through the queue of people standing in the middle of the bus as he tries to alight. Unfortunately, he is too late and the bus starts moving. Alfredo keeps buzzing the indicator and, as the driver ignores his pleas, a static medium long shot shows him pushing to the front of the bus and telling the driver to stop. The same static camera now shows Alfredo as he approaches the front of the bus (the image obstructed at times by a fellow passenger who comes between the camera and the action). As the driver still refuses to stop, Alfredo (now in a medium shot from the same static camera) snaps, grabs the driver by the hair and starts smashing his face against the steering wheel. Once the bus stops, Alfredo gets off and runs back to the bus station, hoping to find the boys (his urgency highlighted by a hand-held long shot as he walks through a labyrinth of green buses). When he finally does so, he begins to follow them from a distance and his body language resembles that of the archetypal psychotic or murderer, stressed through medium close-up low angles of his stern face. At this point, the audience is left wondering whether he has become attracted to the young man who flirted with him, or whether he has finally chosen a victim for the ritual. What is clear, however, is that the film makes a direct connection between his attraction to Gustavo (Miguel Angel Hope) and his newly found 'masculine' assertiveness. Thus the film disavows machismo as a rigid template for heterosexual male sexuality and demonstrates that, as Hector Carrillo rightly points out,

> masculine homosexuals often prove to be as 'manly', or even as macho, as the rest of masculine men, their identities lend validity to a new and growing sense that manhood in Mexico has to be measured by more than masculinity, machismo, or a man's sexual attraction to women. It is in this sense that openly homosexual, masculine men force a redefinition of what being a man in Mexico means. (2002: 353)

However, the narrative will soon provide a peculiar role reversal in which the hunter becomes hunted, or rather the cannibal becomes cannibalised. Although Alfredo believes he has been following the young man discreetly, he is taken aback to discover, when he gets off the metro to which he has followed Gustavo, that the young man and his friends are standing on the platform waiting for him to get off the train. In an over-the-shoulder medium shot from behind Alfredo, the audience see the moment when the protagonist is caught red-handed as Gustavo laughs at him seductively and then he and his friends proceed to run.

The scene continues with Alfredo following the group all the way to a gay nightclub. To his surprise, Gustavo has paid the protagonist's entrance fee and tells the doorman to let him in. Once inside, the two get together and start dancing. After a while, Gustavo tells Alfredo to wait while he goes to the toilet, not without warning him first to keep an eye out as 'hay muchos cazadores y todos quieren comer' [there are too many hunters around and they all want to eat you]. Paradoxically, it is Gustavo who warns Alfredo that he could be regarded as fresh meat in the environment of the nightclub; the director is quick to signal this cannibalisation of the gay club through a series of medium shots of different men dancing (many of them shirtless). Grau seems keen to show how the social dynamic of late capitalism means that at some point everybody becomes a cannibal in their desire to consume (or be consumed by) others. As the director asserts for *Cine Latino en Nueva York,* 'la metáfora que quiero manejar o que intento, es que el único depredador del ser humano es el ser humano mismo' (Del Moral 2011) [the metaphor that I want to use or, at least, I try to use, is that the only predator of humankind are human beings themselves]. In a separate interview he is also quick to point out that 'la metáfora de la película es que el hombre es el lobo del hombre y nosotros somos nuestros propios caníbales, punto. Entonces a mi se me antojaba muchísimo que la metáfora fuera tan obvia que nos preocupáramos más por eso, y luego reflexionar' (Perches Galván 2010) [the metaphor in the film is that mankind is the wolf of all men, and that we are our own cannibals, simple. I just fancied a metaphor that was so obvious that we wouldn't have to worry about anything else, and only later had to reflect upon it]. This is evident in the film when Alfredo is left by himself and, as he looks around, the camera takes his point of view to show different people dancing in the club. At this point the director makes a cultural reference to the gay subculture and the ways in which it objectifies fashion, muscularity and the cult of the body. As such, it could be argued that gay subculture cannibalises the socio-sexual exchanges among its own members. Thus clear similarities are drawn between cannibalism as flesh-eating practice and the cannibalism experienced in modern societies preoccupied with consumerism. Gustavo is no less a cannibal because he does not eat other human beings, since he cannibalises Alfredo, albeit briefly, as a potential sexual partner.

Back in the film, Alfredo decides to search for Gustavo in the toilets. The scene is filmed in a medium long shot that is completely darkened except for the light coming from within the toilets. As Alfredo enters the toilets, Gustavo (who clearly had not gone inside) positions himself outside the door, waiting for Alfredo to come out (with a clear and sexual smirk on his face). The way in which he awaits for his 'prey' to emerge, his body only partially illuminated by a strong chiaroscuro, continues to operate as a diegetic device to depict him as a cannibal and, by default, to victimise the actual cannibal of the film. This is even clearer when Alfredo is about to leave the toilets and Gustavo grabs him, using his free hand to guide Alfredo's head towards his own in a passionate kiss. The camera cuts to a close-up of the two as Alfredo reacts with surprise and Gustavo (without letting him digest what is going on) kisses him again. However, confronting his worst fears—that is, becoming a prey to a form of cannibalisation and, worst of all, assuming his same-sex attraction—proves too much for Alfredo, who ends up running away from the club. The way in which he has been pursued by another man, as well as the moment he was consumed by another person, albeit only through kissing, symbolically disintegrate the safe confines of Alfredo's closet as 'a space to safeguard homosexuality within macho society' (Subero 2014: 58). Whereas the kiss traditionally functions as a trope in folk tales, fairy tales and other media texts that awakens love and goodness, in this film it operates as the catalyst to awaken the protagonist's 'queer' monstrosity. It is a monster that finally emerges as a result of Alfredo's assumption of his queer masculinity. Alfredo's transformation chimes with Creed's assertion that 'the uncanny monstrous male is in many instances akin to a folkloric and mythical shape-shifter who, as he transforms from one state to another, uncovers secrets about man that "ought to have remained... hidden", specially his desire to become "other"' (2005: xv). Although his transformation is not immediate, the kiss is the facilitator that begins the process of transformation through which he realises that his queer masculinity can be accepted and assumed as a valid form of male sexuality, and that it should not handicap his role as the new patriarch in the household (Fig. 3.3).

Fig. 3.3 Confronted masculinities: Alfredo (Francisco Barreiro) and Julián (Alan Chavez) discussing their failures as paterfamilia. *Somos lo que Hay* ©Centro de Capacitación Cinematográfica

To reach this stage, however, Grau incorporates a moment that, although it appears entirely anachronistic within the narrative, serves to complete the rite of passage that Alfredo as a queer monster must experience. After running away from the nightclub, he takes the metro to head back home, his dilemma stressed through a slight high-angle, medium close-up of his face by the carriage window as he sobs. From the back of the carriage he hears a female voice beginning to sing '*Atardecer Huatesco*' and he turns around to locate the source of the singing. The camera switches to a long shot of the entire carriage as a woman walks slowly towards him still singing, and then the camera offers a close-up of Alfredo's face looking back at her. While the singing progresses, the camera cuts from a close-up of a troubled Alfredo—obviously trying to come to terms with his sexual and cannibalistic desires—to a series of vignettes showing all the different dilemmas the family is undergoing. Towards the end of the song the camera returns to the present narrative, with Alfredo in the metro. Once the woman finishes singing, a handheld camera shows her in a medium long shot as she begins to give out messages scribbled on small pieces of paper to the passengers in the carriage. When she reaches Alfredo, the camera changes to a shot reverse shot in close-up as he turns down her offering, but she insists by telling him 'Tómalo! Igual está lo que estás buscando' [Take it. Perhaps it is what you've been looking for]. He proceeds to open the note, now shown in extreme close-up, and reads the words written on it: 'Estás vivo' [You're alive]. This is a turning point in the narrative, since he clearly decides to assume his homosexuality and, by doing so, obliterates the rigid construction of sexuality that he regards as prescriptive within normativity and that is arguably responsible for him repressing his same-sex desires.

By 'coming out', Alfredo triggers the type of crisis of representation that Tim Edwards (2006) sees as paramount in the contemporary crisis of masculinity. In other words, by placing himself within the orbit of same-sex desire, and normalising such desire within the project of the nation, Alfredo demonstrates that machismo—as a template of male heteronormative sexuality—is no longer ubiquitous in the socio-sexual national imaginary. His adherence to gay subculture, as a masculine homosexual, problematises stereotypical images of same-sex desire that circulate in the social, namely heterosexual, imaginary. Coming out, as Rebecca Mark expresses it, 'is never simply personal disclosure, but instead a willingness to align oneself with a certain set of assumptions, stereotypes, inconsistencies, incoherences, irrationalities, and projections' (1994: 245–246). In Alfredo's case, his coming-out points not only to a declaration of a specific sexual preference, but also to an internalisation of self-acceptance of his inner felt sexual preference. This is all the more poignant since it is suggested, at the level of the diegesis, that he will now use both his gay sex appeal and his explorations of the gay subculture as means to attract potential victims for the family's cannibal ritual.

Thus the process of coming out will become a moment of sublimation for the character who will, for the first time in the narrative, show signs of a true sense of identity. This identity will allow him to claim a space of visibility within the microcosm of the family structure, while also providing him with a space of representation in society at large. For Alfredo, coming out will also become a sublimated experience, because it will allow his libidinal desires to be available for other enterprises. In fact, it is this process of coming out that will permit such libidinal desires to emerge and be experienced as the mechanism for assuming his own form of phallic investment. Once this moment of sublimation is reached in the film (after reading the piece of paper given to him on the bus), Alfredo runs back to the nightclub and, as soon as he finds Gustavo, kisses him passionately. His radical change, diegetically triggered by the assumption of his same-sex desires, permits him to challenge heteronormative paradigms of sexuality in which 'the threat of homosexuality lingers, not as a competing life-style but as a symbol of the emasculated *macho*' (Ramírez Berg 2010: 125). The way in which he changes his behaviour—from a docile condition that renders him effeminised to an assertiveness that renders him masculinised—demonstrates that homosexuality, like machismo, is not a quality inherent to a type of sexual identity, but a learnt behaviour that, as Martin Levine and Michael Kimmel argue, 'enacted a hypermasculine sexuality as a way to challenge their stigmatization as failed men' (1998: 5).

Paradoxically, it is also at this point in the narrative that Alfredo becomes a real monster, and thus he can now fulfil the patriarchal role that is expected of him within the household in order to preserve the cannibal ritual. The conflation of his queer identity and his monstrosity reaches its peak in the following sequence, when he takes his new conquest/victim back to the house. At this point the screen frame is shown completely darkened except for the light coming through the door frame, seen on the right-hand side of the screen. Through silhouettes and shadows, spectators can see Alfredo and Gustavo, who are passionately making out and are caught by Alfredo's two siblings, who have come downstairs to check what the noise they could hear was. When the lights are turned on, they discover Alfredo and Gustavo still kissing. The way in which Alfredo is depicted at this point in the narrative shows a radical departure from the type of character development that had been shown earlier in the film. The camerawork now posits him in a position of superiority, conveyed through low angles and medium close-ups. His entire body language and attitude have changed: he is no longer hunched and looking down in submission, but instead he looks straight into his brother's eyes. He is now in control and exercises his role as the new paterfamilias.

> *Sabina*: ¿Conseguiste algo? [Did you find anything?]
> *[Sabina turns the lights on to find Alfredo and Gustavo snogging]*
> *Julián*: ¿Qué estás haciendo? [What are you doing?]
> *Alfredo*: Les traje a Gustavo. [I brought you Gustavo]
> *Julián*: ¿Estás loco? [Are you mad?]
> *Alfredo*: Ésto es lo que vamos a hacer. [This is what we gonna do from now on]
> *Julián*: Tú no eres nadie para decirme que hacer. [You have no right to tell me what to do]
> *Sabina*: Cállate Julián. [Shut up, Julián]
> *Julián*: Yo no me voy a comer un maricón. [I'm not eating a faggot]
> *[Alfredo walks menacingly towards Julián, who begins to walk backwards]*
> *Alfredo*: ¡Tú te vas a comer lo que yo te diga! [You are eating what I tell you to eat]

As an out gay man, Alfredo becomes the monster who 'dares to speak the truth of repressed desire. Whether male or female, the monster speaks the unspeakable, defies order and system, flaunts morality and the law' (Creed 2005: 119–120). His newly emerged monstrous nature guarantees him a space of belonging within the cannibal household and as the new patriarch, while it also has the double function of dismantling machismo as the only socially accepted male force within contemporary Mexican society, because it obliterates the notion of monsters as intrinsically feminine (Creed 1993a) or quintessentially homosexual and queer (Benshoff 1997).

What the film achieves rather poignantly is to confront contemporary representations of masculinity in visual culture alongside the notions theorised by Jonathan Rutherford (1988) of 'retributive' versus 'new' man, and how the two are embedded and represented in the male protagonists. Julián represents a more traditional form of masculinity (retributive), relying on the overt sexualisation of his *hombría* to the extent that it becomes a hypermasculine caricature of manliness itself. On the other hand, Alfredo (new) represents a form of masculinity that speaks more to a modern, liberated and egalitarian society (in terms of gender relations). However, regardless of the point in the narrative at which either character exercises his masculine power, it is undeniable that the film regards prescribed masculinity, in the form of machismo, as a metaphor for a cannibalistic cultural practice—one in which the male subject sets out to consume, at least symbolically, other males in order to exercise his seeming superiority.[5] Cannibalism is, therefore, a basic mechanism of all consumerism based on hierarchical relations between socio-sexual subjects. Thus Joaquin Pedro de Andrade's notion of cannibalism, as explained in the introduction to his film *Macunaíma* (1969), seems rather fitting in the context of *Somos lo que Hay*, since

> every consumer is reducible, in the last analysis, to cannibalism. The present work relationships, as well as the relationships between people—social, political, and economic—are still basically cannibalistic. Those who can 'eat' others through their consumption of products, or even more directly in sexual relationships. (1995: 82–83)

In other words, cannibalism provides an opportunity to create a visual metaphor for the struggle of power in late consumerist society, as all the characters reflect on the consequences of living in a dog-eat-dog society that is also heavily influenced by machismo—or its remnants—as a driving force of all male sexuality.

The film is ironic in its stance on the socio-sexual moral codes that govern society. The consumption of human flesh is not questioned by any of the members of the family, yet the source of such flesh (meat) is highly problematised. If, as Maggie Kilgour suggests, 'cannibalism is a conventional satirical topos, which has been traditionally used for political purposes

---

[5] Such power relations are not only limited to male exchanges, but can also be evidenced in female exchanges within the film. For instance, the tension between Sabina and Patricia is palpable throughout. Although Patricia seems to be at a loss after the death of the father, she seems reluctant to give up power in the household and transfer patriarchal responsibilities to the oldest son or anyone but herself. Meanwhile, Sabina manipulates the two brothers in order to continue the ritual, while altering the status quo of the female relation by taking over as mother/companion figure. The cannibalistic consumption of gender relations can also be seen in the social and moral clash between Patricia and the *putas* [prostitutes], whom she regards as lesser human beings as a result of their engagement in the sex trade. Thus cannibalism operates as a metaphor for all the socio-sexual relationships between individuals in contemporary society, while calling into question the fixity of socio-sexual paradigms. In this light, the prostitutes are as much of a victim as the people eaten by the family, because they are all consumed in order to satisfy a basic need; that is, sex/hunger.

to demonise and attack forces seen as threatening social order' (1998b: 239), then Grau's cannibal narrative successfully provides a filmic voice to segments of society that had remained silenced by their inability to participate more actively in the social and political apparatus accepted and recognised by mainstream culture. That is to say, the moral and ethical dilemmas underlying the cannibal narrative in the film serve to expose the rigidity and ultraconservative nature of the machista (and mariana) sexual paradigms that govern contemporary Mexican culture. This can be evidenced in the reaction of both Patricia and Julián (respectively)—in their symbolic function as the pillars of mariana and machista ideology in the film—towards the two main victims brought into the house; that is, the prostitute and Gustavo. For instance, earlier in the film Patricia shows disgust that the boys have brought a whore to the house. Whores operate in the Latin American imaginary as 'mujeres de la mala vida' [loose women] and, as a result, are regarded as belonging to a lower social stratum that grants them a lesser degree of sexual citizenship (due to their perceived lower morals). Such women are viewed, as Paula Daniela Bianchi (2008) argues in her work on the representation of prostitution in Latin American literature, as 'las figuras de las "mujeres de la calle", del burdel, de la "mala vida", las esclavizadas por el tráfico ilegal de cuerpos, las migrantes, circundan el camino de la periferia y comparten la condición de exclusión social y de indigencia' [the figure of 'street corner women', from the brothel, 'loose women', they are enslaved by the illegal traffic of the body, they are migrants, they operate on the periphery and share their condition of social exclusion and indigence'.

Unsurprisingly, Patricia forbids the family to eat the whore and decides, instead, to disfigure her and then take her back to the corner where the prostitutes gather to pick up new clients. The confrontation between Patricia and the prostitutes is framed in a slight high-angle long shot that shows part of the area as Patricia arrives in a car. Once there, Julián dumps the corpse of the whore while Patricia, now framed in a close-up of her enraged face, warns the other prostitutes that they face the same fate if they dare to go anywhere near her family again:

> *Patricia*: ¿Querían cojerse a mis hijos? ¿No? [You wanted to fuck my kids, didn't you?]
> *[She proceeds to uncover the corpse and shows her disfigured face]*
> *Patricia*: Pues ésto les va a pasar si se vuelven a acercar a mi familia. ¡Cerdas!
> [Well, this is what will happen to you if you come anywhere near my family again. You pigs!]

Although just before this scene, and on the way to drop off the corpse, she admits to Julián 'somos unos monstruos' [we are monsters], Patricia still regards prostitutes as an even lower type of female figure—and arguably also a type of monster—because their social standing opposes and corrupts mariana morality. Undoubtedly, the film evidences a decaying society where authorities, people living in abject poverty and those living on the periphery of social citizenship are all devoid of any form of humanisation. This debut film clearly paints a disturbing picture of Mexican social decay with cinematic strokes that are both poignant and elegant, achieved through dramatic camera angles and a clever use of naturalism, natural lighting and a darkened palette. Unsurprisingly, Grau has mentioned in several interviews that directors such as Guillermo del Toro, Claire Denis and Marina Deban have heavily influenced him, while his film also pays homage to the cinema of George Romero, David Cronenberg and Tobe Hooper, among others. It visualises a metropolis of shocking insensibility, where the authorities are indifferent and passers-by avoid lifeless bodies found in their way. The camera plays an observant role, penetrating the misery of a marginal environment that is always threatened by imminent tragedy. The protagonists are cannibals who belong to an intrinsic, and yet hidden, segment of society: homeless people, prostitutes and homosexuals.

By the same token, Julián shows repulsion towards Gustavo because he is a *maricón* [faggot]. For Julián, eating a *maricón* would be symbolically to penetrate the terrain of same-sex desire as he chewed and swallowed the man's flesh. This makes Alfredo's appropriation of the patriarchal order and his newly assumed role as head of the family all the more disruptive to heteronormative patriarchy, since his homosexuality would be traditionally regarded as a threat to hetero masculinity. Julián's reaction and repulsion towards the gay victim responds to a machista understanding of homosexuality whereby, as Jaime Manrique explains, 'maricón is a word used to connote something pejorative; by implication a maricón is a person not to be taken seriously, an object of derision. Without exception, maricón is used as a way to dismiss a gay man as an incomplete and worthless kind of person' (2002: 12). Despite the fact that the film will ultimately portray Alfredo as a type of 'authentic macho' gay (following Andrade 1992), it cannot be denied that by coming out and assuming his own same-sex desires, he obliterates the notions of machismo that regard homosexuality as a social and moral aberration. This character is all the more significant because Mexico is currently experiencing a historical moment when the gay subculture is surfacing into the mainstream of society, and more positive and visible representations of same-sex desire are being offered in society at large.[6] However, despite the fact that Alfredo's monstrosity is rather humanised within the film, it remains possible to see how the conventions of the horror genre 'still relate homosexuality to bestiality, incest, necrophilia, sadomasochism, etc.—the very stuff of classical Hollywood movie monster movies. The concepts 'monster' and 'homosexual' share many of the same semantic charges and arouse many of the same fears about sex and death' (Vermaak 2008: 3).

In *Somos lo que Hay* Grau seems to offer different degrees of monstrosity closely associated with a number of socio-sexual templates. In this way, while also centering the narrative on an out gay man, the homosexual is rendered more humane than the macho. At the level of the narrative, the film posits same-sex desire in a more positive light by humanising Alfredo's plight from being a submissive closeted gay man to his eventual sacrifice in order to save his sister. Although assuming his homosexuality helps him to become a monster—like the rest of his family—the film constructs him in ways that call for the audience to identify and relate to his dilemma as a closeted gay man. Alfredo's apparent self-loathing and his depiction as a social outcast throughout the story seem to operate at the level of the diegesis as a tool to elicit spectators' sympathy by means of humanising the monster figure. Thus cannibalism is not so much an anthropophagic practice, but a filmic metaphor to convey a deeper social critique of Mexican contemporary society and the values (or lack thereof) of late capitalism. In this sense, the monster and his own monstrosity may reveal the conflicts and contradictions that are latent in a given hypermasculinist society. Grau demonstrates that the monster figure does not necessarily have to be a negative figure, both within the narrative and as part of the conventions of horror. Thus Alfredo represents a positive monster, one whose monstrosity is not necessarily evil or responds to a desire to inflict pain or terror among people around him. He is not presented as a creature that finds enjoyment in killing or murdering others. Instead, the director presents his cannibalism as an ordeal, as part of an unwanted, and

---

[6]A prime example of this integration of queer culture into the mainstream of Mexican society can be observed in the reception of Gerardo Delgado's pornographic film *La Putiza* (2004). After winning best screenplay and best film at the Heat Gay: Festival Internacional de Cine Erótico Gay de Barcelona, the film awakened a wave of interest from the mainstream media and other cultural institutions. The film was then officially released in a screening at the Museum of Art in Mexico, an event that was covered by mainstream media; surprisingly, it was the gay media that remained absent from such events.

yet unavoidable, fate. Henceforth, he becomes a positive monster, 'who, insofar as he becomes positive, ceases to be monstrous, hence no longer frightening' (Wood 2003: 166) (Fig. 3.4).

Alfredo's monstrosity is further recanted, by the end of the narrative, by his decision to sacrifice himself in order to save his sister from death at the hands of the police, once the family have been found out as cannibals. After Gustavo's escape, the police raid the house and break in, aiming to capture the four cannibals, who try to escape by going up onto the roof of their house. However, as they run up the stairs, the police shoot at them and they end up in two separate rooms at either side of the house. Patricia and Alfredo are close to the roof, while Julián and Sabina take refuge in the room opposite. As the shooting continues between Julián and the policemen, the camera cuts between a close-up of Alfredo's face and a medium shot that shows Sabina in a foetal position and crying desperately by Julián's side. Patricia urges Alfredo to escape with her because 'alguien tiene que sobrevivir. Es por el rito' [Someone has to survive. It's all about the ritual]. However, Alfredo feels remorse at leaving his two siblings behind—especially Sabina—and runs into the room to join them. As he does so, framed in a static medium close-up, he gets shot in the

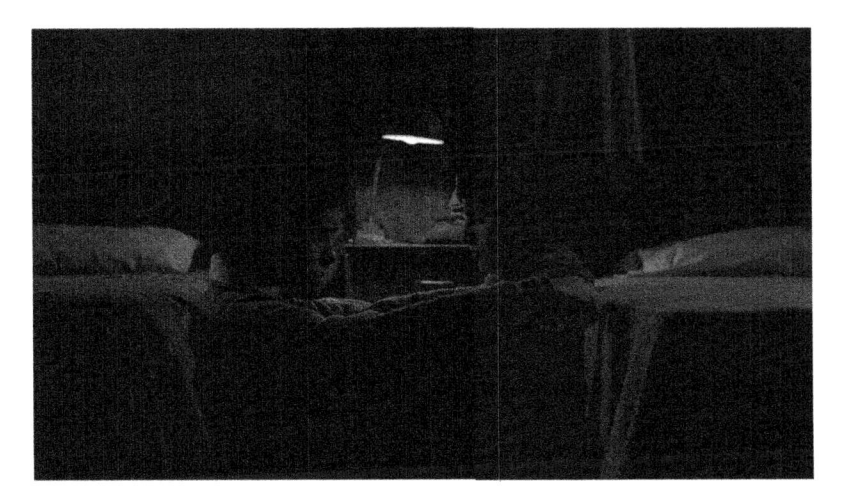

Fig. 3.4 Fighting off machismo: Alfredo (Francisco Barreiro) cries at the metro station after realising he may be gay. *Somos lo que Hay* ©Centro de Capacitación Cinematográfica

shoulder; the camera then cuts to a close-up of him as he falls on the floor, wounded and covered in blood.

It is at this point that Alfredo realises there is no escape for them and, in what seems like a moment of cannibalistic madness captured through a slight low-angle close-up of his face looking up to his brother and straight down to his sobbing sister, he decides to jump over Sabina and bite her on the cheek. The end of the sequence is highlighted by a series of close-ups of Julián trying to pull his brother off his sister, the feet of the policemen going up the stairs and Alfredo's bleeding hands as he puts something into Sabina's hand. In the commotion, Julián shoots Alfredo in order to defend his sister, while at the same time being shot dead by the police who have run up the stairs to intervene. Moments later, the police take Sabina on a gurney to an ambulance, where she is framed in a medium shot starting to unfold a piece of paper in her hands. The camera then cuts to a close-up of her hands—providing a rather symbolic chiaroscuro—as she unfolds the very same paper that her brother was given in the metro and reads the by now prophetic 'Estás vivo'. At the level of the diegesis, one can assume that Alfredo bit his sister so as to pretend she was a victim and in order to save her from being arrested or killed by the police. Thus the film ultimately presents him as a positive monster who makes the ultimate sacrifice—by paying with his own life—in order to save his sister and guarantee the perpetuation of the ritual. In this way Alfredo is the ultimate positive monster, because he not only manages to rebel against heteronormative patriarchy, he also shows signs of humanity towards his own family. In this way, *Somos lo que Hay* could be said to operate, as Bruce F. Kawin asserts in relation to cannibalism in horror cinema, 'to challenge the basis and nature of society, to confront the civilized norm with its opposite and sometimes to criticize the behavior of the civilized' (2012: 188).

KILLING THEM SOFTLY: HOMOSOCIALITY AND THE DEATH OF MACHISMO IN *EL PÁRAMO*

Traditionally, war movies have been regarded as vehicles par excellence to narrate stories of masculinity, male bonding and varied forms of hypermasculinist behaviour, in many instances akin to machismo, both in Latin America and elsewhere (Donald 1992; Smihula 2008). The story of Latin American cinema is intrinsically linked to that of the war soldier and the war hero. Events such as the Mexican Revolutions were among the first cinematographic historical episodes to be recorded in the continent, and the first major armed conflict to be filmed in the world. However, the cinema of Latin America has not exploited the war genre to the same extent as that in Hollywood.[7] In other words, the analysis accompanying many Hollywood war movies has permitted theorists to historicise and understand the changes within paradigms of masculinity that have been experienced in American culture. Although some of these films may try to offer a more humane version of the military forces and those who operate within them, they continue to reaffirm the idea that machismo constitutes a key template of male identity that is vital for the soldier in order to fit in. Recent films such as *Soñar no Cuesta Nada* (Rodrigo Triana 2006) and *Punto y Raya* (Elia Schneider 2005) are clearly set on the idea of humanising the soldier figure, the former by showing him as a victim of his own greediness, the latter by focusing on the formation of brotherly bonds between soldiers of different national forces. It is clear that these films continue to maintain the status quo of a purported hypermasculinity within the military as a key characteristic of those whose embrace such a life. The films tend to be homosocial in nature, as they usually revolve around the emergence of affective ties among men who are not depicted as homosexual. As David Desser aptly observes in his discussion of *The Warriors* (Sol Yurick, 1965), war films offer a 'vision of the all-male group, where men live by a code of professionalism and whose integrity is threatened by the presence of women [...] the hero bonds with a best friend, is a leader of men, and struggles to reconcile heterosexual needs with homosocial communities' (2007: 130).

Desser's words may not be pertinent in relation to Jaime Osorio Marquez's *El Páramo* (2010), a film that arguably shows the dissolution of machismo prompted by the impossibility of homosexual desires as a result of external forces that are both triggered and encapsulated in the figure of a female monster. The film supports the notion that the military constitutes an outlet of institutionalised homophobia, while asserting homosociality as

---

[7] It is worth noting that two major historical events have shaped cinematic representations of war and the military in the United States. First, the scars left by the Vietnam War have been famously tackled by many film directors in a number of genres, with storylines ranging from the simple glorification of war (as in the Rambo films) to the overt criticism of the war and its impact on notions of post-war masculinity in films such as *Platoon* (Oliver Stone, 1986) and *Born on the Fourth of July* (Oliver Stone, 1989). On the other hand, the events of 9/11 and the War on Terror have, once again, propelled an avalanche of films that have deal with the impact on the notion of masculinity of such an episode, including *The Hurt Locker* (Kathryn Bigelow, 2008), *World Trade Center* (Oliver Stone, 2006) and more recently *American Sniper* (Clint Eastwood, 2014).

a mechanism to establish and maintain male relations. In this way, and as Kosofsky Sedgwick has theorised, 'the homosociality of this world seems embodied fully in its heterosexuality; and its shape is not that of brotherhood, but of extreme, compulsory, and intensely volatile mastery and subordination' (1992: 66). However, this homosocial harmony is disrupted by the soldiers' encounter with a woman (Daniela Catz), who is regarded as a witch and whose presence will act as a destructive force among the members of the squad. The remainder of this chapter argues that this female presence operates as a catalyst for the emergence of an inner queer macho monster in the different members of the squad who can no longer disguise their homosexual desires, while making them pass as homosocial.[8]

The death of every male character in this film, in much the same way as happened in *Somos lo que Hay*, can be interpreted as the symbolic death of machismo as a fixed template of masculinity. *El Páramo* recounts the story of a military squad sent to investigate the disappearance of another squad at a military base. After losing contact for several days with a previous squad, nine experienced soldiers are dispatched to the military base in the desolate high-plains moors of Colombia. Once there, they try to figure out what happened to the previous soldiers by going around the camp until they find a woman who has been heavily chained and buried alive behind a wall. As the isolation increases in the camp, a strange fog descends on the soldiers, making escape impossible. The soldiers' sense of duty will be put to the test as they debate whether or not to stay put and await back-up. In the meantime, doubts about the true nature of the strange woman will undermine the men's integrity and mental sanity. One by one, death will claim their lives until only one of them is left alive. Their deaths will operate as the symbolic disintegration of machismo.

Guerrilla warfare operates as the perfect context in which to explore issues of masculinity, machismo and homophobia. Although the film does not deal with the FARC (Revolutionary Army Forces of Colombia), it does hint that the army squad has been sent to deal with what is presumed to be an attack by this guerrilla group. The armed conflict between the FARC and the national armed forces dates back to the civil war between the Liberal and Conservative parties that affected Colombia from 1948

---

[8] This notion of queer monstrosity brings to mind those textual discourses that regard lesbigay characters as somewhat violent or hypervialent in films such as Alfred Hitchcock's *Rope* (1948), John McNaughton's *Henry: Portrait of a Serial Killer* (1986), Patty Jenkins's *Monsters* (2003) or Gus Van Sant's *Elephant* (2003).

until 1958 (commonly known as *La Violencia*). After the end of the civil war, the FARC became disillusioned with the leadership of the group and, led by Manuel Marulanda, turned to communism. It operates in the countryside and subsists through the illegal drug trade, kidnapping and extortion, as well as an 'unofficial' tax it levies on peasants in order to guarantee their protection and other services. Guerrilla actions are also counteracted by paramilitary groups that enjoy the 'unofficial' support of the government's armed forces. All these groups, however, are characterised by an ideological policy of '*limpieza social*' that consists in a form of violence directed towards a specific target group that have as their common denominator belonging to a marginal sector and displaying behaviour that the aggressors regard as dangerous.

Interestingly, the work of Kimberly Theidon (2009) exposes the homophobic junctures and ideologies that abound among members of the FARC. For instance, she argues that among such military and paramilitary groups, men must show ill-tempered and hostile faces, as they are both expressions of machismo. Conveying such facial expressions is something that is taught when joining the group in order to appear more macho among comrades, since 'when people were killing, they changed their faces. You were malencarado [stern face]—pure machismo. Looking like that made you feel like more of a man' (2009: 23). Accordingly, they understand that machismo operates on the basis of a performance of gender and that, as such, is constitutive of the environment in which it is displayed. Thus machismo is not a monolithic paradigm but a set of regulatory norms, based on specific gendered behaviour, that become a necessity in order to be accepted in a specific locus of socialization. This idea chimes with the work of William Payne, who argues that 'cuando existen ejes culturales de homofobia en un lugar determinado, actuar contra esta población es una manera de mostrar una disposición hacia el uso de extrema violencia pero contra personas con menos enlaces en la comunidad que puedan producir resistencia' (2007: 182) [when there are homophobic cultural axes in a particular place, acting against such a population becomes a means to show a predisposition to use extreme violence towards those people who enjoy fewer ties with a community that may offer some form of resistance]. Therefore, the disintegration of machismo as a template of male sexuality among the members of the squad will be tantamount to the infiltration of queer desire within heteronormative society. This is a threat that will jeopardise machismo as the unifying force that sustains the basis of gender relations among the men in the squad.

In the film, machismo constitutes the key element in the narrative and, as Jorge Gissi argues, 'es una realidad social de discriminación social, ligada a una mitología que divide a los individuos en superiores e inferiores, según su sexo, en donde el hombre, por razones "naturales", es superior a la mujer' (1987: 134) [it is a social reality based on social discrimination, one that is linked to a type of mythology that divides individuals between superior and inferior ones. According to a sex typology, it sees men being, for 'natural' reasons, superior to women]. This superiority is also exercised towards all non-masculine figures, including homosexuals and effeminate men, because they are socially and culturally inscribed in the realm of the unmanly. Unsurprisingly, the war narrative in fiction—regardless of the subgenre to which it may pertain—continues to respond to a desire to deconstruct masculinity and to reaffirm or challenge this seeming position of male superiority. The military is then regarded as an outlet of overt homophobia in which men who do not present hypermasculine traits are considered handicapped in relation to other men. As Jan Hopman rightly asserts, 'los excesos dentro de los cuarteles militares tienen su fuente, su desarrollo, su proyección y su sobrevivencia en la cultura machista: las fuerzas armadas son parte de la cultura y refuerzan el machismo que existe en la sociedad civil' (2001: 134) [excesses within military quarters are rooted, developed, projected and depend for their survival on a machista culture. The armed forces are part of culture and reinforce the machismo that exists within civil society].

In *El Páramo*, machismo is shown as a monstrous force from the very beginning of the narrative, as the film centres on a seeming battle of masculinities between the central figures. This is evident from the opening sequence in which all the members of the military squad are being flown to the high-plains moor in a helicopter and the film introduces every character through handheld close-ups of their faces. Furthermore, the tension, and power struggle, between Sergeant Ramírez (Andres Castañeda) and Lieutenant Sánchez (Mauricio Navas) is evidenced by the fact that the members of the squad seem more willing to follow the sergeant's orders.[9] This is further stressed when the sergeant refers to the lieutenant as a 'mariquita' [little faggot] in ways that clearly subvert the hierarchical structure of the military and are intended to challenge the latter's masculinity. Nonetheless, the narrative will privilege the point of view of

---

[9] This type of narrative can also be found in other films such as Claire Denis's *Beau Travail* (1999) or Peter Ustinov's *Billy Bud* (1962).

Ponce (Juan Pablo Barragán), as it is through his eyes and psyche that the audience will discover more about the true and monstrous nature of the soldiers' machismo.

The soldiers in the film become emblematic of what Mark Christopher Straw theorises as a 'damaged male' (2010), since their filmic presence provides a site for the unblocking of all male emotions that are repressed through macho attitudes, while it also makes a spectacle of male suffering. Straw regards the warlike context of such films as a space where 'we have the crucial collision of violence, suffering and masculinity, where the site of this collision is a privileged space in which the representation of the damaged male can flourish' (2010: 10). The film distinguishes males who are damaged not only by the atrocities of war, but by the rhetoric of machismo that is regarded as constitutive of the male psyche of a real Latin American man. Although the film attests to a rather volatile and changing state of machismo for all the male characters, it will not be until the discovery of a female prisoner—who is the only survivor of the massacre that has obviously been experienced at the camp—that what Creed reveals as the 'primal uncanny' (2005) will be unleashed among the squad. Creed points out that if

> the uncanny signifies a disturbance of 'any straightforward sense of what is inside and outside', then the primal uncanny offers an understanding of the nature of that disturbance; it is related to woman, death and the animal—elements that the male symbolic order represents as 'unfamiliar' and 'strange' in its attempt to normalize masculinity as familiar, proper and natural. (2005: 14)

Thus the murders and other monstrous acts experienced in the camp may not necessarily be blamed on the female prisoner found there, who is regarded as a feminine monster, despite being readily labeled as a witch and presented as animalistic in nature. Instead, it could be suggested that the female figure simply operates as the catalyst that disavows the symbolic order of the damaged males in the narrative who, through the diegetic absence of other female figures, seem more free to embrace their homosocial bonds without fear of feminisation or of breaking pre-established socio-sexual taboos. This idea resonates with Ramírez Berg, who argues in relation to Pedro Donoso's *El Lugar sin Límites* (1966) that man's 'flirtation with homosexuality is perceived a threat. To el macho, homosexuals are incarnate negations of his sex, identity and power. Homosexuality counters everything the macho stands for, questions basic patriarchal premises, and—worst of all—lays bare the frightened psychological bases of machismo' (2010: 124).

The overt demonstrations of male solidarity and physical bonding that characterise the members of the squad are, both within the narrative and at a social level, safely justified within the realm of homosocial exchanges. The lack of a feminine figure among the soldiers guarantees that what Kosofsky Sedgwick regards as a 'homosexual panic' (1992) remains under control during the narrative. For instance, the way in which Robledo (Julio Cesar Valencia)—aka El Negro—caresses Parra's (Mateo Silva) forehead after he has been taken injured from a mine explosion shows how such acts of male affection can remain exempt from public sanction in the absence of a female figure who can provide such ministrations. This scene opens with El Negro's gloved hand, framed in a close-up, caressing Parra's ankle through his boot. He proceeds to take his glove off and walk towards Parra, who lies semi-conscious on a stretcher and is now fully framed through a static medium shot, showing El Negro putting his machine gun on the side of the stretcher. El Negro walks closer to Parra's face and sits down. His face comes into full view to the camera in a close-up as he begins to caress Parra's forehead with his fingers. However, this highly homoerotic moment in the film remains unproblematised because it is disguised as purely homosocial. Thus no member of the squad questions the rather feminised way, within the symbolic order, in which the two men show affection to one another; or, as Kosofsky Sedgwick aptly puts it, 'a tendency toward important correspondences and similarities between the most sanctioned forms of male-homosocial bonding, and the most reprobated expressions of male homosexual sociality' (1992: 89). In other words, as long as the demonstrations of affection are kept within the realm of the homosocial, the characters will be able to continue their rather prolonged physical ministrations, even when such ministrations are clearly reminiscent of homosexual bonding. The emphasis provided by the close-up further stresses the character's ambiguity in terms of homosexual desires. Thus it is not surprising that the film very promptly introduces a female force (albeit a non-normative one) in an attempt to even out the shift towards homosexuality that has been experienced by the different members of the squad. The female presence that will eventually be found in the camp, however, will disavow such homosocial bonding, since the soldiers will no longer be able to justify their physical exchanges as necessary or appropriate in the absence of a female figure who can, more naturally, provide such attentions.

This is all the more evident in the scene in which all the soldiers gather to witness the amputation of Parra's leg. Here the camera keeps cutting to medium shots of all the members of the squad, who seem very uneasy and rather squeamish about the procedure that is about to be performed. This seems at odds with the fact that, as soldiers, it is expected that they would be trained to detach themselves emotionally from a situation like this, especially when the wellbeing of one of the squad members is at stake. Instead, the scene presents the soldiers as lacking *hombría*, or without the guts to perform their duty when this may not be such a pleasant task. This sequence is characterised by a handheld camera, a preponderance for medium close-ups, and a lack of focus and zooms that makes a character come in and out of focus in a random manner. As Ramos (Juan David Restrepo) is preparing to cut the leg with a surgical saw, Ponce begins to throw up even before the first cut is made and will continue to do so as the amputation continues. The rest of the sequence will be shown through a series of quick editing cuts that are framed mainly in close-ups, and that range from the moment Ramos makes the first incision, to the different reactions (repulsion, pain, sadness) of every man who witnesses the procedure while Parra moans in agonising pain. As the procedure continues, the camera switches from close-ups of Ramos's face (who seems angered at being forced to perform the surgery) to that of Corporal Cortés (Alejandro Aguilar), who looks at him in a commanding manner since, by this point in the narrative, he has taken control of the squad. Yet both men seem also physically disgusted and repulsed by the whole procedure, like the rest of the men who are by the soldier's side. This behaviour seems to contradict the constant tension between power and pain that Alejandra Brito, as cited by Hopman (2001), regards as paramount within military relationships among men. As she explains,

> aparte de la soledad, la represión de las emociones es una forma de autocontrol para mantener el deseo de control sobre otros; además, están asociadas a la feminidad, rechazada como premisa para la constitución de la masculinidad. Lo peor que puede pasarle a un hombre es mostrar sus emociones, eso es actuar como mujer y tiene una significación muy negativa, un rango parecido a *ser maricón*, a *ser una mina*, y sin duda la homofobia dominante tiene sus repercusiones en el mundo militar. (2001: 137)
>
> [despite the solitude, emotional repression is a mechanism of self-control necessary in order to maintain the desire to control others. Besides, such qualities are associated with effeminacy, rejected as a premise for the constitution of masculinity. The worst thing that could ever happened to a man is

to show his emotions, as this is akin to acting like a woman, and it has a very negative connotation. It is like being a faggot or a woman, thus homophobia has clear repercussions and it dominates the military world]

The aforementioned scene, however, obliterates the idea of self-control as part of the machista ideology promulgated by the military. The behaviour clearly feminises all the members of the squad, as they show a lack of stoicism and of a machista attitude towards life itself. In this sense, the monstrous within the narrative emerges as constituted by the soldiers' repressed feelings and desires, since the fine border that separates their homosocial desires from homosexual enactments becomes more blurred during the story.

Thus by implication the real feminine monster in the narrative, one that is responsible for all the murders in the camp and forces the soldiers to turn on one another, is not the witch. She simply operates as a visual token of a feminine monster that is repressed within the symbolic order of macho mentality. Arguably, the real feminine monster in *El Páramo* is the feminine repressed id that equates its monstrous instinct with a homosexual desire that has been repressed in order to maintain the machista status quo operating within the military squad. As Margaret Tarrat rightly observes in relation to horror films, 'the battle with sinister monsters or extraterrestrial forces are an externalization of the civilized person's conflict with his or her primitive subconscious or id' (2003: 259). In Freudian terms, the id constitutes the site in which the individual's repressed sexual desires, which are incompatible with the moral codes of a civilised culture or society, are stored. Therefore, it is the site in which same-sex desires must be repressed in order to give birth to machismo. The id is monstrous because the repressed desires that are kept in it would jeopardise and threaten the rigidity of heterosexuality as the only accepted sexual template that regulates socio-sexual beings. The witch in the film, as the only feminine Other, makes the soldiers aware that they can no longer justify their homosexual-disguised-as-homosocial bonding as a socially acceptable behaviour, since her presence should, in theory, direct their sexual desires towards her. Instead, the witch as a plot device merely points towards the constructedness of male sexuality—and machismo as its hypermasculine externalisation—while disavowing the assumed naturalness of heterosexuality. As Ramírez Berg points out for el macho, 'his flirtation with homosexuality is perceived as a threat. To *el macho*, homosexuals are incarnate negations of his sex, identity and power. Homosexuality counters everything that macho stands for, questioning basic patriarchal premises, and—worst of all—lays bare the frightened psychological bases of *machismo*' (2010: 124). As a result, it is not surprising that the witch, as a possible projection of the soldiers' repressed id, is presented as a savage and animalistic being who is dispossessed of any form of humanity because she comes to represent their unspeakable desires and inner anti-normative instincts.

The ending of the amputation sequence perfectly exemplifies how the threat of homosexuality and the disintegration of the soldiers' homosocial bond give them all a monstrous quality. The death of machismo is played out on their bodies in a process of physical transformation that occurs as the film progresses, and the boundaries between their homosexually repressed desires and their culturally embedded machismo become more blurred. As already suggested, the fact that this entire sequence is filmed through a medium close shot that lends an intimate feel to the action makes it all the more harrowing to witness the physical and emotional reactions of all the soldiers as the amputation takes place. While Parra's leg continues to be severed, he, in his delirious state, runs his hand over the face of El Negro, who seems to be crying. The camera pans right to Ponce's sickened face and then down to Ramos's hand as he continues to saw the leg off. It cuts to Ramos's face and then to Ponce being sick again, finally resting temporarily on Parra's agonising face. The shot then changes to a close-up of Ramos's face and transitions through a dissolve onto El Negro's face as he begins to weep inconsolably. By panning from face to face, the camera work stresses an overt display of sentimentality and weakness on the part of the soldiers. This shows that Creed is right to suggests that 'whenever male bodies are represented as monstrous in the horror film they assume characteristics usually associated with the female body: they experience a bloody cycle, change shape, bleed, give birth, become penetrable, are castrated' (1993b: 118).

Similarly, the monstrous male body as a penetrable and castrated entity is evidenced in a later sequence in the film when El Indio believes that he has been infected with a sort of plague, which he considers to be the cause of the problems among the squad. In his confused state, he kills Fiquitiva (Nelson Camayo) and then proceeds to take off his own skin in order to rid himself of the monstrous disease. Interestingly, most of the killings in the film happen between pairs of soldiers who were shown from the beginning of the film to have a rather close relationship. The film evidences that in the absence of an outlet into which to channel their homosexual attraction, as well as the impossibility of consummating their same-sex libidinous desires, the id seeks pain rather than pleasure. The repressed id is driven by a desire to experience pleasures that must be concealed within heteronormativity. The men's repressed desires will be under control as long as the social environment guarantees their suppression by providing an alternative outlet for them (in this case a military camp where women would never be expected to be present). The witch, however, disrupts homosocial socialisation and exposes the fissures within the heteronormative system. This idea accords with the thinking of Tony Magistrale, who points out that 'the horror monster signifies abject terror because it violates cultural categories, disrespects organizing principles, and generally serves to present a chaotic alternative to the place of order and meaning, socially as well as biologically' (2005: 7).

The monstrous feminine in *El Páramo* is not a feminine threat but the threat of being seen or read as feminine, the threat of being feminised. The film constructs the monstrous feminine as an active rather than a passive figure. The traditional view of female agency (or the lack thereof) within horror narratives is obliterated in this film, since the witch is not presented as an erotic object—the subject of the erotic gaze as theorised by Mulvey (1989)—or as a fetishistic threat to masculinity through her power of male castration (Creed 1993b). In fact, the diegesis never suggests that the killings and bloody acts occurring in the camp are committed by the witch, but rather by the soldiers themselves. As Creed suggests, it would be erroneous to assume that 'simply because the monstrous-feminine is constructed as an active rather than passive figure that this image is "feminist" or "liberated". The presence of the monstrous-feminine in the popular horror film speaks to us more about male fears than about female desire or feminine subjectivity' (2012: 03). Ultimately, within the narrative it will be machismo that is constructed as the ultimate monster figure and the one that will be responsible for the killing of every member of the squad. Once their repressed desires are unleashed, the men's ids become monstrous and they end up exterminating one another, since there is no space for a female monstrous within the confined parameters of machismo. As Judith Halberstam argues in relation to postmodern horror cinema, the postmodern monster—one that is not easily recognisable but is equally frightening—does not 'scare us from a distance, they are us, they are on us, and in us' (1995: 15). This will become more evident at the ending of the film, which seems to suggest that nowadays machismo cannot escape from the feminine monstrous.

In the final sequence, Lieutenant Cortés finds Ponce as he is trying to run away from the camp. Confronting him, Cortés tells Ponce that he cannot leave him behind: 'Usted no me puede hacer eso, Ponce. Usted no' [You can't do that to me, Ponce. You can't]. The homoerotic tension between the two soldiers, one that had been present all along in the film, reaches an explosive climax when Cortés reminds Ponce that he was the one who had to kill an entire family in a previous mission—one of which the audience is made aware through Ponce's frequent flashback dream sequences. At this point Ponce becomes hysterical and starts fighting Cortés. Cortés overpowers Ponce and begins to strangle him with the body of his machine gun. The homoerotic tone of this scene is intensified by a low-angle, close medium shot that shows Cortés's face very close to Ponce's in what could appear like a desire to kiss him. However, in the struggle Ponce manages to get hold of Cortés's knife and stabs him to death. At this point the narrative seems to suggest that the last bastion of machismo, represented by Cortés, has fallen. Ponce, who has continually been presented as less masculine and macho than the rest of the squad, has come to represent a new type of masculinity, and by this point in the film he is somewhat freed from the social impositions of machismo on his sexual persona.

However, the last image of the film makes it very clear that there is no escape from the monstrous feminine once the dissolution of homosociality is exerted in a masculine locus of socialisation. Here, spectators see a defeated Ponce trying to leave the camp as the sole survivor. The film attempts to create a sense of hope through the mise-en-scène, since the fog that had covered the camp throughout the film begins to disappear and birds can be heard singing in the distance. The camera shows a sobbing Ponce as he walks away from the camp. His face is in close-up and, as the soundtrack increases the diegetic tension, the witch comes into view from her hiding place in a trench behind him. She screams and runs towards the camera (and Ponce) and the film comes to an abrupt end. This open-ended conclusion arguably manifests the impossibility of re-repressing the uncontrollable homosexual (feminised) id once it has been unleashed. In this light, it would be possible to argue that *El Páramo* breaks with the stereotypical horror movie 'as a misogynist genre that provides a showcase for masculine aggression and provokes a sexual response to the spectacle of female mutilation' (Halberstam 1995: 138). Instead, the film creates a spectacle of male transgression brought about by the dissolution of machismo as a sexual template for masculine behaviour and social interaction.

Conclusion

The figure of the monster in the horror narrative has traditionally been regarded as a masculine entity that pursues, abuses and/or kills women and other non-masculine subjects, offered as part of the fetishist imagination of an imagined audience's male gaze.[10] He is depicted as a threat, becoming an instrument to map and act out society's worst misogynist and homophobic fears. Thus horror cinema offers a critical commentary on issues of sexuality and gender relations in contemporary society. In more recent Latin American horror narratives, machismo, and the figure of the macho, have been subjected to a number of (re)evaluations and revisions that arguably equate machismo with monstrosity while opening a space of dialogue with other less rigid paradigms of gender and sexuality. This chapter has shown how machismo, as what is assumed to be the only normative expression of male sexuality in Latin America, is challenged through horror topois, as well as through the psychological responses that the genre provokes in its audiences. The images of machismo that have prevailed in Latin American cinema with figures such as Pedro Infantes, Carlos Gardel and even fictional heroes such as El Santo are now contested by characters who are less radical in the assertion of their masculine behaviour. By the same token, they no longer require queer characters as visual markers of an antithesis of masculinity, or women as objects of their unresolved sexual fixations. As Kyung Hyun Kim explains in relation to Asian cinema, 'the depiction of emasculated and humiliated male subjects set the stage for their remasculinization, and occasioned a revival of images, cultural discourses and popular fictions that fetishized and imagined dominant men and masculinity' (2004: 9–10). Both *Somos lo que Hay* and *El Páramo* examine the ways in which machismo can no longer be regarded as a valid template for male sexuality and invite the audience to re-evaluate such a notion through the diegetic death of macho figures.

The type of machismo embodied by Julián in *Somos lo que Hay* and the members of the squad in *El Páramo* resonates with the ideas of Huang, who points out that 'as long as the killer/monsters are male, the disruptive forces they embody automatically victimize women only or the psychical ambivalence or paradoxical identification they engender serve dominant ideology only' (2007: 42). In both films, the presence of a feminine Other figure is not regarded as a force that must be contained or subjugated,

---

[10] Films such as Alfred Hitchcock's *Psycho* (1960), Werner Herzog's *Nosferatu the Vampyre* (1979) and Mary Harron's *American Psycho* (2000) are but a few of such narratives.

but as a force that has the ability to question and alter the socio-sexual status quo that has been traditionally seen as operating in such societies. In Grau's film, machismo is opposed both by a new sense of radical marianismo (whereby women are more assertive in their roles within the household and are conscious of the power they hold in relation to both decision-making processes and actions that affect the entire family unit) and by the empowerment of the homosexual subject. Alfredo as a queer subject destabilises machismo as a rigid paradigm of sexuality because he exposes its artificiality and its constructedness (through the performance of gender). Alfredo's eventual coming-out, and the ensuing degree of male assertiveness (both physically and psychologically), show that the macho figure stops being an infallible subject as understood in the socio-sexual popular imaginary. Instead, his presence in the film becomes a point of contestation of the rigidity of macho sexuality as a template circulating in Latin American society. In the film, cannibalism is a vehicle to interrogate the dichotomy of active versus passive that has prevailed in the Mexican imagination and in which

> the Mexican concept of masculinity (machismo) requires that the division between male and female be clearly defined culturally as the division between those things passive and female. The ideal male must be tough, invulnerable, and penetrating, whereas the ideal female must exhibit the opposite of these qualities [...] It follows then that only the receptive, anally passive male is identified culturally as effeminate and homosexual. The active male, the inserter, retains his masculinity and therefore cannot be considered homosexual [...] no stigma is attached to the active role. (Carrier 1995, 21)

For Julián, to eat Gustavo would be to accept the symbolic penetrability of his own macho body; a penetration that would render him somewhat effeminised. On the other hand, Alfredo recuperates a crucial role for the male homosexual, who is no longer regarded as a caricature of the feminine or an individual with no *hombría*. Instead, he is portrayed as a masculine figure whose *hombría* is not in direct relation to his sexual orientation and/or his sexual choices.

Conversely, in *El Páramo*, the military squad—with every soldier showing a different type of caricaturised machismo—demonstrates that machismo is structured around a homosocial relationship that verges on the homosexual. The way in which all the male characters interact with one another shows the tensions between male bodies when they become physical with one another. As Cynthia J. Fuchs points out in relation to buddy films, 'yet again, the problem of male self-identity is exacerbated by its apparent resolution. For this conspicuous discharge situates the male couple [or squad] between the representational poles of homoeroticism and homophobia, in love with their self-displays and at odds with their implications' (1993: 195). What is interesting about the film is the fact that the narrative offers many instances of homoerotic physicality between the different members of the squad: they are always embracing, holding each other's faces very close, caressing each other, and yet they fear appearing effeminised or the loss of their own masculinity. These homosexual-disguised-as-homosocial interactions are disrupted by the presence of a female subject who naturally upsets the homosocial dynamics. Her mere presence is enough to dismantle the squad's purported machismo and bring out the soldiers' own inner monstrous feminine (their homosexual desires) and with it their own demise. Machismo is, thus, annihilated by the externalisation of same-sex desires and the impossibility of controlling such desires. The film evidences that the unquestionable omnipresence of macho bravado in environments that are regarded as outlets of overt homophobia simply responds to the needs of many individuals to keep their homosexual desires controlled and closeted.

In short, both films manifest a desire to expose the crisis of representation within Latin American masculinity in which the rigidity of the behaviour and socio-sexual psyche of the figure of the macho is no longer regarded as a fixed entity within the sexual paradigms prevailing in the continent. The horror narrative, by the same token, permits such anxieties to be played out without their becoming a direct attack on the way(s) in which heterohegemonic masculinity circulates in the popular imaginary.

CHAPTER 4

Bloody Femininities: The Horrors of Marianismo and Maternity in Recent Latin American Cinema

In most of Latin America the cult of the Virgin Mary is paramount in the construction of marianismo as a template for female identity and this, in turn, relates strongly to mothering and motherhood as quintessential elements within the process of womanhood. As has been previously discussed, the term marianismo was first coined by Evelyn Stevens (1973) to explain gender relations and spheres of female power among Latin American women, both in the house and in society at large. Stevens claims that this notion travelled to the New World with the conquistadores, eventually becoming part of the mestizo identity in the continent. Marianismo offers a hybrid, complex and idealised notion of femininity through a series of beliefs about women's spiritual and moral superiority to men that have served to legitimise their subordinate, domestic and social roles. It takes at its point of departure an intrinsic relationship between the quality of womanhood and the assumed nature of the Virgin Mary. Unsurprisingly, marianismo relies heavily on the natural ability of women to bear children and be mothers and, like the Virgin Mary herself, to do so in ways that obliterate their ownership of desire, and even their sense of femininity. In other words, women become pregnant and, thus, mothers through a divine act or plan rather than the satisfaction (or fulfilment) of their own sexual desires. Marianismo constitutes the counterpoint to machismo; yet it does not seek to challenge it, but to complement it. Asunción Lavrin views marianismo as celebrating 'the values of patience, stoicism, mediation, and nurturing that are presumed to be the qualities of Mary as preached by the Catholic Church and apply to all women as desirable forms of personal behaviour' (2005: 203). Although it would be rather simplistic to believe that all women follow this idealised form of subservient femininity, it cannot be denied that marianismo has played a crucial role in the Latin American social imaginary by prescribing a form of femininity based on sexual purity, selflessness and blind devotion to husbands and sons.

Motherhood is a key part of the construction of mariana identity. Latin American feminism is strongly related to the notion of motherhood, as in many instances women have claimed social and political adherence via their positions as mothers, such as the Madres [Mothers] de la Playa de Mayo in Argentina. Motherhood has also been used as a political platform by many feminists (unlike in the feminist movements in the West), as it is 'mothers' who have been able to mobilise themselves politically at times of social and political turmoil in Latin America. Lavrin rightly points out in relation to motherhood in the Southern Cone that '[f]eminism oriented toward motherhood was more than a strategy to win favorable legislation, it was an essential component of their [women in the region's] cultural heritage: a tune that feminists not only knew how to play but wished to play' (1998: 10). Within the social imaginary that circulates in most Latin American societies, and that popular narratives in the media as well as folklore perpetuate, mothering defines the essence of womanhood. Thus femininity is defined by essentialists through a woman's ability to bear a child while, at the same time, many female archetypes in contemporary Latin American culture continue to be linked to women's reproductive functions. Undoubtedly, progress made in relation to women's rights, in conjunction with the feminist ideals found outside the continent, has had an impact on the way in which motherhood defines and shapes women's relations. For instance, the image of the *madre abnegada* (self-sacrificing mother) that is often portrayed in film and other media—especially in soap operas—bears no necessary relation to the politicised group of mothers who have mobilised political change in many parts of the continent. For such women, it is their desire to seek justice on behalf of their children and loved ones, or the necessity of defending them from oppression by the political or military system, that has made them unite into a force capable of social and political change.

By the same token, mothering has long constituted a topos of horror cinema whereby the fecund female subject is directly associated with monstrosity through her ability to carry a life within and the bodily changes that occur to her body. As Marilyn Francus discusses, 'the fecund female and her yelping, parasitic progeny evoke the seemingly uncontrollable nature of femininity, and not surprisingly, the image functions as a locus of male disgust with, and fear of, sexuality and reproduction' (1994: 829). For instance, films such as Roman Polanski's *Rosemary's Baby* (1968), David Cronenberg's *The Brood* (1979), Harry Bromley Davenport's *X-Tro* (1982) or Peter Medak's *Species II* (1998) are a few of those that show pregnancy and the process of giving birth as moments of abject femininity. The pregnant woman, within horror narratives, operates at times as a figure that functions as the locus of pre-Oedipal anxieties (usually manifested in unresolved conflicts between the monster and his desire or repulsion towards the mother, as well as his inability to kill her). At the same time, the mother may become a monstrous figure by the embodiment of evil caused by the 'trauma' of being pregnant and the biological and hormonal changes that her body suffers.

Thus this chapter discusses the ways in which mothering and the maternal are problematised as part of an ongoing rhetoric of female subjectivity in the Southern Cone. To this end, the analysis will focus on Pablo Illanes's *Baby Shower* (2011) and Adrián García Bogliano's *Habitaciones para Turistas* (2004) and the way in which these two films' directors posit their maternal protagonists as subjects whose pregnancies are a source of and a magnet for evil. The chapter argues that the anxieties of machista ideology are projected onto the maternal body because it provides a negative reading of fertility whereby the site of reproduction is the site of sin. The female protagonists in these films have defied mariana codes of female sexuality by engaging in sex outside wedlock or by rejecting the support of their male partners during pregnancy. Their pregnant bodies are portrayed as sites of lust that render the mariana figure morally corrupt. Behind the gory deaths of the female protagonists in these films, there is a more latent issue shaped by a misogynist reading of the female ownership of desire, in which women are punished for their attempt to escape from patriarchal domination. Whether or not the films have intentionally set out to deal with the issues of traditional femininity and the ownership of female desire, both share at their core a clear narrative in which women who break the established mariana codes are annihilated. By killing women whose behaviour has clearly challenged the basis of normativity, the films seem to reify the notion that traditional paradigms of female sexuality cannot be questioned or altered by female subjects unless they are willing to pay (with their own lives) for attempting to undermine patriarchal authority.

'DEATH AND THE CITY' OR THE PARADOX OF THE MONSTROUS MATERNAL IN *BABY SHOWER*

Similar to the history of women's participation in the political sphere in Argentina (as will be discussed later in this chapter), Chile has been a country where politics during and after the military junta has been greatly shaped by the role that women played in it. As Lisa Baldez is quick to point out

> women perceived moments of realignment as uniquely gendered opportunities. Women framed their mobilization [either pro/against Allende or pro/against Pinochet as the two most crucial moments in recent Chilean history] in terms of their status as political outsiders, in response to what they perceived as men's characteristic inability to overcome narrow partisan concerns. (2002: 2)

In this light, the maternal and the notion of motherhood became highly politicised within the realm of political mobilisation, in as much as mothers assumed a political role characterised by the enshrining of a new political consciousness (albeit not necessarily a democratic one on all political fronts). Such roles have remained present in the political sphere and have, logically, transferred to the popular imaginary in ways that seem to exalt the importance of socially accepted versions of motherhood (usually regarded as operating within a heteronormative and Catholic paradigm) and to discourage alternative readings of motherhood outside such paradigms. This is evident from the very beginning of Illanes's film, where a number of versions of femininity and motherhood are played out by the different female characters. During the first 20 min of the narrative, one may mistakenly think that the film attempts to be a Southern Cone version of the American hit series *Sex and the City*, aka *SATC* (1998–2004). The premise could not be simpler: four female friends get together to celebrate the pregnancy of one of them. They gather at the pregnant woman's house, located in the country and about an hour from the city (presumably Santiago de Chile). However, Angela (Ingrid Isensee) has an ulterior motive behind letting her friends throw her a baby shower: she wants to know which of them is having an affair with her husband. While living in the country, Angela has become a member of a type of New Age group whose headquarters are next to her property. This group is led by Soledad (Patricia López), a woman who engages in strange ritual and spiritual practices.

Although the film at first seems to celebrate forms of female emancipation, it is soon very clear that, instead, it portrays these women as liberated and with a lack of morals that can be associated with images of anti-mariana femininity that already circulate in popular culture.[1] Illanes resorts to a number of female stereotypes that have prevailed in Western television after the advent of *SATC*; for instance, the four friends are all well off, professional, sexually liberal and physically attractive. They also comply with other stereotypes commonly associated with post-feminist subjects, as two of them play the role of man-eaters and the other acts as the sexually liberated housewife. Similarly, the three cannot make sense of the protagonist's desire to cut herself off from city life (what they deem as civilisation) and move to the countryside. From the outset, these women use their bodies as instruments to externalise their own 'versions' of femininity and as sites to act out their own female desires and values. Like the cast members of *SATC*, these women are hypersexualised in their presentation of self. They all have perfect bodies (which they waste no time showing off in bikinis in an early scene by the swimming pool) and live a life of hedonism and self-indulgence characterised by pre-marital sex and drug consumption. By the same token, throughout the film Angela shows a rather fetishistic fascination with her belly (her body) and can be seen caressing it in most scenes. Maternity—and the maternal body—is what defines the character at all times and allows her to remain embedded within mariana identity. Conversely, her friends' bodies are highly sexualised to mark the distinction between what is morally acceptable and morally corrupt.

Traditionally, 'the horror film has typically been theorised as a misogynist genre that provides a site for masculine aggression and provokes a sexual response to the spectacle of female mutilation' (Halberstam 1995: 138). In *Baby Shower*, female mutilation arguably responds to a desire to punish women for attempting to go against the grain of mariana identity, rather than simply showcasing the visceral pleasures of the traditional slasher film.[2] Although it could be argued that at times the film recuperates

---

[1] As explained in Chap. 1, figures such as La Malinche and La Llorona have become emblematic of this type of anti-mariana identity. Both represent negative aspects of femininity, whereby women are regarded as traitors to their own sex. In both cases these women are driven by lascivious desires and/or jealousy in ways that propitiate the emergence of a dysfunctional sense of motherhood.

[2] These visceral pleasures are characterised by slightly repetitive scenarios that offer audiences a familiar setting for the action to develop. For instance, these films are always set in abandoned locations, onscreen sex is a passport to certain death, the killer is avenging

the gaze for the female and queer audience by offering a spectacle of male nudity—objectifying Angela's handyman Julio (Alvaro Gómez) as the object of the gaze through a series of close-ups of his chiseled and shirtless body (even when the semi-nudity does not appear to be justified in the film's diegesis)—it is the female body as text that will prevail for most of the narrative. Thus the film presents a narrative for an imagined male audience. It makes a spectacle of female nudity—for instance, the scene in which Soledad (Patricia López) and Olivia (Claudia Burr) are getting changed into their bikinis and fighting for the 'right' to seduce Julio— but does so in order to recuperate the narrative for the pleasure(s) of an imagined female audience that see marianismo as a socio-sexual template. Rather than presenting womanliness as a ploy or a front through which an imaginary male audience can experience the forbidden sexual desires procured by the annihilation of the female character, it could be suggested that the film's narrative pleasure is derived from the brutal punishment and gruesome killing of women who uphold anti-mariana values. Ironically, although the narrative never concretely posits Angela as a female monster (a point that will be developed later), the film clearly presents her friends as monstrous because they use their femininity and sexuality either to inflict pain on those around them or for personal gain. As Margrit Shildrick suggests,

> the figure of the monster is particularly rich in binary associations, and, as we have already seen, is characterized variously as unnatural, inhuman, abnormal, impure, racially other and so on. In every case, it is marked against the primary term, the normative standard, as degraded or lacking, an oppositional category that is never of equal value. (2002: 28)

Therefore, Angela's friends are monstrous because they encapsulate all the negative values of a form of femininity that seems unnatural, inhuman, abnormal and impure in comparison with mariana values of abnegation and servitude towards men.

Baby Shower seems slightly ambiguous about the monstrous nature of Angela, despite using many tropes of the horror genre to depict the character and her surroundings: the isolated and remote 'idyllic' location, the cut-off phone line and the lack of mobile reception that prevent people

personal wrongdoing, the killer will use a sharp implement to enact the killings and only one person (in most cases a girl) will survive by the end of the film.

asking for help, the cult group living next door and its strange leader. However, the director seems reluctant fully to demonise or vilify Angela as a monstrous character, despite the existing genre expectations based on motifs that link pregnancy and horror in films such as *Rosemary's Baby*, *The Brood*, *Alien* (Ridley Scott 1979) and *It's Alive* (Larry Cohen 1974) among others. There is a clear ambivalence in the way she is constructed within the narrative. At the beginning of the film, she is presented as the Jungian negative archetype of the mother figure who embodies 'anything secret, hidden, dark; the abyss, the world of the dead, anything that devours, seduces, and poisons, that is terrifying and inescapable like fate' (Jung 1981: 158). It is she who has suggested that her friends throw the baby shower at her place in the country, it is she who continuously exchanges knowing glances with Julio while the friends are visiting, it is she who goes hysterical when Olivia's assistant Ivana (Sofía García) answers the phone, it is she who will eventually cut off the phone line; and yet when her friends start dying she seems rather surprised and taken aback by this turn of events. It is only at this point that audiences figure out that she is not responsible for the killings occurring and that a different monster is hunting them down.

Angela's actions also seem to be directly related to her pregnancy in ways that may suggest that this is the cause of her evilness and, to a greater extent, justifies her seemingly irrational (monstrous) behaviour. The way she continuously touches and caresses her pregnant belly also seems to stress the relationship between her pregnancy and her identity as both mother and monster. Her pregnancy is fetishised to the extent that the fetish is not only the source of pleasure, but also the motivation and drive for her abnormal—that is, monstrous—behaviour. In this way, the film presents her maternal state as both physically and psychologically monstrous. This can be observed from the beginning of the film when the audience first see Angela and Soledad. As the members of the spiritual group leave the former's residence (where they have been practising meditation), the camera presents the two female protagonists in a medium shot as Soledad places her hands on top of Angela's heavily pregnant belly, while Angela herself caresses her belly from the side. The two women take up virtually the entire frame, looking at each other almost with longing. Soledad proceeds to kiss Angela goodbye, on the cheek, and leaves, then Angela turns to face the camera while she continues stroking her pregnant belly. The incidental music turns sombre while the diegetic sound stresses the wind to provide an atmosphere of horror to the scene. At this point,

Angela stops smiling and looks sternly into the distance, as if to foresee the horrors to come. The camera then switches to a long shot of Angela standing by the entrance of her hacienda, then dollies backwards and shows how she continues to caress her belly in an almost obsessive manner.

It could be suggested that Angela is physically monstrous because her physical appearance is incongruent with the sort of images of maternity that circulate in mainstream culture and are reaffirmed by classic film narratives. In such images, pregnancy is understood as a biological stage that provides women with a capacity for nurturing and caring, while the pregnant belly softens the physical appearance of the mother herself. Instead, Angela's pregnancy constitutes the stage during which a temporal and spatial disruption occurs of her more traditional femininity, her mariana identity, and that becomes the moment when she experiences a radical loss of distinction between herself and the Other; or, as Sarah Arnold argues, 'the Bad Mother horrors, when they do offer increased maternal perspective, may encourage [in the public] identification with the mother's transgression (in other words identification with her rejection of essential motherhood). Identification with transgression questions this very subordination' (2013: 71). Angela's pregnancy clearly acts as a force that is opposed to and unsettles her conscious ego (understood as her mariana identity). Therefore, her pregnancy forces her, as Linda Badley suggests in her work on film, horror and the body fantastic, to 'feel trapped in the bod[y] that increasingly determine[s] who we are, projecting a negative or positive image, defining our nerouses as disorders and our rituals and relationships as codependencies' (1995: 27). By the same token, Angela is accepted as psychologically monstrous because the hormonal imbalances that she suffers as a mother figure seem to justify her monstrous instincts at the level of the diegesis. She is monstrous because her maternal body threatens boundaries between the self and the Other. The gestating baby inside her operates as a visual token to explain her monstrous actions; or, as Kelly Oliver explains in her analysis of pregnancy in Hollywood cinema, 'what is horrifying are the ways in which the monstrous is ambiguous— in-between one body (the mother) and another (the fetus); in-between human and animal; even in-between female and male' (2012: 124).

Thus the monstrous mother operates as the antithesis of the mariana figure whose power of address 'spring[s] apparently from primitive awe at woman's ability to produce a live human creature from inside her own body' (Stevens 1973: 5). Angela's pregnancy strips her of mariana agency; in other words of the sense of selflessness and abnegation that the mariana figure culturally displays. Instead, her pregnant body may suggest that her offspring may be poised for evil or is even the son of the devil himself and, by default, forces her to assume a monstrous identity and commit murderous actions. She is, therefore, associated with the negative aspects of the construction of femininity that posit her as anti-mariana, since she lacks the 'spiritual strength [that] engenders abnegation, that is, an infinite capacity for humility and sacrifice' (Stevens 1973: 9). Although most of her actions seem to be justified within the context of the narrative—for instance, evicting her husband from the marital home, or trying to find out which of her friends is having an affair and may even be running away with him—she fails to show the sort of moral code and behaviour that would be paramount for the mariana subject. There is no sense of selflessness in her actions; she is portrayed as callous and monstrous while using her pregnancy as a cover to disguise her evil plans. Although she does not kill or physically torture anyone within the narrative, she is depicted as the most monstrous of all the characters because, as Francus asserts in relation to the monstrous mother and reproductive anxiety, 'since the monstrous mother refuses to be sexually and socially passive, she violates the codes of proper female behavior, which leads to a condemnation of the quality and quantity of her actions' (1994: 830). Angela's thirst for revenge is clearly justified within the narrative (despite her lack of clear actions to assert it), but it is her impassivity and lack of protection of her friends once the killers are discovered that make her monstrous. She may not be the active killer in the film, but the way she seems to enjoy contemplating the gruesome murders of her friends shows a monstrous aspect to her subjectivity. Once again, her pregnancy operates as a trigger to justify her actions and her desire to seek revenge, because she wants to get rid of those who may pose a threat to her and, by default, the babies she is expecting.

Angela's body, unlike that of the mariana pregnant woman, is not disciplined through subordination to macho figures. It is this lack of subordination that, arguably, permits her monstrous nature to surface and to dominate her subjectivity, despite the fact that such a subversive subjectivity will be tarnished and eliminated by the end of the narrative. This idea continues Oliver's analysis when she suggests that there is 'a continued association between pregnancy and insanity. In all of these films [the ones analysed in her study], the protagonists are mentally unstable in ways that suggest their complicity with evil and danger' (2012: 19). However, *Baby Shower* propels a change of narrative subjectivity once it becomes clear that Angela is not behind the disappearances and murders taking place on her property. Nonetheless, her attempt to break free from patriarchal domination makes her somewhat monstrous, as her desire for revenge attests against the role she has been socially assigned as a mariana figure.

By this point in the narrative it is not only Angela who will be punished for going against the grain of mariana identity, but quite logically also all her friends, who are depicted as sexually loose women and, as such, deviate from mariana social norms. All the women in the film appear to be far from the 'mariana's ideal behavior [that] encompasses dependence, subordination, responsibility for all domestic chores, and selfless devotion to family and children. She is also expected to accept and tolerate certain behaviors from her man—aggressiveness, sexual infidelity, arrogance, stubbornness, and callousness' (Sequeira 2009: 30). What the film makes clear is that all deviations from traditional female identity must be punished, and that women must continue to be rendered dependent on men's will and on the pillars that sustain patriarchal order. All the female characters will be depicted, to a greater or lesser extent, as monstrous because their behaviours push against the boundaries of normative patriarchy. However, for most of them their desire to be independent and to rebel against machismo will be viscerally truncated through their gruesome death. Undoubtedly, in *Baby Shower* the narrative follows the tradition described by Carol Clover in her work on slasher films and gender, whereby 'the killer is with few exceptions recognizably human and distinctly male; his fury is unmistakably sexual in both roots and expression; his victims are mostly women, often sexually free and always young and beautiful ones' (1993: 77). Although not one but two girls survive at the end, it could be argued that one of the main failures of the film is the fact that Illanes never empowers the female protagonists beyond a mere caricature of female emancipation. This is also pointed out by Marcelo Morales C. (n.d.), who in his critique of the film asserts that

> aquél reduccionismo y conservadurismo formal va de la mano con el argumento de Illanes, quien con una historia (tal como en las teleseries escritas por él) acude a personajes de clase alta, lleno de histerismos, de ciertos desbordes sexuales o éticos que explotarán brutalmente [...] sorprende por la extraña pacatería con la que castiga a sus personajes.
> [There is a clear reductionism and formal conservatism that go hand in hand with Illanes's plot whose story (in much the same way as the television series written by him) resorts to hysterical wealthy characters, situations that explode brutally through characters who are sexually or ethically deviant [...] while the prudishness with which it punishes some of his characters is also surprising].

As a result, the women in this film are presented as somewhat abject within the context of Latin American sexual culture, because they break with normative stereotypes of femaleness. At the same time, they also posit a criticism of the ideals of female emancipation that is enacted through the violence they endure.

Furthermore, it is possible to suggest that Illanes positions himself, as well as his imaginary audience, in a place that equates any form of femininity—whether mariana or otherwise—with female abjection. Whether the director's understanding of femininity has by this point been heavily influenced by his background as a writer of soap operas and television series (manifested through an excessive use of melodrama as a means to invoke female relations), it is clear that he portrays all women as individuals who are responsible for the temporal and spatial disruption of the life of 'the subject' (attributed as quintessentially male). He clearly regards femininity as an identity imbued with domestic nostalgia, whereby mariana women should find in the maternal home a redemptive space that allows them to escape the chaos and instability of macho culture. In a world of national cultural fictions in which machismo is regarded as an infallible socio-sexual identity, and in which males are always regarded as superior to women, it is only logical that any type of femininity is construed as subversive and becomes monstrous against the seemingly correct functioning of society. In the film Illanes draws a direct correlation between femininity as a whole and abjection, since there are no forms of femininity that are deemed 'natural' within the narrative. Thus, as Imogen Tyler suggests, 'the abject has a double presence, it is both within "us" and within "culture" and it is through both individual and group rituals of exclusion that abjection is "acted out". Abjection thus generates the borders of the individual *and* the social body' (2009: 78).

The female body as abject operates as a key feature in Illanes's film. In one key scene, the three friends come to check on Angela after she has felt slightly faint. The scene, filmed in a static medium long shot, shows Angela's bed occupying most of the frame, the friends sitting around her at different corners. In the middle of the image lies Angela with her enormous pregnant belly as the epicenter of symbolic female abjection: a socio-cultural space where all female subjects are designated to the unlivable and uninhabitable zones of social life. The big pregnant belly of the protagonist is a site of becoming that conflates feelings of repulsion and empathy. Thus the audience are torn between a rejection of her rather monstrous persona and empathy towards her as a maternal subject. In other words, as Oliver explains in her analysis of the work of

Julia Kristeva, 'the pregnant woman or mother is an incarnation of the split body. The pregnant maternal body is a split body' (1993: 40). What makes Angela's body abject is its dual nature, in as much as the abject becomes a constant reminder that the body can be corrupted at any time and that the mariana subject's positionality is not infallible or immutable. As Kristeva herself points out, 'abjection is above all ambiguity. Because, while releasing a hold, it does not radically cut off the subject from what threatens it—on the contrary, abjection acknowledges it to be in perpetual danger' (1982: 13). Furthermore, it is not only the pregnant body that is represented as abject, but the female body at large when posited outside mariana identity. As a result, all the female characters in the film come to represent aspects of femininity that contradict mariana identity—the whore, the neglecting mother, the unsubservient wife—and, therefore, to represent a category of socially excluded bodies. This symbolic abjection is further stressed by the painting hung over the bed (and positioned directly above Angela) that shows a naked woman trying to cover herself in clear fear and shame of an invisible force. It could be suggested that the painting comes to symbolise the abject femininity of the female characters in the film, who are subjected to shame and punishment as a result of their desire to break with mariana ideology. By the same token, this image could be said to anticipate the fatal ending that such women will endure because they inhabit, as Butler rightly suggests in relation to abjection, 'the "unlivable" and "uninhabitable" zones of social life' (1993: xiii). The narrative thus presents the female protagonists as women who have lost their subject positionality within the system of moral and cultural values that would, socially, provide them with a sense of selfhood.

Another such instance in the film occurs in the scene when Angela confronts all of her friends to find out who has been having an affair with her husband. This sees abjection being played out on the pregnant body, but also on the bodies of her friends who, due to their more mature age, are regarded as past their prime. After confronting Olivia, Manuela (Kiki Rojo) and Claudia (Francisca Merino), the women turn to each other and begin to criticise one another in order to avoid becoming the prime suspect of Angela's accusations. At one point Claudia accuses Olivia of being 'ninfómana y vieja' [nymphomaniac and old], yet it is only the fact she has been called 'old' that is taken as a real insult. Olivia is condemned for being selfish and preferring a life of sexual indulgence, a rather hedonistic lifestyle, thereby passing her reproductive prime without a family to speak of. As Lizzy Welby argues, 'at the other end of the age bracket stands the post-menopausal woman whose ageing reproductive body provokes horror and disgust and as such is frequently positioned as abject' (2010: 46).

Interestingly, the camera work continues to construe Angela's pregnancy as abject by stressing her pregnant belly and constructing it as a horror leitmotif throughout the narrative. This is, once again, evidenced when a furious Angela asks her friends to leave her house. There are two short scenes that fetishise her maternal body. The first sees her shutting the doors of the room where the confrontation took place. As she rests against the doors, the camera in a long shot shows her on the left-hand side of the frame, then zooms in towards her body and, more specifically, her pregnant belly. The scene quickly switches to a static long shot of the country house's entrance as the guests leave in a hurry. As they disappear from the frame, the entrance remains in view, darkened by the lack of lighting. The camera zooms in and Angela's silhouette appears in chiaroscuro, as she walks to the entrance while coming into full view with her left hand resting on her pregnant belly.

Arguably, in the film female bodies are scrutinised (as a result of their monstrous nature) by an imaginary, ideal and sexualised mariana female gaze. This gaze is concerned with the ways in which the non-mariana female form operates as a site of transgression and taboo. For instance, the friends' sculpted and fit bodies are seen as transgressive because they evidence an ownership of desire that should be absent from mariana identity, since women should not try to use their bodies in sexual ways or to fulfil their sexual desires without the aim of procreation. Angela's body, on the other hand, renders her a castrating mother, because it is through her pregnant state that she hopes to regain her mariana identity and to disavow the kind of liberal behaviour that the bodies and subjectivities of her friends represent. Angela's body has the power to operate 'as a threat to the stability of the patriarchal symbolic, whose paternal law is dependent on the abjectification of the maternal body, her image is retranslated in, for example, the horror genre as a terrifying negative force with the power to castrate' (Welby 2010: 46). Ultimately, what Illanes does cleverly is to fool the audience into believing that it is Angela who is offered as a *femme castratrice* within the narrative when, in fact, it is Soledad who will ultimately become the real monstrous figure. Soledad's decision to have a monstrous utopic pregnancy manifested through the objectification of Angela's body shows that the abject female body in the film operates at the interstice of macho and mariana identity. Soledad will be the one character who will recuperate mariana identity within the narrative, but in doing so she will embrace a monstrous subjectivity as the mechanism for realigning traditional female subjectivity within the parameters of Latin American patriarchy.

The realignment of the mariana identity at the hands of Soledad can best be perceived in the main torture sequence in the film. This follows many of the conventions of traditional slasher movies, with macabre incidental music, medium close-ups and close-ups and abundance of extreme close-ups, in conjunction with an overt sexualisation of the victims (for the most part female). By this point in the film three of the protagonist's friends have been imprisoned and tortured in one of the stables near the house. Ivana has been forced into a cage after being captured in the woods, trying to run away from the house. In the meantime, Claudia has been dragged out of her room while bleeding from some form of poisoning and has been tied up on top of the cage. During this sequence the way the camera pans up and down Olivia's restrained body, despite the fact that the ropes that keep her tied to the cage seem to be very loose, evidences that she is cinematically offered as the object of the gaze. However, unlike most traditional horror narratives, it could be suggested that she is not fetishised or objectified by a male monster (whose lascivious and murderous desires are equally castrating), but by a female monster. In this case it is Soledad, assisted by the impassive Angela, who punishes these women because she regards their type of femininity as a threat to the status quo of female mariana identity. *Baby Shower* seems to suggest that female emancipation is a synecdoche for a monstrous feminine figure whereby all the female characters in the film are presented through a form of negative feminine excess. As a result, traits such as being excessively sexual, sexually insatiable, manipulative, domineering and economically independent are deemed negative.

Furthermore, the film makes a direct connection between the monstrous feminine and castration. Castration is not the direct result of men's fears of the wholeness of female subjectivity, but the result of female emancipation being construed as a detraction from mariana subjectivity. Unlike many theorists who regard horror cinema as a genre in which violence and danger are exclusive domains of pleasure of an imaginary male audience, *Baby Shower* transgresses the assumed absence of spectatorial female pleasure, as the film posits the mariana female spectator at the centre of the narrative who is asked to derive pleasure from witnessing some forms of male castration and, more importantly, castration of anti-mariana behaviour. However, there is a clear difference between genital castration (as in the scene in which Soledad stabs Claudia in her vagina) and the castration of sexual and gender identity exercised by Soledad's murders and Angela's seemingly sadistic contemplation of them. In contrast to *Habitaciones para Turistas*, this film does not speak to men about their fear of women and, instead, speaks to women about spheres of female power.

The symbolism of female castration can be observed in the scene in which Claudia is chased by Ricardo (Pablo Krogh) after she witnesses Ivana's murder at Soledad's hands. As Claudia runs into the woods trying to escape the killers, a handheld camera shows her through a series of medium shots in which she is nervously trying to reach someone on her mobile phone. She suddenly stops and starts throwing up blood, then begins running again. She is dressed all in white in what can only be described as an ironic take on the purity of female maternal identity, as she is the only one who already has a family. The next sequence begins with Claudia running out of the woods and towards the camera. She stops suddenly and starts shaking and imploring Ricardo, who appears slowly into the frame, not to harm her. He throws her on the floor and asks her to shut up, then proceeds, in a medium close shot, to rape her. What is interesting is that as he rapes her he says, 'Perdón, perdón. Este es tu castigo. Sí, tu castigo... por alabar al gran estafador' [I'm sorry, I'm sorry. This is your punishment. Yes, it is your punishment... for praising the great trickster[3]]. The camera cuts from the medium shot to a close-up of Claudia's face as she screams, and then to an extreme close-up of her mobile phone open on the floor with the images of her children on the call screen. At this point in the narrative, the film simply stresses violence against women by depicting a spectacle of the 'ruined' female body. This is further emphasised when Claudia, semi-naked and with her face covered in blood, walks in on Angela and Soledad having an argument. Rather than assuming that the rape is simply a gratuitous and graphic depiction of gender violence, it could be suggested that by focusing on the image of Claudia's children (the screen of her mobile phone) at the end of the sequence, the director recuperates the narrative for the pleasures of a mariana spectatorship. Claudia has been punished not because of fear of female castration, but because she has neglected her maternal duties. The rape seems to be justified within the narrative—and to the imaginary mariana

---

[3] It can only be inferred that the great trickster to whom Ricardo refers is no other than the type of man who does not follow macho identity and is not capable of controlling women through an excess of patriarchal authority.

spectatorship—because she has not subscribed to 'the three basic images [of marianismo] of woman as virgin, woman as wife and woman as mother, all of which reinforced social, psychological and economic dependency for women' (Nieto-Gomez 1997: 49). Thus the fact that her children become aural witnesses, listening to her rape on the phone line, shows that her punishment is not only physical but also moral, and it is this lack of moral and maternal instinct that will justify her eventual death.

By the end of the film, Angela and Soledad will come to represent two diametrically opposed stances on the maternal abject. As soon as it is discovered that Angela is expecting twins, for both women her unborn babies are not only the platform for some form of socio-cultural redemption, but also the externalization of their subjectivity. They both embody a form of monstrous feminine, but it will only be Angela's body and maternal instinct that will be made abject through her desire to destabilise the mariana symbolic order. Despite the fact that Soledad does destabilise the symbolic order by being a murderous monster—she commits most of the killings in the film—and more importantly by her unfulfilled desire to become a mother and having to resort to a kind of borrowed sense of motherhood through Angela's pregnancy, it is possible to see how she comes to represent a clear form of mariana subjectivity and, in doing so, invites her imaginary mariana audience to relate to her actions. She goes to extreme lengths to protect the unborn babies and to guarantee the perpetuation of the mariana status quo. In this way, she becomes, as Kristeva theorises, 'the other maternal figure [who] is tied to suffering, illness, sacrifice […] This kind of motherhood, the masochistic mother who never stops working is repulsive and fascinating, abject' (1982: 158). She becomes the ultimate monstrous feminine who is, nonetheless, not necessarily transgressive of the codes of normative mariana motherhood, although most definitely transgressive of the codes of human morality.

The Soledad character is presented as the ultimate female monster because she obliterates the kinds of narrative endings usually reserved for traditional monsters, in which they are exterminated, killed or punished. Gérard Lenne, in his study of traditional horror narratives in the 1980s and 1990s, argues that women in horror films are either sexualised victims or lesser monsters that do not have the horror stature of their male counterparts, and are usually depicted as witches and/or secondary monsters. Lenne dismisses the role of the female monster—and its monstrosity— since 'is it not reasonable that woman, who, in life, is both mother and lover, should be represented by characters that convey the feeling of a sheltering peace?' (1979: 35). He sees the maternal figure, in much the same way as Illanes does, as incapable of monstrous acts and continues to assign to her domestic roles that disempower her both within the narrative and as a monster in her own right. Soledad, on the other hand, represents a true female monster whose gory crimes successfully disrupt the phallocentric symbolic order and posit her as a transgressive figure who is a threat to the stability of patriarchy, not because of the changes experienced through her pregnant body (as is the case with Angela), but because her murderous acts are justified within a maternal rhetoric. Soledad is the ultimate abject figure because her levels of subjectivity (as a woman and a mother) are repressed and find an outlet for externalisation in the killings she commits. She is made even more abject by her perverse desire to submit to patriarchy, even though this means a break with the phallocentric order embodied by the two main male figures, and to reject female emancipation by killing those who oppose or become a threat to the mariana social order.

It could be argued that television series such as *SATC*, and more recent examples such as *Desperate Housewives* (2004–2012), *Lipstick Jungle* (2008–2009) and *Cougar Town* (2009–2015), clearly advocate a disruption of the mariana ideology (or traditional femininity) that has characterised filmicn and media texts over the years. At the end of the narrative of *Baby Shower*, the triumph of Soledad (whose murderous actions will go unpunished) posits the mariana subject as a key figure in the socio-sexual imaginary by pointing to the main characteristics of the mariana as key elements of an imaginary social femininity that circulates in Latin American culture. Her triumph may also shed light on the politics of female identity in post-dictatorship Chile, where middle-class women, as Amelia Guy-Meakin (2012) suggests, favoured the sexual politics promulgated by the military junta as 'it secured their privileged position within Chile's existing gender and class hierarchies'. Soledad, as an abject type of mariana subjectivity alongside her murderous actions, demonstrates that when the abject is completely repressed, as Kristeva rightly asserts, 'there is a risk that it will emerge in an entirely destructive, violent, and negative form' (1982: 4). Soledad's actions are aimed at recuperating mariana ideology, albeit through graphic and gory murderous actions, and show a desire on the part of Illanes to reclaim marianismo as a key form of female subjectivity among women in the continent.

The confrontation of mariana and non-mariana identity is clearly evidenced by the end of the narrative in which, through parallel endings, a case is made for a return to the archaic mother (whose subjectivity will be directly associated with that of the mariana). One of the last sequences occurs in the hospital room where Angela awakens after the night of murders and death that makes up the whole of the film and that has prompted her to go into labour. A close shot shows the hospital cot in which her baby has been placed. The camera switches to another close shot of the left-hand side of Angela's face (showing a deep cut from the previous night) as she turns head to the side to look at her baby. Cutting back to the baby, who coos pleasantly, the image then switches to a low-angle, frontal shot of Angela on her hospital bed. When her baby is placed next to her, her slight smile suddenly disappears when she realises that only one baby (instead of two) is by her side. At this point Manuela's hand becomes visible, grabbing Angela's arm in support while the latter starts crying. The camera zooms out slowly as the two women cry and then pans right to show the nurse placing the baby back in his cot and taking him out of the room, the sobbing of the two women continuing.

The next, and final, scene opens with an extreme close-up of a baby sucking a woman's breast, then the camera moves to a close shot of her upper torso as it pans up to her face. A cut to a medium shot of the back of the woman (by this point it is clear it is Soledad) shows a breathtaking natural landscape—a lake, a forest and snowy mountains—and the camera begins to zoom out to show more of this peaceful landscape as the film comes to an close. This ending serves to reify the relationship between the monstrous feminine and maternal authority, in which the female body becomes the locus on which is mapped the notion of the horrific. Through Soledad's act of breastfeeding, Illanes forces the audience to conflate horror and maternity. On the one hand, the spectator is expected to react in disgust to Soledad's thirst for blood, but on the other, her maternal instinct reinforces the notion that there is a fusion between mother and nature. The act of breastfeeding operates as a reminder that the maternal body, as discussed by Creed following Kristeva, exposes 'the way in which the fertile female body is constructed as an "abject" in order to keep the subject separate from the phantasmatic power of the mother, a power which threatens to obliterate the subject' (1993a: 25). In the end, Soledad reclaims a space for mariana identity in which the search for maternal subjectivity justifies her monstrous killings as a way to restabilise the patriarchal symbolic order.

Mothers of the Plaza of Horror: Motherhood and Female Agency in the Argentinian Slasher Film

The notion of motherhood is intrinsically embedded in the Argentinian social, political and cultural imaginary. The Madres de la Plaza de Mayo can be regarded as one of the most successful social and political movements in the country since the time of the military junta in the 1970s. By staging their silent protests and with the subsequent political mobilisation to press for a governmental response in relation to the *desaparecidos* (disappeared), the Madres managed both to politicise motherhood as an institution and to provide a voice of dissent against the repressive military regime. These women's maternal instincts and their desire to unearth the truth about the disappearance of their children acted as a catalyst to mobilise them to political action. As Gisela Norat rightly asserts, 'maternity had been the Argentine women's sole motivator and their sole ammunition' (2008: 219). This is a country in which motherhood has operated as an institution, albeit characterised by the traumatic scar left by a socially recognised absent motherhood that had to be experienced by those women whose children were taken from them, their whereabouts never known. Motherhood in this sense is about not only the ability to bear children, but the multiple possibilities of female identity shaped by the act of bearing and raising children by playing the role of the mother. The institution of motherhood, as Adrienne Rich proposes,

> is not identical with bearing and caring for children, any more than the institution of heterosexuality is identical with intimacy and sexual love. Both create the prescriptions and the conditions in which choices are made or blocked; they are not 'reality' but they have shaped the circumstances of our lives. (1976: 42)

The Madres did not set out either to challenge the status quo of patriarchal sexism characteristic of Argentinian culture, or to claim allegiance with any branch of the feminist movement. Instead, their power of address derived from their position—and identity—as mothers. The Madres as a movement reinterpreted the role of women as activists and utilised their inscription to the domestic sphere as a platform from which they effectively call for answers from the government in relation to the atrocities committed during the regime, while not posing an imminent threat to the regime itself.

The Madres have exercised what Sara Eleanor Howe regards as a type of 'motherist' politics in Argentina through the adoption of 'a strongly maternalist role, focusing their opposition to the regime through their role as mothers, and the rights and responsibilities inherent to motherhood' (2006: 43). They were quick to separate themselves from other feminist movements as a result of the 'seeming incompatibility of the Madres' identity with the equality and freedom from traditional roles as sought by feminism' (2006: 43). For the Madres, their roles as mothers, nurturers, carers, protectors and guardians of the household were not ones they intended to challenge or change. However, the moment the state invaded their private sphere—by means of kidnapping, torture and assassination of their children; that is, political dissidents and other individuals who were deemed subversive—they felt the need to get organised and sought by means of pacifistic protest to gain a governmental response to the atrocities committed. The success of the marches they staged did not only bring visibility to the political and social unrest that dominated the country from the time of the junta, but also cemented the importance of motherhood in the nation's socio-cultural imaginary. The Madres, as Adrián Pérez Melgosa asserts, 'transform[ed] traditional notions of motherhood into a powerful tool of political resistance, both women and symbols of the feminine have been at the forefront of every major popular protest denouncing the abuses, crimes, and injustices of a corrupt political class in Argentina' (2005: 151). Arguably, the legacy of a widespread marianismo and the key role that these women played in guaranteeing the return to democracy in Argentina have secured the figure of the mother a prominent space in which motherhood is revered as an aspiration in its own right.

Motherhood as a form of rhetoric (and even a trope) has also shaped the Argentinian filmic social imaginary in key films[4] in which the figure of the mother is depicted as the moving force that guarantees progress and socio-political stability in the country. Although Pérez Melgosa is quick to point out that a number of films made after the return to democracy have depicted 'the figure of the upper-middle-class mentally ill mother,

[4] Adrián Pérez Melgosa regards *La Historia Oficial* (Luis Puenzo 1985), *El Hijo de la Novia* (Juan José Campanella 2001), *Apartment Zero* (Martin Donovan 1988), *La Ciénaga* (Lucrecia Martel 2002) and *Animalada* (Sergio Bizzio 2001) as key films that study motherhood in contemporary Argentinian cinema. The list could also be extended with the inclusion of *La Mujer sin Cabeza* (Lucrecia Martel 2008) and *Leonera* (Pablo Trapero 2008).

whose illness seems to originate in her inability to cope with physical ageing and economic decadence' (2005: 152), it is clear that the abnegated and pious mother continues to be regarded as the quintessential form of Argentinian motherhood. It is from this point of departure that the rest of this chapter will provide an analysis of Adrián García Bogliano's *Habitaciones para Turistas* (2005), and will demonstrate how the film can be read as the backdrop to an institutionalised motherist socio-political agenda in contemporary Argentina that has—by its sheer exaltation and reverence of a nationalistic notion of motherhood—repressed the ownership of the female body by women in the country. In the film, five women in their early 20s find themselves stranded in an isolated rural town outside Bueno Aires after missing their connecting train to the town of Trinidad. They have no other option but to spend the night in a hostel for tourists owned by two brothers. However, as the night goes on, they become victims to the dark side of local hospitality and a twisted sense of bloody justice.

What makes García Bogliano's film particularly poignant is the fact that the gruesome killings—albeit lacking quality in the execution through special effects and make-up—occur, as audiences soon realise, as a result of the girls' intention to have an abortion for their unwanted pregnancies. Halfway through the film, spectators learn that all the girls had arrived at the town of San Ramón for the same purpose: to visit an abortion clinic in a remote town and get rid of their unborn babies without their families finding out. Although the film follows the pattern of misogyny characteristic of other slasher films, in which rather vulnerable girls are persecuted and gruesomely killed by one or more male psychopaths (who are depicted as monsters), it would be possible—and it is the contention of the argument here—to see the girls as somewhat monstrous as a result of their determination to get these abortions. It is their 'unnatural' desire to get rid of their unborn babies that makes them monster figures, thus justifying their killing.

This would challenge D. Bruno Starss's argument that 'in most mainstream horror films the woman is depicted as the victim, frequently punished for her unrestrained libido, because, according to psychoanalytic theory, at the heart of horror lies a patriarchal fear of female sexuality' (2006: 22). However, in *Habitaciones para Turistas* the girls are not necessarily presented as undeserving victims. Instead, it could be suggested that they come to symbolise the embodiment of unrestrained libido, since their pregnancies challenge national discourses of motherhood that have been perpetuated through patriarchal structures of power and oppression (usually enacted in the form of anti-abortion laws) and social movements such as the Madres. Despite Argentina's return to democracy in 1983 and the legalisation of divorce in 1980, Argentina is still to this day one of the few Latin American countries where, as Merike Blofield points out, 'abortion remains illegal except to save the life of the woman. Even in the legally permitted cases, however, the courts and public health system have denied the procedure to women in need' (2006: 15). Thus the film clearly reifies the notion that motherhood is an intrinsic part of the national imaginary, and that its repulsion goes against the grain of the country's gender and social paradigms that have been prevalent since the return to democracy. It could be argued that, to a great extent, motherhood in Argentina is not an individual choice, but a social imposition. The traumatic scar left by the *desaparecidos* could be said to have institutionalised a sense of patriotic motherhood whereby mothering children is regarded as a national duty. Unsurprisingly, Julio Malfud asserts that it 'would be difficult to encounter other peoples where the maternal cult enjoys such protection and transcendence as it does among the Argentine' (cited in Malin 1994: 191).

In *Habitaciones para Turistas*, García Bogliano exploits a number of tropes that not only create the perfect environment for widespread killings (the isolated rural town, the chief of the fanatical religious sect, the strange brothers who own the hostel), but also confront national paradigms for the audience—mainly the notion of *civilización y barbarie* [civilization and brutality] and, as previously suggested, the motherist identity embedded in the national consciousness. For instance, at the beginning of the film, during the bus trip to San Ramón, Elena (Jimena Krouco) and Theda (Elena Siritto) become acquainted as they sit next to each other on the bus. It becomes clear that they are both concealing the real reason for their journey to Trinidad (their fictitious final destination): Elena looks flummoxed and hesitates when asked about her reasons for travelling, while Theda simply responds that the whole journey may have been a mistake on her part. However, the conversation also illustrates the dichotomy of rural versus urban life that will become a latent theme throughout the narrative. As the bus journey continues, Elena asks Theda what the landscape inspires in her. When the latter pauses to think about her answer, the director offers panoramic shots of peasants working the land. Ironically, the camera returns to Theda, who says she is not very keen on the countryside, to which Elena responds 'a mí me encanta, pero para verlo desde la ventanilla de un micro' [I love it. But only to be seen from the window of a bus]. Their disdain for rural life and the characters' pregnancies, suggesting an implicit lasciviousness derived from a life of permissiveness in the city, are what, in the end, justify their annihilation from the narrative.

In many horror films, the countryside is depicted as a space in which death is part of a process of purification of the natural corruption of urban life. Although such films do not necessarily ask the audience to identify with the killer and his or her methods of killing, the narrative implies that urban spaces corrupt people, thus justifying the character's murderous actions. The urban metropolis constitutes a space in which moral codes have been relaxed or eroded from the national consciousness, as well as the regulatory practices that govern mariana identity. The film suggests that sex outside marriage is a symptom of the careless nature of the sexual practices and moral codes operating in those loci of socialisation where machismo is no longer a controlling force. By doing so, García Bogliano's film turns on its head the notion of *civilización y barbarie* in which, although people living in rural Argentina continue to be depicted as barbaric as a result of their murderous tendencies, their actions are regarded as somewhat necessary to cleanse those who live in urban spaces. Thus Jonathan Risner is right to signal that

> social relations play a crucial role in determining space, gender, and gender relations, and the cinematic landscapes in Bogliano's films are not solely about images of pampas or streets. The landscapes are also shaped by the relations between characters of different genders, which in the context of a horror film, often acquire a violent dimension. (2011: 5)

It is not surprising, then, that the people portrayed within the narrative as living in rural Argentina will hold more traditional values in relation to gender politics and the individual's ownership, or lack thereof, of the politics of desire. Like the countryside, the female body is constructed as part of a national imagery that seeks to place motherhood at the centre of discourses on national identity and pride (Fig. 4.1).

The horror genre has traditionally operated as an outlet that seeks to explore the relationship between monstrosity and notions of female identity and motherhood. Christopher Sharrett has claimed that the slasher

Fig. 4.1 The protagonists arrive at their final destination: Silvia (Mariela Mujica), Lidia (Victoria Witemburg), Elena (Jimena Kruoco), Ruth (Brenda Vera) and Theda (Elena Siritto). *Habitaciones para Turistas* ©Pauraflics

movie is 'explicitly about the destruction of women' (1996: 254). Similarly, Sarah Trencansky argues that 'women are repeatedly killed, apparently in conformance to the monster's attempt at repressing the dangerous sexuality they exhibit [...] or seek out during the course of the film' (2001: 64). However, García Bogliano's film does not portray the annihilation of the female characters as a sign of a latent misogyny embedded in the narrative, but as a sign of a desire to align the film with a national discourse that sees reproduction as part of a motherist national agenda. *Habitaciones para Turistas* could be said to respond to the anxieties evoked by the current climate of reproductive rights that, to a great extent, reaffirms the notion of motherhood that has shaped politics, as well as the socio-cultural imaginary, in the country after the return to democracy.[5] This

---

[5] Josefina Leonor Brown (2008) explains that on the return to democracy in the 1980s (marked by the imposition of a new economic system and the establishment of new social networks) the country also embraced a neo-conservative discourse that promoted the return of women to more traditional roles. She had begun to elaborate this view in an earlier paper (2004) in which she claimed: 'hablar de derechos (no)reproductivos supone poner en el centro de la escena cuestiones largamente silenciadas, tales como la anticoncepción y el

pro-motherist agenda begins to filter through the narrative in an earlier scene in which Elena, after having a shower, steps on some bathroom scales (shown through a close-up of her feet on the scales, which switches to an extreme close-up of the markings on the scale). Through a series of consecutive close-ups of her face looking down at the reading on the scales, her hands caressing her belly, her breasts, and ending on a medium shot of her staring at her reflection in a three-sided mirror, her body is already encrypted as part of the motherist agenda prevalent in the social, political and cultural imaginary. However, the female bodies of the protagonists (as an allegory of the purity of mariana identity) in terms of both object of desire and the sadistic gaze of the male monster will soon be obliterated after the women's real intentions are made explicit within the story. Thus once it is revealed that the protagonists' true aim is to rid themselves of their unborn babies, the film positions them as anti-mariana figures and, by doing so, lessens the degree of empathy from the audience when they are killed (Fig. 4.2).

The women's pregnant bodies highlight an ownership of desire that remains excluded from mariana identity. Meanwhile, their rejection of their unborn progeny reifies an anti-motherist position that seems at odds with the social and political notions of motherhood put forward by the government and other social and religious institutions. It could be argued that the abortions sought by the protagonists in a remote part of the country equate with the atrocities commited by the military junta. The extermination of the anti-motherist young women begins with the death of Silvia (Mariel Mujica). The director's use of black and white throughout the film, the preponderance of chiaroscuro that makes some images quite hard

aborto, así como otras formas de ejercicio de la sexualidad que exceden la heterosexualidad, poniendo en tela de juicio los roles de género estereotipados y largamente naturalizados' [Talking about (non)reproductive rights supposes to place centre stage issues that have been largely silenced such as contraception and abortion, as well as other ways to exercise one's sexuality that question stereotypical gender roles that are largely naturalised]. These ideas chime with those expressed by Lynn M. Morgan (2015), who declares that 'conservative religious activists increasingly adopt the secular language of "rights" to advance their "pro-life" and "pro-family" policies. Rather than arguing for womens rights, abortion rights, and the right to choose, the conservatives argue for natural rights, parental rights, and fetal rights.' At the time of writing the debate about reproductive rights in Argentina continues to be at the forefront for both conservatives and liberals, while abortion is still excluded from any legislative protection unless the wellbeing of the mother is at stake (and in such cases both the right-wing and Catholic press and conservative politicians continue to stigmatise and denigrate women who want to exercise their right to control their reproductivity).

Fig. 4.2 Girls as object of the murderous gaze: Silvia (Mariela Mujica) discovers a camera watching over Ruth (Brenda Vera) in the brothers' room. *Habitaciones para Turistas* ©Pauraflics

to distinguish and the extensive use of close shots and close-ups give the film a more terrifying tone. For instance, in one sequence Lydia (Victoria Witemburg) hears a strange noise coming from underneath her bedroom and decides to investigate by putting her face against the floorboards. Through a series of flash edits, the film proceeds to show a close shot of her face against the floorboards, her back and shoulders, the blade of a butcher's knife, a close-up of her face in terror, a wound on her body, her body rolling on the floor, her hands grabbing the blade of the knife in an attempt to stop the murderer inflicting any more damage, the knife going into her body, her eyes opened wide in sheer terror and her face being splattered with her own blood. Once the rest of the girls are awakened by Silvia's screams, they all run out of their rooms and end up bumping into one another in the hall. After checking Silvia's room and finding a pool of blood on the floor, the girls try to escape, only to discover that all the windows are locked and they are trapped in the house. Simultaneously, the lights go off and the girls are left in total darkness.[6] As the women wander around the house in order to look for an escape route, Ruth (Brenda Vera) stays behind, because she has dropped the lighter she was using to illuminate the way. Through a medium shot spectators see Ruth bending over to pick up the lighter and when she disappears from the screen, a shirtless masked man is viewed in the background. A series of close-ups then shows Ruth being caught with a piece of rope around her neck and dragged away from the rest of the group and up some stairs. However, before the man can kill her, Lydia comes from behind and kicks and punches him. To the average observer these scenes may be reminiscent of classic horror films in which the 'male audience members cheer on the misogynous misfit in these movies as they rape, plunder, and murder their screaming, writhing female victims [...] these same men cheer on (with renewed enthusiasm, in fact) the heroines, who are often as strong, sexy, and independent as the victims' (Schoell 1985: 55). However, it will be soon after this encounter with the murderous monster that the narrative turns on its head to suggest that perhaps the victims and the final girl do deserve to be punished and eliminated from the narrative, because they have attempted to rebel against the established paradigms of female identity through the notion of motherhood.

Soon after this episode, and after taking Nestor (Rolf Garcia) hostage, the four women try to make sense of what is happening to them. By

---

[6] Technically speaking, this is perhaps one of the least effective narrative devices in the film, since it is almost impossible to differentiate between the lighting work before and after this moment due to the use of black-and-white film and the constant use of chiaroscuro in many other sequences.

comparing their stories, they soon realise that it is more than a coincidence that they all have the same amount of money with them ($1500), and this leads them to work out that they all had the same purpose for their trip; that is, to get an abortion at a remote clinic. At this point, it becomes clear that the female victim of *Habitaciones para Turistas* is no longer a random woman who embodies the sexual frustrations or becomes the object of the perverse desire of the killer, but a woman who must be punished for attempting to strike the basis of normative femininity. Thus it is possible to suggest that the real monsters in the films, when reading it from a motherist perspective, are not the men who carry out the murders but the girls who decide to terminate their pregnancies. Their annihilation from the narrative simply reinforces the notion that abortion, as Kevan M. Yenerall asserts in her analysis of *Revolutionary Road* (Sam Mendes 2008), 'is an abhorrent and abnormal practice that signals deep underlying emotional and mental deficiencies' (2011: 12). The rejection of the maternal imperative provides a narrative justification to the killing of the women and the punishment of the final girl (which in itself obliterates the conventions of the traditional horror narrative). By making the girls' intention to get an abortion explicit within the story, the director disavows two elements of the cultural construction of maternal femininity as understood in the popular imaginary. On the one hand, they overturn the passivity of the body in possession of a child, and secondly, they push to actively reject the fulfilment that emotive mothering—that is, gestation and pregnancy—evokes.

In other words, the girls in the film become monstrous because they purposely and unremorsefully set out to kill their unborn babies. The transformation into monstrosity is marked by the physical change undergone by Elena during the scene in which she, Ruth and Silvia are looking for Theda. As the three girls gather to plan their next move, Elena, hearing Theda yell for help, runs to a wall and puts her ear next to it to try to hear better. As she does so, she is framed in a slight low-angle, close medium shot that shows her face changing from fear to pain. As her expression changes, Ruth comes closer and asks her what is going on. Elena simply runs away and locks herself in a convenient empty room. At this point the camera switches to a low-angle, medium shot as she takes her pants off and remains in her underwear, then she touches her stomach in pain and takes her underwear off. The camera moves to a close-up of her agonising face and then switches, zooming in to a close-up of her underwear stained in blood. She looks down to realise that blood is pouring down her legs and forming a small pool by her feet. The camera returns to her face to show her crying in distress. It is clear that the scene suggests that Elena is having a miscarriage; however, this episode only serves to make her even more abject compared to the normative and motherist femininity the film seems to purport. The blood-stained underwear represents, hyperbolically, the corpse killed by the monstrous feminine in which, as Kristeva theorises, 'the corpse (or cadaver: *cadere*, to fall), that which has irremediably come a cropper, is cesspool, and death; it upsets even more violently the one who confronts it as fragile and fallacious chance' (1982: 3). The bloody transformation of the character(s) into monstrous feminine abject form seems to adhere to a desire to denounce abortion as a political strategy that destabilises the basis of post-dictatorial Argentina. As Osiel Gutierrez asserts,

> movies don't represent females as horrifying for their femaleness; however, females are horrifying to the extent they lose their femaleness […] The reality is that female monsters are horrifying because they project an image of femininity that is contrary to the way man's desire constructs them. The desirability of femaleness is altered once the female character undergoes a physical transformation of her beauty. (2001: 6)

Elena's miscarriage evidences her shift from innocent female to monstrous feminine whereby the bloodstained underwear becomes a signifier of her unmotherly monstrous nature. Her miscarriage is both a punishment for her attempt to go against female norms (motherly instinct) and an external sign of her perverse nature. Thus it could be argued that her body is preempting her anti-mariana psyche, as it rids itself of the unborn baby through a spontaneous abortion. In this light, she shows an innate (and uncontrollable) ability to kill that does not necessarily depend on her direct actions.

The girls' detachment from a supposedly maternal instinct, at least at the level of the diegesis, renders them monstrous, because they are deemed selfish and see abortion as an easy way out of having to accept responsibility for their own actions. The killing of the girls, whose unborn babies also vanish with them, could also be regarded as a synecdoche for the disappearances during the years of the dictatorship. Like the *desaparecidos*, the unborn babies disappear without leaving any trace of their whereabouts, in much the same way that Karen A. Foss and Kathy L. Domenici describe the social and political vacuum left by the forced disappearance of youth in Argentina who 'lost all of the usual forms by which social and political identity are represented' (2001: 243). The girls' decision to go to a remote town to seek an abortion is influenced by their desire to avoid official records, funerals, memorials and, more importantly, naming the baby, thus stripping the foetus of any form of identity.[7] Their killings may therefore be regarded not as murderous acts, but as an act of justice on behalf of the babies/disappeared who have been denuded of any form of social identity and any sense of citizenship (and whose deaths will remain unaccounted for).

García Bogliano's slasher movie could be said to challenge both national discourses regarding motherhood and some aspects of the cinematic genre itself. On the one hand, *Habitaciones para Turistas* reconsiders the role of maternity within the country's national politics and highlights the importance of mothering as part of a national political strategy. The girls in the film represent a shift in current attitudes towards the politics of the female body, in which bearing children is no longer regarded as paramount for the construction of femininity. Although this research does not attempt to suggest that such a shift should be regarded as a national problem, the film seems to align itself with this line of thought by justifying the protagonists' deaths as punishment for their desire to break away from the motherist politics sought by and campaigned for by the Madres and other official voices. By the same token, the notion of *civilización y barbarie* is reimagined as, arguably, it is the city girls who are constructed as barbaric due to their desire to rid themselves of their unborn babies. Despite the fact that some characters and tropes are used to stress the relationship between rural spaces and psychopathy—for instance, Maxi (Alejandro Lise) as the deformed brother and Flora (Mariana Pacotti) as the blind girl—it is the protagonist women who can be regarded as impure (and therefore barbaric) because they have obviously engaged in pre-marital sex and are now trying to cover up the evidence of their unmariana actions. As a result, the men's actions in trying to kill the girls may find justification when Judith Halberstam claims that 'the act of murder is merely a moral necessity, a compulsion to save the world from the contaminating potential of a "race of devils"' (1995: 48).

---

[7] However, it would be possible to consider the dynamics restricting women's reproductive rights in Argentina, especially abortion (as explained earlier), given which the film could also be read to function as a denouncement of conservative politics in the country. Despite such a potential reading, it could be insisted that the tacit monstrous nature of the female protagonists is really brought to the front of the narrative, as theorised in this chapter.

Finally, the film also speaks against the cinematic genre itself, since the final girl, Theda, does not manage to escape unharmed at the end of the narrative. According to Clover (1993), the final girl is the surviving female character who, unlike the rest of the 'gang of friends' to which she will undoubtedly belong, will manage to make sense of the horror surrounding her and fights back against her attacker in order to defeat him. This character, as Trencansky admits, 'is the undisputed main character, both because of increased character development afforded to her throughout the film and because of her early discovery of the killer, evident to the viewing audience from the beginning of the film' (2001: 64). However, in *Habitaciones para Turistas* Theda is the least developed of all the characters and her luck seems to be more fortuitous than a matter of working out the best way to deal with what is happening around her. The fact that she is the sole survivor does not come as a surprise, because she is the only one who has, from the beginning of the narrative, expressed some doubts about the real purpose of her trip. In this way, she is slightly more aligned with the motherist politics of contemporary Argentina that the film is trying to put forward, albeit through the killing of women who do not embrace such a political agenda. This is all the more obvious during the last scenes in the film when Theda tries to save Elena and herself from their persecutors and manages to arrive at the station hoping to catch the train to San Ramón. When they arrive Theda asks Ruben (Abel Ponce) to call the police to report what has happened, and to get a doctor to help Elena. As she waits while Ruben makes the call, the camera zooms in rapidly from a close-up of Ruben with the handset by his face to the actual phone over a table. The camera then pans right in an extreme close-up along the phone cable, alternating between this image and low-angled extreme close-ups of Theda's face, until it stops where the cable has been cut through. At this point the audience sees Theda's face through a shaky hand-held, close-up shot showing sheer panic. Theda tries, once more, to escape with Elena and manages to get back to the town. However, she will soon be caught by Horacio (Oscar Ponce), the town's priest, and the other men they had encountered the previous day (Fig. 4.3).

After a short exchange between Horacio and Theda, she soon realises that she is about to be killed. However, at the last minute she hears a phone ringing, stabs Maxi in the throat with a knife and runs towards the place where the ringing is coming from. She manages to get to the phone in the nick of time and tells her dad about her pregnancy (she had phoned the previous day and asked her sister to have her father call her on that

Fig. 4.3 Escaping machismo: Theda (Elena Siritto) helps a wounded Silvia (Mariela Mujica) find a safe hideout. *Habitaciones para Turistas* ©Pauraflics

number); she also tells him about the people she has met (without making them sound like psychopaths), that she has decided to keep the baby and that Horacio will drive her home. She finishes the conversation and gives the phone back to Horacio, who had stopped the men from trying to kill her, and walks out in an act of defiance when she, for the first time, looks her attempted killer right in the eyes. At this point the film seems to imply that Theda has managed to become the final girl by overcoming the horrors of the night before. However, if according to Clover one precondition of the final girl is her ability to remain virginal, or at least somewhat chaste, during the whole narrative—whereas her female counterparts all engage in intercourse—then Risner is right to assert that 'with all the young women in *Habitaciones* already having engaged in intercourse, not only is their survival put into doubt, but also the possibility of any final girl emerging unscathed' (2011: 10).

Theda's pregnancy is a clear sign of her unchaste condition, and it is obvious that her decision to keep the baby at the end of the film has more to do with escaping her killers than a real desire to be a mother. Although her baby will not become a *desaparecido*, as do those of the other girls in the film and indeed of any woman who has to seek an illegal abortion in

Argentina, Theda does not embrace motherhood as part of her mariana identity. Ariel Dorfman's words in his article on Mother's Day best exemplify the way in which the film deals with the issue of motherhood and its impact on the national imaginary. The relationship between Argentina's gender politics, heavily shaped by a motherist mentality, the trauma left by the *desaparecidos* and the notion of abortion in the film demonstrates that

> the ambiguity that surrounds the missing person goes, however, further than death: What is being denied, ultimately, is his birth, the fact that he had a mother. It is as if he never existed. [...] What is really being ravaged is the meaning of motherhood itself. It is as if the hours of labor needed to bring each of the desaparecidos into the world had been erased. (1983)

For this reason, Theda's apparent redemption at the end of the narrative is not regarded as an honest attempt to re-engage in the motherist politics of the country, but as a stratagem to preserve her life.

The director decides to obliterate the fate of the final girl by allowing her, and the film audience, to believe that she will leave the narrative unscathed, and then, at the very last minute, still exercise a form of physical punishment. As Horacio drives Theda home, he tells her: 'Si, pensás que somos sólo unos locos de pueblo, tengo que decirte que no entendiste nada. Y no creo que hayas entendido nada en realidad. Así que tarde o temprano, sé que vas a terminar pagando' [If you think we are just a bunch of crazy townies, then you haven't understood a thing. And I don't think you have understood anything at all. So, sooner or later, you are gonna pay the price for your actions]. Theda quickly leaves the car and runs to hug her dad, who is awaiting her return. However, as they hug, she hears over the road someone preaching in much the same way as Horacio did back in San Ramón. Looking over, she realises that there is a temple of the Iglesia Jesucristo es Vida like there was in the town from which she has just escaped. As she hears preaching from inside the church, the camera cuts to the preacher shouting "arde, arde, arde" [burn, burn, burn] and back to Theda, who is then bumped into by a passer-by. When she kneels down to pick up a medallion that has fallen from her chain, she panics at the realisation that she has not really escaped her persecutors, then turns to notice her father lying on the pavement and bleeding from a wound in his neck. She goes to scream and the camera cuts to a slight high-angle shot of her face. As she looks up, a hand is seen covering her mouth and then the camera cuts to a close-up of the other hand wielding a knife and making two stabbing moves. The camera finally cuts to a close medium shot of Theda covering her eyes as blood pours profusely from her fingers and she falls on her back, bringing the film to a close.

This ending clearly breaks the tradition of the final girl as the only survivor in the slasher film; Theda simply becomes the last victim in the narrative. By doing so, the film maintains a position of male hegemonic supremacy, whereby women are not allowed ownership of their bodies or control over their own gender politics, since their bodies are regarded as national property. The murders in the film become the natural (re) action to the girls' attempt at transgressing patriarchal normativity and imply that motherhood should be at the forefront of their social identity, as is the case with the Madres and other political and religious groups who continue to deny access to clinical termination for women in Argentina who do not want to become mothers. Thus Risner is able to claim that 'Theda's survival as a maimed final girl speaks to a hopelessness of political action to change abortion laws in Argentina in the face of a powerful Catholic church [and other institutions]' (2011: 14) (Fig. 4.4).

Fig. 4.4 Victims of machismo: Lidia (Victoria Witemburg) and Theda (Elena Siritto) run into one of the crazy church-goers while escaping from the killers. *Habitaciones para Turistas* ©Pauraflics

Conclusion

The image of the pregnant woman has long fascinated the popular imagination in many cultures. From the abnegated and selfless mother who will sacrifice herself for the benefit of her family, to the monstrous mother who will inflict pain and suffering on her family and others, the mother operates as a figure who is, more often than not, made abject through a lack of identity beyond motherhood. Oliver explains that in many film genres, but especially in horror, 'women's fertility is not only metaphorically threatening and excessive but also a danger that literally comes to life in the demon or alien seed that inhabits or possesses these (usually) unsuspecting pregnant women' (2012: 111). However, in the two films analysed in this chapter, fertility is threatening to the extent that it either subverts the notion of motherhood that is embedded in the national imaginary through the perpetuation of mariana identity, or makes an attempt against the basis of motherist politics whereby the government regards motherhood as a national institution in need of protective social surveillance. What is clear about both films is that the female protagonists are depicted, mainly due to their pregnant state, as monsters.

In *Baby Shower*, Angela's pregnancy is regarded as the evil force that drives her to plot against her best friends in order to find out who has destroyed her marriage. She clearly uses her advanced pregnancy both as a bait—to invite her friends to join her and celebrate the shower from which the film derives its title—and as a shield, to invite empathy from the audience and avoid an overt demonisation of her character. She shifts from monster feminine to mariana during the narrative and, ultimately, fails at both, since she never fully adheres to either as a pre-emptive identity. The film, nonetheless, seems to be fascinated with the punishment of those manifestations of female identity that deviate from the traditional mariana role. At the same time it rewards the character—despite this being the most monstrous of all—who is the only one to regard motherhood as 'no longer as a restrictive label but instead as a positive force believed to be exemplary of particular qualities such as an "especially ethical and responsible (attitude) to life"' (Howe 2006: 44).

Similarly, in *Habitaciones para Turistas*, mariana identity and the role of the mother are both brought to the forefront of the narrative, since it is the lack of either on the part of the female protagonists that will justify their eventual annihilation. The film clearly engages with gender politics and reproductive rights in contemporary Argentina, since a national audience may not read the film outside the context of the illegality of clinical terminations and the motherist politics prevalent in the country. The film clearly follows the formula whereby premarital sex is punished by death, at the expense of the life of its own final girl, who does not manage to survive the narrative untouched and is seriously harmed (although it remains unclear whether she dies from being stabbed in her eyes) by the end of the film. Unlike the final girls of more recent horror cinema, the girls in this film all die once stripped of agency, as the 'male monsters' are not necessarily evil, but work in order to maintain the status quo of patriarchal domination over the female body. This film, ultimately, creates a dilemma for the viewer, who is split between rejecting the monstrosity of the killings perpetuated by the men and seeing such killings as the natural punishment for transgressing the tenets of normative motherhood.

In a country in which contemporary motherhood has been greatly shaped by the actions of the Madres and their unique way of placing motherhood in the limelight of contemporary politics, it is impossible to avoid a more politicised reading of the narrative. Furthermore, Argentina possesses the highest level of female representation in politics in the whole of Latin America, with women forming 39% of the national congress. Thus, the greater number of female politicians in the country, including until the end of 2015 the president, Cristina Fernández de Kirchner, connotes that female legislators have a bigger impact on policy than in other parts of the continent and, as a result, that women's issues remain at the forefront of policy-making and politics in society and, naturally, will also permeate the socio-sexual imaginary. As a result, the film clearly displays the maternal body as an entity that taps into male anxiety surrounding birth and reproduction, while showing how the horror narrative serves as an excellent vehicle for addressing issues of reproductive rights.

CHAPTER 5

Bromance, Homosociality and the Crisis of Masculinity in the Latin American Zombie Movie

Simon Pegg (2008) has famously written, 'as monsters from the id, zombies win out over vampires and werewolves when it comes to the title of Most Potent Metaphorical Monster'. The 'modern' zombie—one that is 'literally' a living-dead creature and who is hungry for human flesh—has come both to represent and to play out society's fear of death, the loss of a sense of collective belonging in contemporary culture and the effect of consumerism as part of late capitalism. Cultural theorists may argue that, today more than ever, individuals are being 'zombified' by a society that strongly fosters taking a break from other individuals and from the act of socialisation itself, especially after the advent of social media. The zombie as a contemporary monster owes its current incarnation—as a kind of somnambulistic walking corpse with glaring eyes, emitting grunting sounds and pursuing human flesh to eat—to George Romero's *Night of the Living Dead* (1968). Earlier representations of the zombie were directly connected to voodoo practices in Haiti and responded to the miscegenistic anxieties of an American population, regarded as exemplary of the Western world, that regarded black Caribbean cultures as intrinsically retrograde and dangerously primitive. In the Latin American filmic imaginary, zombies are seen as early as Benito Alazakri's *Santo contra los Zombies* (1962); however, in this film zombies are more Frankenstein-like creatures who are provided with an electronic mechanism that brings the dead back to life and controls them at the same time. Regardless of the type of zombie portrayed on screen, it is undeniable that June Pulliam is right when she asserts:

> the zombie itself is a malleable symbol—representing everything from the horrors of slavery, white xenophobia, Cold War angst, the fear of death, and even apprehensions about consumer culture—and has become an icon of horror perhaps because it is quite literally a memento mori, reminding us that our belief that we can completely control our destiny, and perhaps through the right medical technology, even cheat death, is mere hubris. (2007: 724)

The zombie narrative, thus, could be regarded as a metaphor for reflecting on and externalising social anxieties in relation to the loss of individuality, a trope that has figured prominently since 9/11 in popular films such as Danny Boyle's *28 Days Later* (2002), Ruben Flieischer's *Zombieland* (2009) and Marc Foster's *World War Z* (2013), and that constitutes the ultimate Other monster figure.

Unlike alternative monster figures, zombies have an uncanny ability to be both scary and funny, because they lack the refinement, sophistication and level of humanity of other popular monsters. It is this level of malleability that permits them to fit just as easily in horror-gore narratives as well as horror-comedy narratives. The child-like behaviour of the zombie, in his/her rather infantilised instinct for survival through mere eating and grunting, offers an ideal outlet for comedy. Since they can only be killed at the head, zombies can endure a great deal of pain as well as physical injuries to their bodies, therefore the narrative can be quite inventive in finding ways to exterminate them. For instance, in films such as *Shaun of the Dead* (Edgar Wright, 2004) the protagonists use everyday items such as LPs, darts, a toaster, a cricket bat and tennis balls to try to annihilate the zombies. The humour derives from the actual use of such items and their deployment as weapons of destruction.

At the same time, many zombie narratives also revolve around a love triangle in which the zombie becomes the opposing figure to the fulfilment of a happy relationship between the protagonists. The zombie presence adds a new dimension to traditional rom-coms (romantic comedies) in which the couple not only has to try to overcome the obstacles posed by social values at large, or friends and family, or social, economic and even religious status, but also needs to confront the zombie invasion and manage to materialise from the narrative unscathed. The rom-zom-com (romantic zombie comedy), a term coined by Peter Dendle (2001) and further theorised by Kyle William Bishop (2006), emerges as a highly hybrid genre that combines love relationships, the absurd, the ridiculous and the horrific. With the exception of *Zombies of Mass Destruction* (Kevin Hamedani, 2009) and the hardcore satire *L.A. Zombie* (Bruce La Bruce, 2010), most rom-zom-coms tend to centre on heterosexual couples whose love is disrupted by the appearance of zombies who threaten to separate them or become an obstacle to their happiness.[1] More importantly, men tend to play a more pivotal role in these films, while women are usually relegated to secondary roles, or are somewhat fetishised as the object of an imaginary male gaze audience.

Thus most traditional zombie narratives (especially those from the 1960s to the early 2000s) show a seeming aversion to lead female characters who can oppose and/or fight against zombie invasions.[2] Most zombie films tend to play with the anxieties of an imaginary male audience whose sense of sexual identity—understood as inherently heterosexual—seems to be in direct correlation to the male protagonist's fate. Their heterosexual identity appears to be at stake during the narrative and is somewhat jeopardised by the imminent threat of the protagonist becoming a zombie at any given point. Although the rom-zom-com's narrative may ultimately centre on the emergence and development of an affective relationship between a heterosexual couple, this very same narrative tends to pay more attention to the way(s) in which male-to-male relationships develop and evolve in the advent of a zombie plague. With such an emphasis on male relationships, it is possible to argue that the imminent possibility of the disappearance of humankind becomes the catalyst for the emergence of homosocial feelings among such men and, as a result, the emergence and development of bromance narratives. The zombie comedy, especially, appears to operate as the bromantic and homosocial narrative per excellence, in which male characters can finally express their mutual 'love' in the disguise of brotherly banter while using jokes as a shield to cover up their, perhaps, real feelings for one another. In such films, comedy operates as a

---

[1] Although, most recently, Jonathan Levine's *Warm Bodies* (2013) breaks with this type of narrative by focusing on the relationship between a still-living teenage girl and an oddly introspective teenage zombie boy (who lives in a world mostly dominated by zombies) as they fall in love.

[2] It is only more recently that zombie movies such as *28 Days Later*, Francis Lawrence's *I Am Legend* (2007), Paul W. S. Anderson's *Resident Evil* (2002) or the hit television series *The Walking Dead* (2010–present) have embraced female figures who play a more active role in helping rid the world of the zombie plague.

twofold strategy whereby the homosocial bromance is kept separate from feelings of homosexual desire by means of fraternal mockery, while the film's audience remain safe in their position of 'imagined' heterosexuality by literally laughing off homosocial advances between such characters.

As has been discussed in Chaps. 2 and 3, machismo operates, culturally, as a template and driving force of all male sexuality in Latin America (Andrade 1992; Gutmann 1997; Carrillo 2002) and is based on the externalisation of hypermasculine behaviour and the conscious avoidance of any feminine traits that could call into question the *hombría* of a macho man. 'Real men' should only show such traits when mocking the behaviour of those believed to be homosexual in ways that can merely reinforce their own sense of heterosexual masculinity (Lancaster 1997). However, the bond between seemingly heterosexual male characters in most zombie narratives seems to operate at the border of hetero- and homosexuality, since their close relationship is tested, retested and will usually constitute a turning point within the narrative. Two recent Latin American zombie movies seem to attest to the fact that, as Patrick D. Hopkins argues,

> the gender category of men constructs its member around two conflicting characterizations of the essence of manhood. First, your masculinity (being a man) is natural and healthy and innate. But second, you must stay masculine—do not ever let your masculinity falter. So, although being a man is seen as a natural and automatic state of affairs for a certain anatomical makeup, masculinity is so valued, so valorized, so prized, and its loss such a terrible thing, that one must always guard against losing it. (1998: 179)

In Pablo Parés and Hernán Sáez's trilogy *Plaga Zombie* (1997, 2001, 2011), the main preoccupation of the films is not so much how to survive the zombie plague that has stricken a fictional town in Argentina, but the survival of the friendship between the three main male characters. Similarly, in Alejandro Brugués's *Juan de los Muertos* (2011), although the two main characters must fight the zombie plague that has recently attacked La Havana, the film seems to be more preoccupied with a friendship that has an overtly homosocial nature and explores clear moments of homoeroticism. In all these films, the affective relationship between the main male characters is shielded under the guise of a very strong friendship. These friendships are put to the test once one of the characters has potentially contracted the zombie 'virus' and risks becoming a zombie himself. At this point, the potential break in the male-to-male heterosexual friendship has the capacity to destabilise the pillars that sustain machismo as a rigid sexual template, thus forcing the characters to lose their macho masculinity and enter the terrain of the homoerotic by and through overt displays of male affection. This chapter, therefore, will explore the mechanisms whereby the zombie movie constitutes a queer narrative with the potential to destroy the basis of hetero-machismo, while contagion or zombie mutation seems ubiquitous with the loss of macho identity itself. This in turn demonstrates that the sense of masculinity of the male protagonists in these films is continuously in peril, and that becoming a zombie equates to a disavowal of the naturalness of machismo as an innate form of masculinity.

The analysis that follows will provide an exploration of the zombie comedy narrative as a genre that subverts gender codes of sexuality within Latino and Caribbean (hetero)sexual culture by promoting the emergence of a type of brotherly romance narrative or bromance in which a number of male protagonists create strong relationships that seem to break with established codes of male bonding and friendship and may border on the amorous. It will demonstrate that these films present narratives in which aspects of homosociality soon become intermingled in the sort of relationships that show more of a tendency towards romance between buddies (even when one of the parties is already engaged in a sentimental relationship with someone of the opposite sex). These are films that have quite an overt homoerotic tone in terms of the interaction among the men while, at the same time, using either toilet humour or some form of physical aggression/banter as the only permitted way of manifesting their physical desire and attraction. Arguably, the desire of film directors to obliterate the 'loving' physicality of the relationships between the male characters simply derives from a necessity to perpetuate the status quo of the basis of machismo. However, what it truly achieves is to manifest a crisis of masculinity within Latino and Caribbean cultures in which the 'innate' nature of male heterosexuality is called into question and the characters' sexuality becomes more multiple and fluid (although it is still framed within a machista sexual paradigm). Despite the heterosexual tribulations that are present in the storylines of these movies, the turning point in every film will be the moment when the relationship between the male protagonists is at stake or is challenged by external forces (the zombification of a character) and there is the possibility of a rupture in the 'normal' (albeit homosocial) nature of the relationship between the male protagonists. In short, this chapter will argue that these rom-zom-coms defy the familiar codes of the zombie genre and, by doing so, offer a rather subtle commentary on national (and arguably continental) cultural fears in relation to competing gender parameters.

The evolution of the male hero within zombie narratives in Latin American cinema has been marked by a shift in the way in which machismo, as a template for male sexuality, has been understood and has come under scrutiny in society at large. For instance, at the end of *Santo contra los Zombies*, the highly erotic Gloria Sandoval (Lorena Velásquez), on being rescued by the hero, ponders out loud who El Santo really is while the camera eroticises the hero's body through a long shot of his muscled body as it becomes enveloped, at times, by his own cape in a rather ethereal manner. The Detective Chief Almada (Dagoberto Rodríguez) simply replies, 'Una leyenda. Una quimera. La encarnación de lo más hermoso, el bien y la justicia. Ese es El Santo, el enmascarado de plata' [A legend. A dream. The incarnation of that which is most beautiful, good and just. That is Santo, the silver masked hero]. El Santo comes to represent the incarnation of the best characteristics of a purported masculinity. In this film, as in most of the films in this saga, he remains sexually neutral, as he develops affective relations with neither women nor men (and the closest audiences get to see him exerting any form of physical exchange is when he is wrestling other men in the ring). El Santo, as a precursor to the contemporary rom-zom-com heroes analysed in this chapter, manages to safeguard his macho identity by keeping his male and female admirers, colleagues and villains all at bay. By his being a lone hero, El Santo's masculinity is safeguarded from any deviation from standard masculinity. By asexualising the male protagonist in such films the narrative ensures that, as Matthew Stern suggests,

> there is an essential, clear-cut connection between sexual identity and behaviour, in practice there are many men who flout traditional heterosexual codes of behaviour while adopting specific strategies to avoid being publicly labelled gay, queer, or bisexual, thereby preserving their social status as masculine heterosexuals. (2010: 145)

However, unlike El Santo, the male protagonists in the films under scrutiny in this chapter become entangled in a type of camaraderie that goes far beyond mere friendship and, arguably, shows clear signs of sexual attraction (even if sex is never consummated within the narrative). In fact, a common diegetic device in all of these films is that at the critical point in the narrative when the subversion of heterosexual identity is about to be consummated, the male protagonists make a joke of the desire to subvert sexual identity in order to maintain the status quo of normative sexuality. By doing so, they intend to sustain the basis of hetero-patriarchy and avoid the transgression of normative sexuality; and, more importantly, they evidence that machismo continues to prevail as a driving force for male sexuality in the continent.

A closer look at these storylines, nonetheless, demonstrates that these films rely heavily on bromance narratives to justify the type of interaction and level of closeness that occurs between these men. More importantly, these films illustrate that the bromance scenario is capable of dismantling the tight parameters that regulate machismo in such societies. Since the zombie narrative usually implies the potential end of humankind and, by default, the end of the world, this apocalyptic scenario makes it more permissible for men to forget about the institutionalised machismo (or rigid masculinity as it may be in non-Latino or Caribbean contexts) that governs male relations. Such a bleak scenario makes it ideal for seemingly heterosexual men to shift their desires to one another and for a film to develop a more romantic narrative where amorous and affective relations, as well as sexual intercourse, are possible without threatening purported machismo.

For instance, the possibility of the bromance becoming homoerotic and potentially homosexual is depicted in films such as *Shaun of the Dead*. Although the storyline, on the surface, focuses on Shaun's (Simon Pegg) quest to ensure that his girlfriend Liz (Kate Ashfield) is safe from the zombie plague, the real dramatic tension emerges when Ed (Nick Frost) is bitten by a zombie. Therefore, the transition from human to zombie will change the nature of the relationship between the two male protagonists. The scene following Ed's contagion will be framed through a medium close-up of the two men talking (providing an atmosphere of intimacy to their exchange). After they disclose their feelings for one another, the director resorts to an instance of humour (albeit toilet humour) in order to avoid ending the sequence with a display of physical affection. Instead of the traditional kiss that would seal such an exchange in most romantic comedies (involving a heterosexual couple), the two male protagonists seal their display of affection by smelling each other's flatulence. Arguably, this activity becomes the closest to any expression of intimacy that will be permissible to both male characters, a way to sustain heteronormativity as an operating force within the narrative. The film concludes happily when, once the zombie invasion is under control, Shaun manages to keep the Ed-zombie character in his shed in order to rekindle the relationship with him at his leisure. As will be shown in the following analysis, this type of romantic interlude is replicated to a greater or lesser degree in the films studied here, where the climax of the film will be triggered by the fact that the homosocial relationship runs the risk of turning homosexual.

Bromancing the Zombie Movie in the *Plaga Zombie* Trilogy

In all the aforementioned films, the climatic moment of homoerotic desire is overturned by the use of comedy as a device that guarantees the safeguarding of masculinity. The humour in comedy operates as a ubiquitous force that has the ability to 'overturn (at least momentarily) official institutions and hierarchies of power' (Matthews 2000: 2). What the zombie film achieves, however, is to draw the narrative away from the possibility of romantic engagement that would otherwise ensue between the male protagonists. The addition of the zombie narrative permits attention to be diverted to the ways in which the protagonists will try to overcome the zombie attack rather than thinking about their feelings for one another. The level of physicality that is depicted in these films—especially when it comes to the rather imaginative and comedic ways in which the zombies are exterminated—opens up a space of physical and verbal intimacy between men that is regarded as less threatening to hegemonic masculinity. Drawing from other buddy narratives and the types of masculinities at play, the humour in zombie narratives helps to legitimise tensions arising from male-to-male physicality and intimacy.

In the *Plaga Zombie* trilogy, for instance, the audience sees the relationship between two of the main protagonists—John West (Berta Muñiz) and Max Giggs (Hernán Sáez)—develop beyond bromance into something that, although never consummated, has many aspects of homoerotic and homosexual desire. There is a clear evolution of the homoerotic bromance that develops between John and Max over the course of the trilogy, in which Max takes a positively female role (despite lacking any effeminacy in his personal appearance or mannerisms). Their bromance tends to be dictated by situations that arise between the characters and the obstacles they must overcome in order to continue together as a kind of single unit. In fact, most of the narrative is structured around Max and John working as an unbreakable team, while Bill Johnson (Pablo Parés) operates as a lone warrior against the zombies. The films follow the adventures of the three misfit heroes, who uncover an alien government conspiracy after a zombie outbreak begins in their hometown. The first film is confined to Bill's house, where the three protagonists are attacked by the zombies and are forced to hide in an upstairs bedroom and devise ways to kill the invaders. The second film is set just hours before the first instalment and follows the three heroes when they discover that an Argentinian government agency is working with the aliens in exchange for protection from the zombie virus. The three will then have to avoid the zombies and also a government death squad while trying to find a way out of the town. In the final film of the trilogy, set 3 days after the original two, they develop a plan to capture an infected human, feed it large amounts of gunpowder and lure the aliens into taking it aboard their spacecraft. Once aboard, the 'trojan zombie' would explode and destroy the alien mothership.

The films portrays a number of symptomatic aspects of a modern crisis of masculinity as experienced in Latin American and Caribbean societies. As such, these texts utilise the bromance narrative as the perfect mechanism for men to attain and display a higher degree of physicality among themselves without jeopardising the sense of male identity that is presented in society at large. For instance, in *Plaga Zombie: Zona Mutante* (the second film in the trilogy), a great deal of the storyline is devoted to the imminent possibility of a rupture in the bromance between Max and John. This bromantic break-up is triggered by the sudden introduction of another male character that will disrupt the homosocial dynamic that has characterised the relationship between the two protagonists thus far. In order to highlight further the threat that this character will pose to the bromantic relationship, his name will be the same as that of the character he may come to substitute for within the narrative. Max (Paulo Soria), who also happens to be an adoring fan of John's wrestler persona, will temporarily become the object of John's homosocial affection. Naturally, this new character soon becomes a disruptive element and causes Max to resort to violence in order to re-establish the harmony in the bromance between the two male protagonists.

It is possible to argue that this episode of the trilogy is the one that most directly refers to a possible bro-zom-com (as a direct derivation of the romantic zombie comedy already explained), since the narrative focuses on the bromance developed by the male protagonists and how the zombie invasion becomes an obstacle to the fulfilment of such a relationship. In this sequel, after an earlier encounter with the zombies, the three protagonists decide to carry with them a body bag that they rescued from the zombies, who clearly wanted to eat the corpse that lay within. After many tribulations, the men, and their accompanying corpse, manage to arrive at an empty house where they hope to seek refuge from the zombies. While looking round the house for supplies or weapons to try to defeat their foe, John and Max stumble across a room that belonged to an unknown and clearly hardcore fan of John's star persona (this is demonstrated by the fact that the room is fully decorated with memorabilia from John's days as a professional wrestler and the fact that he proclaims his delight at such a high degree of fandom). This rather long sequence, which serves no real purpose in the overall narrative, only reinforces the bromance between Max and John and calls into question the fixity of machismo as a governing force for all male relations.

The opening of this sequence already borrows some of the tropes of traditional horror cinema by placing the camera at a very low angle—over a crane and tilted slightly right—that shows the room where the action will develop in semi-darkness, with toys hanging from the ceiling that in the gloom confer a terrifying look to the space. The moment Max turns the light on, the camera cuts to a very high angle then begins to zoom in on Max's face as the incidental music changes from the macabre to a more 'celestial' or 'heavenly' tone, with the protagonist's face showing a big smile of surprise. The camera, in a less emphatic high angle, begins to pan slowly right across the room, displaying the walls covered in drawings, photos and other memorabilia from John's wrestler days, ending in a close-up of Max's face as he admires the place in awe. However, just before Max can rip a drawing off the wall (under which can be seen a newspaper cutout covering John's career demise), shown through an extreme close-up, the camera swivels to a medium shot of John standing by the door frame watching Max approvingly and telling him to feel free to look around. The following shot reverse shot goes from John standing by the door to a medium shot in a slight low angle of Max, who gestures as if asking for approval to rummage around the room, and back to the medium shot of John, who starts walking towards Max. The camera then cuts to a medium close-up in a slight high angle of Max, clearly using the camera frame to depict John's narrative point of view. He puts his hand on Max's shoulder and tells him: '¿Sabes Max? Creo que este es el comienzo de una gran amistad' [You know what, Max? I think this is the beginning of a great friendship]. Interestingly, these images are then contrasted with a short sequence of Bill trying to use a fork and a spoon, the only things left in the house, as possible weapons against the zombies while executing what appear to be martial arts moves.

When the action returns to the two men in the room, the directors offer another bromantic instance in which the line that divides macho identity from same-sex desire is blurred. The sequence opens with Max sat on the floor (shown in a medium, slight low-angle shot), examining some of John's boxed toys. Max's image is then framed in a kind of triangle by John's legs, the latter standing in front of him. This is further reinforced by a medium shot with a very low angle of John, who looks down on Max in a rather menacing manner; however, the tone of the sequence changes very quickly when he produces a mini LP (with his face on it) and shows it to the camera in a close-up. Once the LP is played, the musical sequence that develops sees John depicted as the clear object of a bromantic and homosocial gaze. While the music exalts John's many physical and personality attributes—'John West, John West, es el campeón. John West, John West, es el mejor' [John West, John West is the champion. John West, John West is the best]—the camera work fetishises his masculine body through the excessive use of medium close-ups and close-ups of his body. The song also praises John's *hombría* in ways that resonate with Mara Vivero Vigoya's analysis of football chanting, since 'through these songs fans dramatize gender identity and establish the limits of positive and negative aspects for what is supposedly defined as masculine' (2003: 44). The song becomes a vehicle to validate the protagonist's masculinity, as it expresses a man's quest for status and social recognition. Through the song, the film establishes an 'us' versus 'them' paradigm in which the person celebrated (in this case John West) through chanting exhibits more masculine qualities than the rest of the other characters. However, although the chanting and dancing between the two men may be meant to be read as a form of masculine camaraderie, it cannot be denied that there is a homoerotic undertone evidenced through the men's infantilised and rather campy singing and dancing. For instance, one of the many instances of homoeroticism during the song focuses on John's big butt, wearing his feline-printed wrestling leotard, and emphasised through a very low-angle, medium close-up of his butt as he shakes it. Towards the end of the song, the camera keeps cutting between close-ups of cut-out pictures, drawings and posters of John West and a medium close-up of the real John flexing his muscles and dancing. Once the song is over, the camera cuts to a low-angle shot of Max who applauds his buddy's performance enthusiastically, and almost hysterically.

The narrative clearly tries to construct John as a hypermasculine individual, whose physicality leaves very little space to cast doubt over his alleged *hombría*. This is reinforced by the pastiche, in the form of an anachronistic amalgamation, of different pieces of costume that he wears to construct his star persona. For example, the cowboy hat he wears is clearly borrowed from popular films of the 1990s such as *Crocodile Dundee* (Peter Fairman, 1986) as well as Pixar's *Toy Story* (John Lasseter, 1995), which the directors confessed speaking on behalf of FARSA to *Argentina Sc-Fi* (2001). By the same token, his masculinity is also highlighted by the wrestling singlet he wears that emulates that of a caveman. Such items of clothing constitute a visually economic means of manifesting the character's masculinity. However, despite the way he is depicted and the manner in which he behaves, it is possible to argue that the relationship between John and Max could be regarded as that of a 'crypto gay couple', as theorised by Markus Rheindorf (2007), who observes that narratives such as the one in *Plaga Zombie* are characterized by 'two ostensibly heterosexual men who displace their desire for each other in the homosocial construction of their masculinities. But they are also, on a more obvious level, opposites of each other in their performance of masculinity' (2007: 132). For the two characters the only way to maintain their homosocial bond is to cut all ties with any subject or situation that could call into question the naturalness of their heteromasculinity and, instead, could evidence its constructedness. In other words, the narrative must ensure at all times that every situation the characters face guarantees the heteronormative status quo on which machismo relies. Both the heteronormative and homosocial paradigms that are maintained throughout the narrative in the first instalment will be under scrutiny in the two sequels by means of adding a third party to the bromantic dynamics operating between the two characters.

In *Zona Mutante*, the slippage from homosocial to homosexual occurs shortly after the previous episode. While John and Max are singing and dancing, Bill is downstairs preparing to go and get provisions for them all. He notices movement from the body bag that they have brought with them into the house. As the music reaches its climax, the 'corpse' appears to sit and Bill is surprised to discover that the body in the bag is actually alive. As Bill checks whether the man is unharmed, the camera, once again through a very low angle, shows a set of stairs in the background that John will eventually be seen coming down. The camera quickly cuts to a high-angle shot that frames in a close-up the new man's face (looking in awe as John makes his way down the stairs). The quasi-choral, non-diegetic music in conjunction with a blurred image of John conveys an immediate idealisation of him (and his masculinity) in the eyes of the new Max. Such an idealisation or adoration does not escape the old Max, who takes an immediate dislike to the newcomer, and this disruption of the bromantic dynamics will culminate when the old Max, driven by jealousy, murders the new Max while John and Bill are out of the house trying to find supplies.

The killing of Max and John's eventual reaction to it leave no doubt that a transgression of the codes of heteromasculinity has occurred within the narrative, and that machismo as a template of male sexuality has been highly threatened. Although the storyline wastes no time in chastising and punishing Max for his transgression of social and heteromasculine codes, the film fails to reinsert the whole narrative into the safe ground of heteromasculinity and to eliminate the threat of queerness from its core (a narrative strand that is further developed in the third instalment of the trilogy, which will be discussed later in this chapter). John and Max constitute embodiments of adverse masculinity that are in constant conflict, because at no point does the film offer a safe outlet for their same-sex desires to be fulfilled and, instead, continues to suggest that macho (hypermasculine) behaviour should not break the continuum of heteronormative sexuality. In the film, this is evidenced when, on returning from their short trip out, John discovers that the new Max has been murdered—in fact brutally dismembered—by the old Max. This sequence sets out to portray Max as a queer psychopath by using tropes that are commonplace—the scratched LP that repeats the same segment of the record incessantly, the static camera that shows the character in a medium shot becoming psychotic and then stays in the same static place while the character disappears from the frame as he commits the murder—in traditional horror films such as *Psycho* (Alfred Hitchcock, 1960), *The Shining* (Stanley Kubrick, 1980) and *Funny Games* (Michael Haneke, 1997 and 2007). Although within the *Plaga Zombie* trilogy there are some battles between zombies and humans that serve as slapstick violence and are at times fairly graphic, this is one of the most explicit scenes of gore. Once John is back, the camera follows him as he goes up the stairs to check on the newcomer. When he gets to the landing, the camera cuts from a medium shot of John's body to a close-up of a bloodied photograph on the floor. When John picks it up, the camera shows from a very low-angle medium shot John's face being replaced by his own face on the photograph, which then zooms in on his own face and cuts to a medium long shot of the room where the dismembered remains of the newcomer are sprayed all over the floor.³

However, John will not have the chance to confront Max about this social transgression because, almost immediately after this discovery, the house is attacked by the zombies. As the fight begins and the lights go off, Max is heard shouting to the zombies not to throw him out of the window. Once the lights are back on, John hears a noise and runs upstairs to witness from the first-floor window Max being attacked, dismembered and partly eaten by the zombies. Max's cries for help remain unattended by John who, obviously, decides that this is a fair price to pay for Max's murderous actions and his clear attempt at breaking the heteronormative social order that operated among the triad. John's decision not to help Max becomes a mechanism through which he can attempt to reinsert his 'wounded' masculinity back into the terrain of safe machismo by positing himself as a just man whose behaviour does not contravene prescribed heteromasculinity. His actions chime with the ideas theorised by Markus Rheindorf when he asserts that 'men define their masculinity not so much in relation to women, but in relation to each other. Masculinity, therefore, is largely a homosocial enactment, and most of the policing is done by other men' (2007: 133). As a result, the two characters become embroiled in a queer conflict that can only be solved by the intervention of the zombies who, inadvertently, act as 'father' figures by punishing one of the pair (in this case the one whose action directly threatened the laws governing homosocial desire) and thus resolving the imminent queer conflict. In this sense, the zombies facilitate social control by attempting to eliminate those individuals who do not display the 'ideal' characteristics of purported masculinity that circulate in the popular imaginary.

The zombies in this trilogy differ from those seen in early voodoo zombie narratives that 'represent the slave of a colonial society', or those post-modern zombies who 'do nothing beyond attacking humans and eating their flesh; they represent consumers on the most fundamental and primitive level (all they do is take, and what they take is food)' (Bishop

---

³ This component of the narrative could also be regarded as a commentary on fandom and the homosocial aspects of bromance. The type of blind devotion that both the unknown owner of the room and Max show towards the wrestler demonstrates that the male-to-male dynamic operating within male-to-male fandom reconceptualises heterosexual masculinity through, as Garry Whannel points out, 'a new repertoire of cultural practices which seek to demarcate, through space and ritual, a distinctive, defensive yet celebratory mode of being male' (2008, 191).

2010: 236). The zombies in the *Plaga Zombie* trilogy have the ability of almost rational thought, to communicate with one another, show and express their feelings; as a result, they have the ability to operate as the controlling force that shapes, regulates and sanctions masculinity. Unsurprisingly, in this trilogy the vast majority of the zombies, especially those who tend to have a more starring role, are all male, while the narrative itself is devoid of any female figures. The films permanently consider and reconsider contemporary masculinity as seen through the bromance lens in which machismo must be continually tested against the corrupting forces of same-sex desire that are prevalent in an apocalyptic world where women are completely absent. Thus the main problem with Max's actions is that, by killing the newly found Max, he externalises his queerness and makes it evident that the relationship between him and John, in much the same way as Kayley Thomas discusses about the fictional characters Sherlock Holmes and Watson, goes beyond 'back-and-forth banter, a love-hate dynamic, codependency, masculine physicality and action, male camaraderie and loyalty, and potential homoeroticism' (2012: 38). John's decision to remain an impassive witness to Max's demise at the hands of the zombies demonstrates that machismo, as Marvin Leiner argues, 'requires individual men to make a display of physical power and social domination, and to disdain any feminine, or supposedly feminine traits' (1994: 79). Since Max's actions can be read as a sign of female hysteria, it is unsurprising that John realises the importance of eliminating Max in order to guarantee the permanence and immutability of his own macho persona. Homosexuality remains latent in the film, despite the multiple attempts at neutralising or debunking it from the narrative through the zombie invasion, and evidences a clear crisis of masculinity in which the bromance no longer remains a safe terrain in which to express homosocial feelings.[4]

The instances of bromance in the film are characterised by a sense of *compadrismo*, and in them, as Sergio de la Mora suggests in his analysis of Pedro Infantes and buddy movies, 'the sexual ambiguities and anxieties surrounding the social institution of compadrismo, a close-knit friendship bond and a form of extended family, and the ties between men register a

---

[4] This crisis of masculinity is all the more evident in the third instalment of the saga (*Plaga Zombie: Revolución Tóxica*), in which a great part of the storyline centres on John losing quite a lot of bodyweight and, therefore, regarding himself as less of a man, while Max becomes a mother figure to one of the zombies. Interestingly, the director chooses two situations of conflict that are more commonplace in chick flicks or female dramas and that clearly feminise the male protagonists.

[twofold] crisis: first, a crisis in Mexico's patriarchal system; [and] second, a crisis in the nation's official "macho" identity' (2006: 70). Although de la Mora's analysis centres on Mexican male sexual identity, it is possible to translocate this notion to other Latin American sexual cultures where machismo continues to shape the male sexual imaginary of the nation. The patriarchal system, in itself, is threatened throughout the *Plaga Zombie* trilogy by the impossibility of maintaining the 'appearance' of heterosexual masculinity when female subjects are excluded from the narrative. In fact, only a handful of female zombies are seen in the three films and it appears that the zombies are the only characters that are capable of maintaining the status quo of heteronormativity. Although the films could not be regarded as rom-zom-coms (in the way that *Shaun of the Dead* explicitly advocates), it is clear that the narrative in these films remains in a constant battle to avoid homoeroticisation of the relationship between John and Max. The zombies are, thus, of prime importance within the narrative, as their inclusion will guarantee that all attempts at romantic involvement and male sexual physicality can be channelled through the combat and killing of the monsters.

Another such instance of bromoerotic desire is evidenced in one of the key sequences towards the end of the third instalment of the trilogy. Here, the three heroes find themselves surrounded by all the zombies in what appears to be a preamble to meeting their own end. However, at the last minute John asks his companions to imitate and follow his own actions. As the zombies—led by Junior (Paulo Soria), a zombie that has been nurtured by Max—get ready to attack the protagonists, the camera in a very slight low-angle medium shot shows the moment when John hands a piece of paper to his two companions. The camera quickly switches to a close-up of his face as he says, 'Bien muchachos. Es con ritmo de balada en Fa. Observen los cambios y traten de seguirme, ¿de acuerdo?' [OK, guys. This is a ballad in D. Pay attention to the changes and try to follow me, OK?]. The camera quickly moves to a medium shot of Max and then Bill, who both shrug their shoulders, unclear what is coming next. At this point the sequence cuts to a close-up of John's hand as he takes his hat from behind him and puts it on his head, stressed by a low-angle close-up. What ensues is a musical number in which the three protagonists dance as a chorus line, with umbrellas, while being showered with zombie vomit, and they even get the rest of the zombies to dance around them. This last part of the sequence is further stressed by a high-angle, craned, medium shot showing the three men occupying almost the totality of the screen space while the zombies dance behind them. This type of un-macho sequence justifies male-to-male interactions that fall outside the realm of heteronormativity. It is clear that the only way for the men to express their feelings (towards each other or the situation at hand) is by means of a subtle feminisation of their persona.

The *Plaga Zombie* trilogy evidences a national crisis of masculinity in which the figure of the macho, or his more romanticised counterpart the Latin lover, is disavowed as an epitome of masculinity, as the protagonists do not respond physically or intellectually to such masculine prototypes. This crisis of masculinity can arguably be linked to a specific number of conditions that Argentinian society has undergone since the financial crisis in 2000. A correlation can be seen between the demise of the free-market state and the type of masculinity that was usually associated with a specific social stratum, albeit it affected middle-class men most significantly. The discourses of hegemonic masculinity, and especially of machismo as a template of male sexuality, evolved both in society at large and, more importantly, within the popular imaginary. As a result, they have come to encapsulate images that, as Natalia Milanesio points out in her study of advertisements in Argentina, 'invert gender expectations but were further based on the derision of male characters. Ad-makers portrayed men as emasculated, subjugated, and miserable, removed from traditional male occupations and unprepared to fulfill domestic roles' (Milanesio 2013: 112).

This seems all the more pertinent to the analysis of the bromance between the two male protagonists discussed here. John's version of his own masculinity is both jeopardised and questioned by living in the shadow of his former self (evidenced by his demise as a famous wrestler), in ways that remove him from his traditional male occupation. By the same token, Max's inability to raise or look after his zombie offspring evidences his failure as a paternal figure. The bromance between the two characters ultimately reflects on a broader crisis of masculinity in which men's 'loss of social status and privilege translated into a diminished sense of authority in both the public and private spheres [...] unemployment, lack of prestige, and the inability to achieve both glory and status made Argentine men feel emasculated' (Rocha 2012: 12). In many ways it is possible to suggest that the zombie invasion is a necessary evil, as combating it becomes the only vehicle for the protagonists to regain their sense of loss of masculinity. The men's bodies and their bodily interactions, within the framework of the bromance narrative, also highlight narratives of disintegration that express the absence, loss and disintegration of the once-pivotal figure of the macho.

The trilogy proves that the protagonists' 'complex bodies are thus affected not wholly or in entirety, but by a vast number of internal and external relations at any one time, which impact upon and transform them in partial and selective ways according to the nature of the elemental connections and disjunctions' (Bignall 2010: 13). Since zombie films rely on a high degree of gore both to attract and to repulse the audience (and even the characters who inhabit such stories), it is possible to understand why the protagonists' bodies are a key element in the figuration of their own identities. The different, diverse and, at times, highly allegorical ways in which the three protagonists try to defeat—that is, dismember or kill—the zombies demonstrates a crisis of masculinity that is externalised through a crisis of representation of the male body, but one that uses the dismembered bodies of the zombies as a decoy to divert attention to the actual crisis of the body suffered by the human male protagonists. These betamales illustrate the transformation of a 'typically strong and confident connotation of masculinity into one that displays a severe lack of confidence, especially concerning women, and a desperate need to compensate for inadequacies in traditional masculinity' (Bignall 2010: 25). In other words, the zombies, or rather fighting against them and finding ways to exterminate them, become the perfect smokescreen for the bromantic and homosocial anxieties of the John and Max characters whose (b)romance cannot be crystallised, so as to maintain the sense of hetero-hegemony within the narrative and for the imagined audiences at which the film is aimed.

NIGHT OF THE LIVING DEAD MACHOS IN *JUAN DE LOS MUERTOS*

Machismo, as has been suggested throughout this study, has played a key role in shaping the socio-cultural imaginary of most societies in Latin America in relation to masculinity and male desire. In Cuba, the work of Arés (1996) theorised a number of seizures of masculinity whereby a man was expropriated of his emotions and sentiments (showing them was a sign of vulnerability), expropriated of personal validity (through allowing women to make most of the decisions at home) and expropriated of paternity (as men do not get involved with the upbringing of their own children). Whether men have actually been dispossessed of such aspects of their own identity or have, instead, happily assumed them as part of their persona as a mechanism to perpetuate hegemonic power, it is possible to discern a crisis of masculinity for those men who do not embrace such monolithic notions. Nonetheless, machismo continues to be 'validated in Cuba as a form of culture [that], despite being subjected to much criticism in the last two decades, seems to enjoy deep roots in different social groups, both on the island and in the Cuban diaspora' (González 2004: 1). It is here that machismo becomes intrinsically entwined with the male body and with performativity, as it demonstrates that certain patterns of hegemonic masculinity continue to circulate in the socio-sexual imaginary, especially those that rely on the performance of a certain type of (hyper)masculinity. Cuban *compadrazgo* as an early step on the path to bromance will rely heavily on bodily interactions, whereby men establish and follow a number of socially accepted norms to justify the way in which they interact with one another without calling into question their own masculinities (assumed to be heterosexual in nature).

The Cuban-Spanish co-production *Juan de los Muertos* clearly borrows many elements of Wright's *Shaun of the Dead*, while it also sees the bromance narrative reach new heights as the sexual tension between the two male protagonists is more explicit and latent throughout the storyline. In the film, Juan (Alexis Díaz de Villegas) and Lázaro (Jorge Molina) are two slackers living in today's Havana. As the city, and eventually the whole of the country, seems to fall under a zombie attack, they seize the opportunity to start a company that will be in charge of killing people's loved ones after they have turned into zombies. Enlisting the help of Juan's daughter Camila (Andrea Duro), Lázaro's son Vladi California (Andros Perugorría), a transvestite known as La China (Jazz Vilá) and a bodybuilder who goes by the nickname of El Primo (Eliecer Ramírez), they will try to survive the zombie apocalypse. The film plays to most of the stereotypes found in the Caribbean sexual culture; stereotypes that have been a point of contestation in Cuban filmmaking since the advent of the New Latin American Cinema. As Guy Baron suggests in relation to machismo and the Cuban cinema of the Revolution, in most Cuban films 'the illusion of equality is created as the status quo remains intact' (2010: 364). As will be argued in this section, characters such as La China and El Primo primarily serve as smokescreens for traditional notions of machismo and *compadrazgo* as they are understood in mainstream society. The type of queer masculinity that such characters display will ensure that homosocial relations between the two main male protagonists, in other words their bromance, always remain at the interstice of, or beyond, same-sex desire (Fig. 5.1).

Fig. 5.1 Bromanctic interactions: Juan (Alexis Díaz de Villegas) and Lázaro (Jorge Molina) walk among the zombie devastation. *Juan de los Muertos* ©La Sanfoña Producciones

The excessive and rather caricaturised version of machismo that the two male protagonists display continues to support the notion of machismo as theorised by Carlos Alberto Montaner and discussed in Chap. 3. Although the film's protagonists show a more tolerant attitude towards sexual minorities—gays and transvestites—same-sex desire is still regarded as less normative than the purported heterosexuality that circulates in the national imaginary as the ideal form of human sexuality. In a similar fashion to Wright's *Shaun of the Dead*, the two protagonists here maintain a high level of homoeroticism that is evidenced in their desire for hyperbolic sexual penetration (despite how obliquely such penetrations may be performed and consummated within the narrative) and a fascination for each other's sexual adventures that goes beyond mere brotherly interest. As previously suggested, in Wright's film the way in which the two male protagonists engage in an oblique form of sexual intercourse is by smelling each other's flatulence. Although Nick Haslam argues that one characteristic of heteronormative male transactions is that 'men at times seem to actively flout social norms governing faecal matters and doing so seems to be a way of performing their masculinity' (2012: 65), it seems that for the characters in this film, smelling each other's farts allows them a level of intimacy that they never seem to consumate, but that determines most of their actions within the film. Farting occurs at two key points in the narrative in which the two male protagonists use this faecal strategy in lieu of the sexual penetration that would be socially forbidden to them. However, it is ironic that they express so blatantly their revolt, tinged by admiration, at the smell of the fart in ways that do not disguise their satisfaction at being the recipient of someone's 'masculinity'. Similarly, in *Juan de los Muertos* the relationship between Juan and Lázaro seems to be marked by Lázaro's homoerotic and overt desires towards his friend.

Although the notion of bromance, as has been previously theorised, conveys a non-physical and non-sexual relationship between males, it would be argued that most bromantic narratives tend to 'hide'—or rather suppress—an underlyng sexual tension between men who, perhaps for fear of social rejection and ostracism or as a result of adhering to social and cultural conventions, are either discouraged or forbidden from acting on their attraction for one another. However, and as previously suggested, all social and sexual barriers are dismantled through the imminent presence of zombies. The prospect of an apocalyptic zombie holocaust is enough for men to forget the rigid parameters that regulate heteromasculinity and to propitiate a slippage into the realm of the homoerotic. As Peter Dendle argues, the zombie operates as a barometer of cultural anxiety since 'it has become, in recent years, increasingly nihilistic. It is the sign of an over-leisurely society lacking in broader spiritual or communal purpose, left to the impulses of its unchecked power and its desires for consumption' (2007: 54). However, rather than the zombie narrative highlighting moral issues (or the lack thereof) in contemporary society, it could be suggested that the necessity of returning to a more primal state (in order to defeat the zombies) operates as a mechanism that unleashes the 'impulses' and 'unchecked powers' of homoerotic desire. It is not surprising, then, that the narrative in *Juan de los Muertos* centres on Lázaro's physical obsession with his friend and his need to use Juan's recounting of his sexcapades as an outlet for externalising and acting on his own sexual desires. For instance, very early in the film, and after narrowly escaping being caught by the husband of one of Juan's lovers, the two protagonists get together in their hideout at the top of their building. Lázaro asks for a very detailed account of events and while Juan tells him, Lázaro turns to face the veranda as he masturbates, obviously aroused by the story he hears. Lázaro is depicted as a beta-male; that is, a man who shows a severe lack of confidence in relation to women, who tries desperately to compensate for his inadequacies in both traditional masculinity and, more often than not, physical appearance, and who clings to his alpha-male buddy in the hope that his friend's idealised form of masculinity will somehow rub off on him. However, by the same token he also seems somewhat erotically obsessed with his friend.

Lázaro's adulation of Juan goes beyond pure masculine idolatry and moves readily into the terrain of overt homoerotic desire (despite the fact that for most of the narrative Lazaro's adoration appears to be one-sided). To some extent, the two protagonists in this film parallel the relationship between Diego (Jorge Perrugoria) and David (Vladimir Cruz) in *Fresa y Chocolate* (Tomás Gutiérrez Alea and Juan Carlos Tabío, 1993), regarding which David William Foster argues that the reasons behind the fact that the two characters 'never fuck' (2003: 149) remain unclear throughout the narrative. Foster is right to signal that the characters cannot consummate their alleged desires because the society in which they operate does not provide a system of socio-sexual values in which same-sex desire can be expressed and manifested. Similarly, in *Juan de los Muertos* the two protagonists can never consummate their desires because machismo as a force that drives and regulate sexuality and sexualised behaviour forces men to (re)duplicate fundamental assumptions in relation to how man-to-man relationships ought to be publicly displayed in ways that are socially acceptable. Thus it is not surprising that Lázaro sees Juan's recounting of his sexcapades as an outlet for both internalising and externalising his own same-sex desires. This is evidenced by the fact that Lázaro not only asks the most minute and intimate details, but also furiously masturbates during the narration of Juan's sexcapade. This type of meta-bodily interaction supports Strikwerda and May's (1992) claim that among men, and as part of a homosocial and macho paradigm, crudeness has become a cover for sensitivity.

Juan de los Muertos reproduces a trifold strategy that seeks to compensate for the loss of machismo, and in turn evidences a crisis of masculinity in contemporary Latin American culture. First, the film hypersexualises most female characters to the point that, at the beginning of the film, it is hard to distinguish whether Camila is one of Juan's many sexual conquests or, as she turns out to be, his own daughter. Similarly, Lázaro's obsession with the exuberant Sara (Blanca Rosa Blanco) further reinforces his role as a beta-male whose masculinity is always questioned by the rejection he suffers from most female characters and by his sense of inadequacy in portraying his own masculinity. It is this failed sense of masculinity that runs throughout the narrative and keeps pushing Lázaro into the terrain of the homoerotic. For instance, after the zombie attacks become widespread, the two male protagonists break into Sara's flat after hearing grunting noises coming from within. Once inside, they find her in a foetal position and covered in blood, hiding inside a closet. However, while Sara recounts what occurred in the apartment, Lázaro appears transfixed and hypnotised by the sight of her naked breasts. It could then be suggested that the sight of female nakedness is enough for Lázaro to stop functioning like a rational being and instead instils fear in him. Furthermore, Sara's character also slightly complicates the pretended heterosexual dynamic because she is in a lesbian relationship. Therefore the film seems to suggest that Lázaro's masculinity (queer or otherwise) can only operate when subordinated to the main protagonist's own masculinity. As Brian Orndorf (2012) asserts in his review of the film, 'the character of Lazaro is employed repeatedly as a sight gag, observing the creep publicly masturbate while peeping in open windows, deal carefully with topless victims, and wear short shorts without the protection of underwear. He's a prankster, yet utterly devoted to Juan.' (Fig. 5.2)

Secondly, the film fails to spell out what constitutes machismo, as the characters continually play out and negotiate different versions of masculinity that range from respect and veneration of motherly figures, to the degradation and objectification of women seen as prospective

Fig. 5.2 A bromosocial moment interrupted by zombies: Lázaro (Jorge Molina) harpoons a zombie about to attack Juan (Alexis Díaz de Villegas). *Juan de los Muertos* ©La Sanfoña Producciones

partners or love interests. To this end, the film relies on a number of caricaturised stereotypes of masculinity (including queer masculinity) in which machismo is no longer a rigid identity to which men must adhere, but becomes fluid in its own understanding of maleness. As previously suggested, Brugués presents some versions of 'queer' masculinity in the character of La China, the viperine transvestite, and El Primo, the colossal bodybuilder who faints at the sight of blood. However, as Antonio Cardentey argues,

> paradójicamente en *Juan de los Muertos* el gay es dilucidado como parte de la degeneración social y no tanto una ganancia en términos de apertura mental. Además, el negro forzudo manifiesta la persistencia del racismo—uno de los supuestos males superados por la Revolución—porque encarna la fuerza bruta en tanto metonimia de la esclavitud y del sistema económico de la plantación. (2013: 4)
> [paradoxically, in Juan de los Muertos the gay character is portrayed as part of a social degeneration, and not so much in terms of mental openness. Furthermore, the black muscled man manifests the persistence of racism—one of the alleged social ills removed by the Revolution—as he embodies a brute force as a metonymy of slavery and of the plantation economic system]

Thus these two characters provide a stark contrast to the relationship between the two male protagonists, while they also provide diegetic justification for the protagonists' homosocial identities. Hyperbolically, the scene in which Juan, Lázaro, La China and El Primo are detained and strip-searched naked by the police best exemplifies the undercurrent of tension in the different versions of machismo that exist both within the film and in society at large. Once undressed, the group are ordered to get in the back of the police van; at this point La China has a furtive look at Juan's *hombría* and remarks, 'Oye Juan, a eso tú le pones una pañoleta y es un boy scout' [Juan, listen, if you put a neckerchief on that [his penis] you'll get a boy scout out of it]. The camera immediately proceeds to a long shot of all the men seen from their naked backs as they walk towards the police van, and then switches to a medium shot of Lázaro, who had stayed behind, looking puzzled and then glancing down at his manhood with obvious disapproval. In this sense the film already feminises Lázaro by evidencing that he has no phallic power of address—as derived from his penis—and, naturally, can only enjoy sexual fulfilment through his secret desire for his friend. Lázaro's small penis (suggested by his facial expression) confirms that, as Richard Dyer has pointed out, it is 'crucial that the penis provided the model for [the phallus]' (1992: 116). Thus the suspicion implied throughout the diegesis that Lázaro is less of a man (based on a hetero-hegemonic model) is confirmed by the implication that his penis is much smaller than his friend's. The penis, then, becomes the instrument for asserting masculinity and, since Lázaro's is not big enough for him to be considered a real man, the transition to the realm of the homoerotic appears justified within the narrative (Fig. 5.3).

Thirdly, the necessity of the two male protagonists boasting and challenging each other's maleness clearly demonstrates 'that manhood's center cannot hold, that manhood is split, that the warring elements of manhood spill out beyond the individual subjectivity of the star-protagonist, and that the burden of male representation must be carried by two stars rather than one' (Greven 2009: 125). This is evident in the key bromantic scene in the film, which sees the two men declaring their feelings for one another, while almost hinting at the realisation of their physical and sexual desires. The climax of the film, as well as of the bromance between the two main protagonists, commences the moment that, after finding a place to hide and plan a counterattack against the zombies, Lázaro, in a medium shot, shows Juan what appears to be a bite on his arm. The following

Fig. 5.3 Versions of Caribbean masculinities: Juan (Alexis Díaz de Villegas), Lázaro (Jorge Molina), Vladi (Andros Perugorría), La China (Jazz Vilá) and El Primo (Eliecer Ramírez) are stopped by the police. *Juan de los Muertos* ©La Sanfoña Producciones

shot-reverse-shot dialogue is framed in a close medium shot with a low angle of Juan sitting on the bonnet of a car, while Lázaro's face, slightly out of focus, appears in the right-hand corner of the frame. Despite it being Lázaro who carries the nuanced plot of the narrative at this moment, the camera continues to build Juan as the supreme male character while his friend is relegated to a secondary role. Lázaro, then, makes Juan promise that he will kill him once he turns into a zombie. As a final wish, he asks Juan to accompany him to the roof of the building in order to see the sun rise. If there was any doubt that the relationship between Lázaro and Juan was portrayed as a queer bromance, this sequence leaves no doubt that the two are somewhat entwined in a relationship that goes beyond pure masculine camaraderie or friendship. Despite the fact that the sequence offers a comic pastiche of similar love scenes in many romantic comedies, it is undeniable that it also involves a level of sexual ambiguity that makes it almost impossible to determine whether the director is simply mocking the tropes (ab)used in traditional romantic comedies or seriously portraying a romantic scene between the two men. As will be seen, the camera work, lighting and dialogue lend themselves to blurring the lines separating homosociality from same-sex desire to the point that, by the end of the sequence, it comes as no surprise that Lázaro makes an overt sexual request of his friend.

The sequence starts with an extreme long shot of the two friends sitting on the edge of the building facing in different directions. The camera switches to a medium close-up of the men with their faces only slightly illuminated by natural moonlight. They do not look at each other—as if dealing with their internal turmoil—yet the conversation centres on Juan asking Lázaro how he wants to be killed. Lázaro asks to be bludgeoned with an oar, but stresses that he wants Juan to kill him 'por la cabeza, con el remo. Pero por favor no me toques la cara. Me metí en más de veinticinco broncas y nunca nadie me tocó la cara' [on the head, with the oar. But make sure you don't touch my face. I got into more than twenty-five fights and no one ever touched my face]. Once again Lázaro shows a preoccupation with an aspect of his persona that would socially and culturally be considered feminine and puts into question his own machismo. As Roger Lancaster suggests, 'whoever fails to keep an aggressively masculine front will be teased, ridiculed and ultimately stigmatized' (2002: 48). Lázaro's preoccupation with his physical appearance only serves to stress a sense of machismo that is eschewed by an imagined heterosexual audience, even if this serves the comic purpose of the film. The combination of his already acknowledged penis envy (from the sequence with the police) with this point in the narrative shows the split in the representation of the penis/phallus in which the beta-male always carries within his persona some form of 'small dick joke'. However, what is truly interesting about this sequence is that Lázaro cleverly manages to turn the symbolic meaning of the phallus, as represented by his best friend's penis, into a role reversal that will empower him, albeit only temporarily. Peter Lehman has developed the notion of the melodramatic penis, one that is 'neither the phallic spectacle nor its pitiable and/or comic collapse, [which] on the one hand challenge conventional representations, and on the other constitute a troubled site of representations that contains disturbing contradictions' (2001: 235). Following from such theorisation, it can be proposed that *Juan de los Muertos* resorts to what could be deemed the melocomedic penis as the quintessential site of representation for the development of the bromance narrative. This melocomedic penis can be found in many horror narratives in which the relationship of the male protagonists is portrayed as a bromance within the storyline, but requires a moment of dramatic intensity finally to trigger feelings of same-sex desire.

This is all the more obvious towards the end of the sequence, when Lázaro appears to reveal that he has been in love with Juan all along. The camerawork in unison with the dialogue further supports this notion. The two men can be seen talking through a static medium shot reverse shot, with their bodies barely illuminated by moonlight in a way that lends a rather romantic tone to the sequence:

> *Lázaro*: Juan. Hay una cosa que siempre quise decirte. [Juan. There's something I've always wanted to tell you]
> *Juan*: Dime. [Tell me]
> *Lázaro*: Te quiero. [I love you]
> *Juan*: Yo tambiém te quiero brother. [I love you too bro]
> *Lázaro*: No, no me entiendes. [No, you don't understand me] [Emphatic whisper] ¡Te quiero! [I love you!]
> *Juan*: [Sniggers] ¡Ah, no jodas Lázaro! [Fuck sake, Lázaro]
> *Lázaro*: Todo este tiempo te lo oculté. Pero ya que más da. ¡Te quiero y bien! [I've hidden it from you all this time. But now I don't care any more. I love you and that's it!]

Although Juan's first reaction is incredulity, he soon becomes enraged when Lázaro boldly asks him 'me dejarías que te la chupe?' [would you let me suck you off?]. However, it does not take Juan long to agree and he gets ready to engage sexually with his bromantic partner. Juan's decision to grant his friend his 'final wish' demonstrates that, as Jeffrey Pilcher comments with regard to Cantinflas as a Latin American icon that conforms to a non-machista masculinity, these types of character represent 'the ambivalent nature of masculinity' (2001: xvii). As a result, macho identity—one that seems paramount to the construction of Juan's masculinity in the film and is continually reaffirmed throughout the narrative—cannot be regarded as a fixed identity. Instead, it is multiple and fluid to the extent that Juan does not seem to need much encouragement to engage in same-sex sex with his best friend. Despite Juan's initial outrage at his friend's request, once he changes his mind the camera cuts to a long shot of the two men as Juan unzips his trousers. Immediately, it cuts back to a medium shot of Lázaro, who stares at Juan's crotch and after a long pause, bursts out laughing and lightly scolds his friend: 'Te jodí brother. Usted es tremendo maricón [...] chama, tu eres tremendo bugarrón' [I got you. You're such a faggot [...] girl, you are a big puffter]. Although the sexual act is not consummated in this sequence, the sexual tension between the male lead characters remains paramount throughout this scene and the film as a whole. The return to the terrain of homosociality at this critical point in the narrative can be seen as a necessity for Lázaro to reclaim a space of male hegemony, since the film has repeatedly bashed his masculinity by comparing his inadequate—read small—penis to his friend's.

Once again, the penis becomes the focal point of the narrative. However, this time the possession of a seemingly large penis, and the phallic empowerment that Juan has enjoyed throughout the film as a result of his endowment, has not guaranteed that his masculinity remained unscathed. Lázaro's practical joke (or his last-minute conscious denial of his own same-sex desires) demonstrates that machismo continues, to a great extent, to shape power relations among men in Latin America and the Caribbean. These power relations have become more and more fluid, to the point that behaviours that would otherwise be considered unmanly are now becoming more accepted. As a result, homosociality, as famously theorised by Eve Kosofsky Sedgwick (1985), allows ties between males to rely on the assumption that the more closely men associate in their relations, the more they are expected to express their disdain, hatred and fear of homosexual desire and behaviour. It is for this reason that Lázaro makes a joke at the expense of Juan's *hombría* and, finally, manages to level himself with his friend, who has so far operated as both an object of desire and an object of phallic envy. It is possible to suggest that the zombie narrative within the comedy genre both permits the externalisation of same-sex desires to be diffused from the core of the narrative and conceals the bromantic interest of the male protagonists as homosocial bonding. Yet Lázaro's obsession with the sexual life of his friend (as an outlet for his own sexual desires), his male inadequacy as portrayed by his inability to match up to other men's *hombría* and his slight feminisation as a beta-male throughout the narrative are effective at eliciting laughter, and most definitely put into question the fixity of normative male heterosexuality.

CONCLUSION

Much has been theorised about how zombies act as a metaphor for the state of contemporary society, in order to offer a critique of how consumerism and capitalism have spread in most Western(ised) societies in much the same way as zombie plagues spread in living-dead narratives. Most of George Romero's work, as well as that of many other zombie movie directors, continues to see the zombie figure as a representation of the state of mutism and capitalist somnambulism in which societies are submerged. However, it could be argued that, as Bishop points out, zombies 'also act as the catalyst that reveals the true problem infecting humanity' (2010: 235). In this chapter, the zombie narrative has operated as the catalyst for the dismantling of machismo as a template for male sexuality in the Latino-Caribbean context. It would be pertinent to suggest that zombie narratives offer a safer ground in which feelings of same-sex desire and homoeroticism can be more overtly displayed, because the attention in such texts is diverted to the personified abjection embedded in the zombie figure, whose body is a constant reminder of bodily transgression. In this way, the transgression(s) of male identity and behaviour, and more importantly the transgressions of macho behaviour, can easily be overlooked by the physical and bodily transgressions of the zombies themselves. Since these films are much more preoccupied with how the zombies will be exterminated, and most of the scopophilic pleasure is derived from the way(s) in which the annihilation of the monsters will be achieved, homosocial relations between male characters that break with the established parameters prescribed by machismo remain somewhat unscrutinised by the audience and the films themselves.

The zombie narrative also guarantees that there is no serious risk that 'homosociality is threatened by an underlying current of homosexuality'

(Wyat 2001: 62). By dedicating a great deal of the narrative to the means by which the zombies will be annihilated, these films make it possible to avoid any serious underlying tension over whether the male characters may end up getting involved sentimentally or emotionally—let alone sexually. In the *Plaga Zombie* trilogy, the relationship between Max and John, centred on Max's obsession with his friend, makes it evident that Max's interest goes beyond pure comradely admiration and shows signs of real sexual attraction. He will kill, betray and even father a zombie in order to show that he is ready to be John's ideal partner and will do anything to gain his trust and love. At the same time, in Parés and Saez's trilogy women remain absent from the whole narrative (apart from a couple of female zombies), which in itself further stresses the fact that affective relationships can only be established among the three men who have survived the zombie apocalypse. As a result, the films disavow the possibility that, as Sharon Bird argues in relation to homosociality and hegemonic masculinity, 'through male homosocial heterosexual interactions, hegemonic masculinity is maintained as the norm to which men are held accountable despite individual conceptualizations of masculinity that depart from that norm' (1996: 120). The films in this trilogy distance themselves from the main characteristics of homosocial identity: the possibility of emotional detachment (the tensions between Max and John are clear throughout the narrative and episodes of blind male jealousy, break-ups and reconciliation abound), male competitiveness (zombie narratives stress the requirement to work as a team and put aside the need for individual success) and the objectification of women (there are no women to objectify nor references to any female partners, past or present).

By the same token, *Juan de los Muertos* follows pretty much the same line of argument, whereby homosociality becomes entangled in a bromantic narrative that is blurred by homosexual desire. Unlike the *Plaga Zombie* trilogy, in which the bromantic undertone of the film is more subtle and there is an absence of overt intimate physicality between the male protagonists, *Juan de los Muertos* relies to a great extent on the tacit physicality of the two male protagonists. Their relationship seems to be based on Juan's rather explicit recounting of his sexual escapades while Lázaro uses such stories as a platform to bridge the gap between the two men and achieve a level of physical intimacy. Juan and Lázaro constitute a crypto-gay couple, since they continue to embody the values and—still important to Latin American sexual culture—the mechanisms whereby machismo is socially constructed, while displacing their desire for one another within a homosocial apparatus that both validates their masculinity and conceals their homosexual desires. The film persists in eliminating from the narrative all the opposite-sex characters who could, potentially, get entangled emotionally or physically with the male protagonists and become their prospective partners. In this way, it would seem that the two characters are destined to become each other's substitute for a romantic partner. The zombie plague constitutes the external force that will push them together since, by the end of the narrative, no female alternatives are left alive (except for Juan's daughter, who has been spared for Lázaro's son's benefit and, more importantly, for the preservation of the human race).

In short, zombie movies could be regarded as the perfect platform from which to address male homoerotic desire without the fear of embodying a queer or homosexual identity. The protagonists in such films are not gay, but they develop emotional homoerotic desires and identities as a result of the lack of female figures who can become recipients of their *hombría*. Thus they find themselves with no other choice but to turn to one another in order to maintain a system that resembles the construction of sexuality and gender that they knew before the zombie invasion.

FILMOGRAPHY

28 Days Later (dir. Danny Boyle, 2002)
A Árvores dos Sexos (dir. Silvio de Abreu, 1977)
A Meia-Noite Levarei Sua Alma (dir. Jose Mojica Marins, 1964)
Alien (dir. Ridley Scott, 1979)
Alucarda, la Hija de las Tinieblas (dir. Juan López Moctezuma, 1978)
American Psycho (dir. Mary Harron, 2000)
American Sniper (dir. Clint Eastwood, 2014)
Amores Perros (dir. Alejandro Gonzalez Iñárritu, 2000)
Animalada (dir. Sergio Bizzio, 2001)
Apartment Zero (dir. Martin Donovan, 1988)
Baby Shower (dir. Pablo Illanes, 2011)
Beau Travail (dir. Claire Denis, 1999)
Billy Bud (dir. Peter Ustinov, 1962)
Born on the Fourth of July (dir. Oliver Stone, 1989)
Cougar Town. TBS (2009–2015)
Crocodile Dundee (dir. Peter Fairman, 1986)
Dawn of the Dead (dir. George A. Romero, 1978)
Dos Monjes (dir. Juan Bustillo Oro, 1934)
El Espejo de la Bruja (dir. Chano Urueta, 1962)
El Fantasma del Convento (dir. Fernando de Fuentes, 1934)
El Hijo de la Novia (dir. Juan José Campanella, 2001)
El Misterio del Rostro Pálido (dir. Juan Bustillo Oro, 1935)
El Páramo (dir. Jaime Osorio Marquez, 2010)
El Vampiro (dir. Fernando Méndez, 1957)
El Vampiro Sangriento (dir. Miguel Morayta, 1962)
Elephant (dir. Gus Van Sant, 2003)

© The Editor(s) (if applicable) and The Author(s) 2016
G. Subero, *Gender and Sexuality in Latin American Horror Cinema*, DOI 10.1057/978-1-137-56495-5

Encarnação do Demônio (dir. Jose Mojica Marins, 2008)
Esta Noite Encarnarei no Teu Cadaver (dir. Jose Mojica Marins, 1976)
Fresa y Chocolate (dir. Tomás Gutiérrez Alea & Juan Carlos Tabío, 1993)
Funny Games (dir. Micheal Haneke, 1997 and 2007)
Habitaciones para Turistas (dir. Adrián García Bogliano, 2004)
Henry: Portrait of a Serial Killer (dir. John McNaughton, 1986)
Histórias que Nossas Babás não Contavam (dir. Oswaldo de Oliveira, 1979)
I Am Legend (dir. Francis Lawrence, 2007)
I Spit on Your Grave (dir. Meir Zarchi, 1978)
It's Alive (dir. Larry Cohen, 1974)
Juan de los Muertos (dir. Alejandro Brugués, 2011)
L.A. Zombie (dir. Bruce La Bruce, 2010)
La Bruja (dir. Chano Urueta, 1954)
La Ciénaga (dir. Lucrecia Martel, 2002)
La Historia Oficial (dir. Luis Puenzo, 1985)
La Llorona (dir. Ramón Peón, 1933)
La Llorona (dir. René Cardona, 1960)
La Maldición de la Llorona (dir. Rafael Baledón, 1963)
La Mujer sin Cabeza (dir. Lucrecia Martel, 2008)
Leonera (dir. Pablo Trapero)
Lipstick Jungle. NBC (2008–2009)
Macunaima (dir. Joaquim Pedro de Andrade, 1969)
Monsters (dir. Patty Jenkins, 2003)
Mulher Objeto (dir. Silvio de Abreu, 1981)
Night of the Living Dead (dir. George Romero, 1968)
Nosferatu (dir. F. W. Murnau, 1922)
Nosferatu the Vampire (dir. Werner Herzog, 1979)
O Cangaceiro (dir. Lima Barreto, 1953)
O Ritual dos Sádicos (dir. Jose Mojica Marins, 1970)
Pixote (dir. Hector Babenco, 1981)
Plaga Zombie (dir. Pablo Parés & Hernán Sáez, 1997)
Plaga Zombie: Zona Mutante (dir. Pablo Parés & Hernán Sáez, 2001)
Plaga Zombie: Zona Mutante: Revolución Tóxica (dir. Pablo Parés & Hernán Sáez, 2011)
Platoon (dir. Oliver Stone, 1986)
Psycho (dir. Alfred Hitchcock, 1960)
Punto y Raya (Elia Schneider, 2005)
Rebecca (dir. Alfred Hitchcock, 1940)
Resident Evil (dir. Paul W. S. Anderson, 2002)
Revolutionary Road (dir. Sam Mendes, 2008)
Robot Monster (dir. Phil Tucker, 1953)
Rope (dir. Alfred Hitchcock, 1948)

Rosemary's Baby (dir. Roman Polanski, 1968)
Rudo y Cursi (dir. Carlos Cuarón, 2008)
Santa Sangre (dir. Alejandro Jodorowsky, 1989)
Santo contra las Mujeres Vampiro (dir. Alfonso Corona Blake, 1962)
Santo contra los Zombies (dir. Benito Alazakri, 1962)
Sex and the City. HBO (1998–2004)
Shaun of the Dead (dir. Edgar Wright, 2004)
Sisters (dir. Brian De Palma, 1973)
Somos lo que Hay (dir. Jorge Michel Grau, 2010)
Soñar no Cuesta Nada (dir. Rodrigo Triana, 2006)
Species II (dir. Peter Medak, 1998)
The Brain That Wouldn't Die (dir. Joseph Green, 1962)
The Brood (dir. David Cronenberg, 1979)
The Curse of Frankenstein (dir. Terence Fisher, 1957)
The Exorcist (dir. William Friedkin, 1973)
The Hurt Locker (dir. Kathryn Bigelow, 2008)
The Shining (dir. Stanley Kubrick, 1980)
The Walking Dead (dir. Various 2010–present)
The Warriors (Sol Yurick, 1965)
The Wolf Man (dir. George Waggner, 1941)
Toy Story (dir. John Lasseter, 1995)
Warm Bodies (dir. Jonathan Levine, 2013)
World Trade Center (dir. Oliver Stone, 2006)
World War Z (dir. Marc Forster, 2013)
X-Tro (dir. Harry Bromley Davenport, 1982)
Y Tu Mamá También (dir. Alfonso Cuarón, 2001)
Zombieland (dir. Ruben Fleischer, 2009)
Zombies of Mass Destruction (dir. Kevin Hamedani, 2009)

BIBLIOGRAPHY

Anaya, R. 1996. 'I'm the King': The Macho image. In *Muy Macho: Latino men confront their manhood*, ed. R. González, 73–89. New York: Anchor/Doubleday Books.
Andrade, R. 1992. Machismo: A universal malady. *Journal of American Culture* 15(4): 33–41.
Anselmo-Sequeira, D. 2013. The country bleeds with a laugh: Social criticism meets horror genre in José Mojica Marins's a Meiia-Noite Levarei Sua Alma. In *Transnational horror across visual media: Fragmented bodies*, ed. D. Och and K. Strayer, 141–155. New York/London: Routledge.
Arboleda, M. 1995. Social attitudes and sexual variance in Lima. In *Latin American male homosexualities*, ed. S Murria, 100–110. Albuquerque: University of New Mexico Press.
Arés, P. 1996. Virilidad ¿Conocemos el costo de ser hombres? *Revista Sexología y Sociedad* 2(4): 137–149.
Argentina Sci-Fi. 2001. Entrevista a FARSA Producciones: Hacer ciencia-ficcion no es serio en Argentina. [online] http://www.argentinasci-fi.com.ar/Web%20-%20Arg%20SciFi/farsa1024.htm. Last accessed June 2015.
Arnold, S. 2013. *Maternal horror film: Melodrama and motherhood*. London: Palgrave Macmillan.
Badley, L. 1995. *Film, horror and the body fantastic*. California: Greenwood Publishing Group.
Bakhtin, M. 1968. *Rabelais and his world*. Cambridge/London: The MIT Press.
Baldez, L. 2002. *Why women protest: Women's movements in Chile*. Cambridge: Cambridge University Press.
Barcinski, A. and Finotti, I. 1998. *Ze do Caixao: Maldito - A Biografia*. Rio de Janeiro: Dark Side.

Baron, G. 2010. The illusion of equality: Machismo and Cuban cinema of the revolution. *Bulletin of Latin American Research* 29(3): 354–366.
Beattie, P.M. 2002. Beyond machismos: Recent examinations of masculinities in Latin America. *Men and Masculinities* 4(3): 303–308.
Beeler, K. 2005. *Tattoos, desire and violence: Marks of resistance in literature, film and television*. North Carolina: McFarland and Co. Publishers.
Benshoff, H.M. 1997. *Monsters in the closet: Homosexuality and the horror film*. Manchester: Manchester University Press.
Berenstein, R. 1995. *Attack of the leading ladies: Gender, sexuality, and spectatorship in classic horror cinema*. New York: Columbia University Press.
Bianchi, P. D. 2008. La subjetividad y el goce femeninos. Las nuevas representaciones de las prostitutas en la literatura latinoamericana contemporánea. Cuerpos, placeres y alteraciones. *Hispanet Journal 1*.
Bignall, S. 2010. Desire, Apathy and Activism. *Deleuze Studies* 4: 7–27.
Bird, S. 1996. Welcome to the men's club: Homosociality and the maintenance of hegemonic masculinity. *Gender & Society* 10(2): 120–132.
Bishop, K. 2006. Raising the dead: Unearthing the non-literary origins of Zombie cinema. *Journal of Popular Film and Television* 33(4): 196–205.
Bishop, K.W. 2010. The idle proletariat: Dawn of the dead, consumer ideology, and the loss of productive labor. *The Journal of Popular Culture* 43(2): 234–248.
Bitel, A. 2012. Santa Sangre review. [online] http://www.littlewhitelies.co.uk/theatrical-reviews/santa-sangre-21912. Last accessed July 2014.
Blofield, M. 2006. *The politics of moral sin: Abortion and divorce in Spain, Chile and Argentina*. New York/London: Routledge.
Brintnall, K.L. 2007. Re-building Sodom and Gomorrah: The monstrosity of queer desire in the horror film. *Culture and Religion: An Interdisciplinary Journal* 5(2): 145–160.
Brito Peña, A. undated. *La Masculinidad: Una construcción simbólica en las fuerzas armadas chilenas*. Mimeo.
Brown, J.L. 2004. Espacios y Actores: Derechos, ciudadanía y mujeres en Argentina. SciELO. Política y Cultura. No. 21. [online] http://www.scielo.org.mx/scielo.php?pid=S0188-77422004000100008&script=sci_arttext. Last accessed Jan 2015.
Brown, J. L. 2008. (No)reproductive rights in Argentina: Theoretic and political struggle. SciELO Cadernos Pago. [online] http://www.scielo.br/scielo.php?pid=S0104-83332008000100015&script=sci_abstract. Last accessed Jan 2015.
Bueno, E.P. 2012. *Amácio mazzaropi in the film and culture of Brazil: After cinema Novo*. New York/Basingstoke: Palgrave Macmillan.
Butler, J. 1993. *Bodies that matter: On the discursive limits of sex*. New York/London: Routledge.
Cagle, R.L. 2009. The good, the bad and the South Korean: Violence, morality and the South Korean extreme film. In *Horror to the extreme: Changing boundaries in Asian cinema*, ed. J. Choi and M. Wada-Marciano, 123–144. Hong Kong: Hong Kong University press.

Cantú, L. 2000. Entre Hombres/between men: Latino masculinites and homosexualities. In *Gay masculinities*, ed. P. Nardi. Thousand Oaks/London/New Delhi: Sage Publications.
Cardentey, A. 2013. La Revolución zombificada. La alegoría del trauma cubano en Juan de los Muertos, de Alejandro Brugués. *Alambique: Revista Académica de Ciencia-Ficción y Fantasia/Jornal académico de ficção científica e fantasia* 2(1): 1–13.
Carreiro, R.O. 2013. O problema do stilo na obra de José Mojica Marins. *Galaxia* 26: 98–109.
Carrier, J. 1995. *De los Otros: Intimacy and homosexuality among Mexican men*. New York: Columbia University Press.
Carrillo, H. 2002. Neither Machos nor Maricones: Masculinity and emerging male homosexual identities in Mexico. In *Changing men and masculinity in Latin America*, ed. M.C. Gutmann, 351–369. Durham: Duke University Press.
Carroll, N. 1990. *The Philosophy of Horror or Paradoxes of the Heart*. New York and London: Routledge.
Cerdán, J., and M. Fernández Labayen. 2009. Arty exploitation, cool cult, and the cinema of Alejandro Jodorwsky. In *Lastploitation, exploitation cinemas, and Latin America*, ed. V. Ruétalo and D. Tierney, 102–114. New York/London: Routledge.
Chant, S., and N. Craske. 2003. *Gender in Latin America*. London: Latin American Bureau.
Chromik-Krzykawska, A. 2010. Flowing subjectivities: Vampires, femininity and jouissance. In *Creating humanity, discovering monstrosity: Myths and metaphors of enduring evil*, ed. E. Nelson, J. Burcar, and H. Priest. Oxford: Inter-Disciplinary Press.
Clover, C. 1993. *Men, women, and chain saws*. New Jersey: Princeton University Press.
Collier. 1986. From Mary to modern woman: the material basis of Marianismo and its transformation in a Spanish village. American Ethnologist. 13(1): 100–107.
Craton, L. 2009. *The Victorian freak show: The significance of disability and physical differences in 19th-century fiction*. New York/London: Cambria Press.
Creed, B. 1993a. *The monstrous feminine: Film, feminism, psychoanalysis*. New York/London: Routledge.
Creed, B. 1993b. Dark desires: Male masochism in the horror film. In *Screening the male: Exploring masculinities in Hollywood cinema*, ed. S. Cohan and I.R. Hark, 118–133. London/New York: Routledge.
Creed, B. 2002. Horror and the monstrous-feminine: An imaginary abjection. In *Horror, the film reader*, ed. M. Jancovich, 67–75. New York/London: Routledge.
Creed, B. 2005. *Phallic panic: Film, horror and the primal uncanny*. Melbourne: Melbourne University Publishing.
Creed, B. 2012. *The monstrous-feminine: Film, feminism, psychoanalysis*. London/New York: Routledge.

Crhová, J., and A. Escandón. 2011. Conceptualizing Malinche in discourse: An analysis from a sociocultural perspective. [online] http://www.interdisciplinary.net/wp-content/uploads/2011/04/escadronepaper.pdf

Cruz, M. 2000. Gay male domestic violence and the pursuit of masculinity. In *Gay masculinities*, ed. P. Nardi. Thousand Oaks/London/New Delhi: Sage Publications.

De Andrade, J.P. 1995. Cannibalism and self-cannibalism. In *Brazilian cinema*, ed. R. Johnson and R. Stam, 81–83. New York: Columbia University Press.

De la Mora, S. 2006. *Cinemachismo: Masculinities and sexuality in Mexican film*. Austin: University of Texas Press.

De la Torre, M.A. 2009. Marianismo. In *Hispanic American religious cultures*, vol. 1, ed. M.A. de la Torre, 346–348. Santa Barbara: Greenwood Publishing Group.

Del Moral, C. 2011. Entrevista: Jorge Michel Grau, Somos lo que hay. *Cine Latino en Nueva York*. [online] http://cinelatinony.blogspot.co.uk/2011/02/entrevista-jorge-michel-grau.html. Last accessed Dec 2014.

Delgao, K.K. 2008. José Mojica Marins: el anticristo del cine sudamericano. *Cineforever: cine de ayer, hoy y siempre*. [online] http://www.cineforever.com/2008/10/11/José-mojica-marins-el-anticristo-del-cine-sudamericano/. Last accessed July 2014.

Dendle, P. 2001. *The Zombie movie encyclopedia*. Jefferson, NC: McFarland.

Dendle, P. 2007. The Zombie as barometer of cultural anxiety. In *Monsters and the monstrous: Myths and metaphors of enduring evil*, ed. N. Scott. Amsterdam: Rodopi Publishing.

Desser, D. 2007. When we see the ocean, we figure we're home: From ritual to romance in the warriors. In *City that never sleeps: New York and the filmic imagination*, ed. M. Pomerance. New Jersey: Rutgers University Press.

Discépolo, A., and R. Cossa. 2008. *El grotesco criollo: Discépolo-Cossa*. Buenos Aires: Ediciones Colihue SRL.

Donald, R.R. 1992. Masculinity and machismo in Hollywood's war film. In *Men, masculinity and the media*, ed. S. Craig, 124–135. London: Sage Publications.

Dorfman, A. 1983. *Mother's Day*. The New York Times. [online] http://www.nytimes.com/1983/05/07/opinion/mother-s-day.html. Last accessed January 2016.

Du Maurier, D. 1938. *Rebecca*. London: Gollancz.

Dyer, R. 1992. *Only entertainment*. London: Routledge.

Dyer, R. 2013. *The matter of images: Essays on representations*. New York/London: Routledge.

Ebert, R. 2003. Santa Sangre. [online] http://www.rogerebert.com/reviews/great-movie-santa-sangre-1989. Last accessed July 2014.

Edwards, T. 2006. *Cultures of masculinity*. London/New York: Routledge.

Eljaiek Rodríguez, G.A. 2011. "Tropicalización" en tres películas de horror colombianas. In *Horrofílmico: Aproximaciones al Cine de Terror en Latinoamérica y el Caribe*, ed. R. Díaz-Zambrana and P. Tomé, 163–182. San Juan: Isla Negra Editores.

Eljaiek Rodriguez, G.A. 2012. *Transilvania-Cali-Bogotá "Tropicalización" en tres películas de horror colombianas* in R. Diaz'Zambrana and P. Tome (eds.) Horrofílmico: Aproximaciones al Cine de Terror en Latinoamérica y el Caribe. San Juan: Isla Negra Editores.

Fergusson Ellis, K. 1989. *The contested castle: Gothic novels and the subversion of domestic ideology*. Illinois: University of Illinois Press.

Ferreira, J. 2000. *Cinema de Invenção*. São Paulo: Limiar.

Fiedler, L.A. 1960. *Love and death in the American novel*. Champaign: Dalkey Archive Press.

Foss, K., and K.L. Domenici. 2001. Haunting Argentina: Synecdoche in the protests of the mothers of the Plaza de Mayo. *Quarterly Journal of Speech* 87(3): 237–258.

Foster, D. 2003. *Queer issues in contemporary Latin American cinema*. Austin: University of Texas Press.

Francus, M. 1994. The monstrous mother: Reproductive anxiety in swift and pope. *English Literary History* 61(4): 829–851.

Fuchs, C.J. 1993. The Buddy Politics. In *Screening the male: Exploring masculinities in Hollywood cinema*, ed. S. Cohan and I.R. Hark, 194–211. London/New York: Routledge.

Gibron, B. 2011. In god's hands: 'Santa Sangre' (Blue Ray). [online] http://www.popmatters.com/post/136759-in-gods-hands-santa-sangre-blu-ray. Last accessed July 2014.

Giffney, N. 2004. Denormatising queer theory: More than (simply) lesbian and gay studies. *Feminist Theory* 5(1): 73–78.

Girman, C. 2004. *Mucho macho: Seduction, desire, and the homoerotic lives of Latin men*. London/New York: Routledge.

Gissi, J. 1987. *Identidad latinoamericana: psicología y sociedad*. Santiago: Impresión Gráfica Andes.

González, J. 2004. Género y masculinidad en Cuba: Teorizando: Macho, varón, masculino y algo más. *Cuba Literaria*. [online] http://www.webcitation.org/6OUb2pqpP. Last accessed June 2015.

Greven, D. 2009. *Manhood in Hollywood from bush to bush*. Austin: University of Texas Press.

Grobet, L. 2006. *Espectacular de Lucha Libre*. UNAM: Mexico D. F.

Gutierrez, O. 2001. *The horrifying transformation of the female monster*. California: San Jose State University.

Gutmann, M. 1997. Trafficking in men: The anthropology of masculinity. *Annual Review of Anthropology* 26: 385–409.

Gutmann, M. 2006. *The meanings of macho: Being a man in Mexico City.* California: University of California Press.

Guy-Meakin, A. 2012. Augusto Pinochet and the Support of Chilean Right-Wing Women. *E-International Relations Students.* [online] http://www.e-ir.info/2012/09/17/augusto-pinochet-and-the-support-of-chilean-right-wing-women/. Last accessed Jan 2015.

Haggerty, G.E. 2006. *Queer Gothic.* Illinois: University of Illinois Press.

Halberstam, J. 1995. *Skin shows: Gothic horror and the technology of monsters.* Durham: Duke University Press.

Halberstam, J. 1998. *Female masculinity.* Durham: Duke University Press.

Hart, L. 2005. *Fatal women: Lesbian sexuality and the mark of aggression.* London/New York: Routledge.

Haslam, N. 2012. *Psychology in the bathroom.* Hampshire: Palgrave Macmillan.

Heasley, R. 2005. Queer masculinities of straight men: A typology. *Men and Masculinities* 7(3): 310–320.

Heiland, D. 2008. *Gothic and gender: An introduction.* Hoboken, NJ: Wiley.

Hopkins, P. 1998. Gender treachery: Homophobia, masculinity and threatened identities. In *Race, class, gender and sexuality: The big questions*, ed. N. Zack, L. Shrage, and C. Sartwell. West Sussex: Wiley-Blackwell Publishing.

Hopman, J. 2001. El machismo: su relación con los excesos al interior de las fuerzas armadas. In *Hombres: Identidad/es y Violencia. 2o Encuentro de Estudios de Masculinidades: Identidades, Cuerpos, Violencia y Políticas Públicas*, ed. J. Olavarría, 133–146. Ñuñoa: FLACSO-Chile.

Howe, S.E. 2006. The Madres de la Plaza de Mayo: asserting motherhood, rejecting feminism. *Journal of International Women's Studies* 7(3): 43–50.

Huang, H. 2007. *Horror and evil in the name of enjoyment: A psychoanalytic critique of ideology.* Schweiz: Peter Lang AG.

Ingham, J.M. 1986. *Mary, Lichael, and Lucifer: Folk Catholicism in Central Mexico.* Austin: University of Texas Press.

Jaquez, A. 2010. Somos lo que hay: Canibalismo despiadadamente humano. *Revista Medina.* [online] http://medinamag.com/2010/11/somos-lo-que-hay-canibalismo-despiadadamente-humano/. Last accessed Dec 2014.

Johnson, R. 1995. 'Cinema Novo and Cannibalism: Macunaíma' in R. Johnson and R. Stam (eds.) Brazilian Cinema. New York: Columbia University Press, 178–190.

Jung, C.G. 1981. *The archetypes and the collective unconscious*, vol. 9. New Jersey: Princeton University Press.

Kahane, C. 1985. The Gothic mirror. In *The (M)other tongue: Essays in feminist psychoanalysitc interpretation*, ed. S. Nelson Garner, C. Kahane, and M. Sprengnether. Ithaca: Cornell University Press.

Kaiser-Lenoir, C. 1977. *El grotesco criollo.* La Habana: Casa de las Américas.

Kawin, B.F. 2012. *Horror and the horror film.* London/New York/Delhi: Anthem Press.

Kilgour, M. 1998a. Dr. Frankenstein Meets Dr. Freud. In *American Gothic: New interventions in a national narrative*, ed. R.K. Martin and E. Savoy. Iowa: University of Iowa Press.
Kilgour, M. 1998b. The Function of Cannibalism at the Present Time. In *Cannibalism and the colonial world*, ed. F. Barker, P. Hulme, and M. Iversen, 238–259. Cambridge: Cambridge University Press.
Kim, K.H. 2004. *The remasculinization of Korean cinema*. Durham: Duke University Press.
Kimmel, M.S. 2006. *Manhood in America: A cultural history*. New York: Oxford University Press.
Kirtley, B. 1960. "La Llorona" and related themes. *Western Folklore* 19(3): 155–168.
Korolczuk, E. 2004. One woman leads to another – Female identity in the works of Margaret Atwood. *The Americanist* XXI: 35–52.
Kosofky Sedwick, E. 1985. *The epistemology of the closet*. New York: Harvester Wheatsheaf.
Kosofsky Sedgwick, E. 1992. *Between men: English literature and male homosocial desire*. New York: Columbia University Press.
Kristeva, J. 1982. *Powers of horror: An essay on abjection*. New York: Columbia University Press.
Kulick, D. 1998. *Travesti: Sex, gender, and culture among Brazilian transgendered prostitutes*. Chicago/London: The University of Chicago Press.
Kulick, D. 2000. Gay and lesbian language. *Annual review in Anthropology* 29: 243–285.
Kulick, D. 2002. The gender of Brazilian transgendered prostitutes. In *The masculinity studies reader*, ed. R. Adamas and D. Savran. London: Blackwell Publishing.
Lancaster, R. 1997. Guto's performance: Notes on the transvestism of everyday life. In *Sex and sexuality in Latin America*, ed. D. Balderston and D. Guy. New York/London: New York University Press.
Lancaster, R. 2002. Subject honor, object shame. In *The masculinity studies reader*, ed. R. Adams and D. Savran. London: Blackwell Publishers.
Langman, L. 2003. The Ludic Body: Ritual, Desire, and Cultural identity in the American Super Bowl and the Carnival of Rio. In *The politics of selfhood: Bodies and identities in global capitalism*, ed. R. Harveybrown, 64–86. Minnesota: University of Minnesota Press.
Lavrin, A. 1998. *Women, feminism, and social change in Argentina, Chile, and Uruguay: 1890–1940*. Lincoln: University of Nebraska Press.
Lavrin, A. 2005. Latin American women's history: The national period. In *Women's history in global perspective*, vol. 3, ed. B.G. Smith, 180–221. Champaign: University of Illinois Press.
Lehman, P. 2001. *Masculinity: Bodies, movies, culture*. New York/London: Routledge.

Leiner, M. 1994. *Sexual politics in Cuba: Machismo, homosexuality and AIDS.* Boulder: Westview Press.
Lenne, G. 1979. Monsters and victim: Women in the horror film. In *Sexual stratagems: The world on women in film*, ed. P. Erens, 31–40. New York: Horizon Press.
Levine, M.P., and M.S. Kimmel. 1998. *Gay macho: The life and death of the homosexual clone.* New York: New York University Press.
Li-Vollmer, M., and M.E. LaPointe. 2003. Gender transgression and villainy in animated film. *Popular Communication: The International Journal or Media and Culture.* 1(2): 89–109.
Long Hoeveler, D. 1998. *Gothic feminism: The professionalisation of gender from Charlotte Smith to the Brontës.* Liverpool: Liverpool University Press.
Lozano-Díaz, N.O. 2002. Ignored virgin or unaware women: A Mexican-American protestant reflection on the virgin of Guadalupe. In *Blessed one: Protestant perspectives on Mary*, ed. B. Roberts Gaventa and C.L. Rigby, 85–96. Louisville: Westminster John Knox Press.
Luengo López, J. 2008. Ídolos populares de latina masculinidad. Valentino, Gardel y, otros 'violeteros modernistas': *Culturas Populares. Revista Electrónica* 7. [online] http://www.culturaspopulares.org/textos7/articulos/luengo.htm. Last accessed Dec 2014.
Lumsden, I. 1996. *Machos, maricones, and gays: Cuba and homosexuality.* USA: Temple University Press.
Magistrale, T. 2005. *Abject terrors: Surveying the modern and postmodern horror film.* Schweiz: Peter Lang AG.
Malin, A. 1994. Mothers Who won't disappear. *Human Rights Quarterly* 16(1): 187–213.
Mallan, K. 2000. Witches, bitches and femmes fatales: Viewing the female grotesque in children's film. *Papers: Explorations into Children's Literature* 10(1): 26–35.
Manrique, J. 2002. *Eminent maricones: Arenas, Lorca, Puig, and Me.* Pennsylvania: University of Wisconsin Press.
Mark, R. 1994. Teaching from the open closet. In *Listening to silences: New essays in feminist criticism*, ed. E. Hedges and S. Fisher Fishkin, 245–259. Oxford: Oxford University Press.
Matthews, N. 2000. *Comic politics: Gender in Hollywood comedy after the new right.* Manchester: Manchester University Press.
Melchor Iñiguez, C. 2007. La Llorona, la Malinche y la mujer chicana de hoy. Cuando ceda el llanto. *Acciones e Investigaciones Sociales.* Julio 2007: 151–172.
Melgosa Pérez, A. 2005. Imaging crisis in contemporary Argentina: mothers on the street and mothers on the screen. *Studies in Hispanic Cinemas* 1(3): 151–168.
Mendès-Leite, R. 1993. A game of Appearances: The "Ambigusexuality" in Brazilian Culture of sexuality. *Journal of Homosexuality* 25(3): 271–282.

Metz, C. 1982. *The imaginary signifier: Psychoanalysis and the cinema*. Bloomington: Indiana University Press.
Milanesio, N. 2013. *Workers go shopping in Argentina: The rise of popular consumer culture*. Albuquerque: UNM Press.
Mohr, R.D. 1992. *Gay ideas: Outing and other controversies*. Boston: Beacon Press.
Molloy, S. 1998. The politics of posing. In *Hispanisms and homosexualities*, ed. S. Molloy and R. McKee, 141–160. Durham: Duke University Press.
Montaner, C. 2001. *Las Raíces Torcidas de América Latina: Como la historia y la cultura contribuyeron a moldear la región más pobre, inestable y atrasada de occidente*. Madrid: Plaza and Janes Editores.
Moon, M. 1998. *A small boy and others: Imitation and initiation in American culture from Henry James to Andy Warhol*. Durham: Duke University Press.
Morales C.M. n.d. Baby Shower, de Pablo Illanes. *Cinechile*. http://www.cinechile.cl/crit&estud-145. Last accessed Dec 2015.
Morgan, L.M. 2015. Reproductive rights or reproductive justice? Lessons from Argentina. *Health and Human Rights* 17(1). [online] http://www.hhrjournal.org/2015/04/16/reproductive-rights-or-reproductive-justice-lessons-from-argentina/. Last accessed Jan 2015.
Mulvey. 1989. Visual Pleasure and Narrative Cinema in J. Evans and S. Hall (eds.) *Visual Culture: The Reader*. London, Thousand Oaks and New Delhi: SAGE Publications, 381–389.
Murray, S. 1995. Machismo, male homosexuality, and Latino culture. In *Latin American male homosexualities*, ed. S. Murray. Albuquerque: University of New Mexico Press.
Navarro Arias, R. 1999. *Las Emociones en el Cuerpo*. Editorial Pax Mexico: D.F. Mexico.
Nieto Gómez, A. 1997. La Chicana – legacy of suffering and self-denial. In *Chicana feminist thought: The basic historical writings*, ed. A.M. García, 48–50. London/New York: Routledge.
Norat, G. 2008. Women staging coups through mothering: Depictions in Hispanic contemporary literature. In *Feminist mothering*, ed. A. O'Reilly. New York: SUNY Press.
Nowell, R. 2010. *Blood money: A history of the first teen Slasher film cycle*. New York/London: Bloomsbury Publishing.
Oliver, K. 1993. *Reading Kristeva: Unraveling the Double-bind*. Washington: Georgetown University Press.
Oliver, K. 2012. *Knock me up, knock me down: Images of pregnancy in Hollywood films*. New York and West Sussex: Columbia University Press.
Orndorf, B. 2012. *Juan of the Dead Preview*. [online] http://www.blu-ray.com/Juan-of-the-Dead/125704/#Preview. Last accessed Jan 2015.
Parker, R. 1985. Masculinity, femininity, and homosexuality: On the anthropological interpretation of sexual meanings in Brazil. E, Blackwood (Guest Editor). *Journal of Homosexuality* 11(3/4) (New York: The Haworth Press).

Parker, R. 1991. *Bodies, pleasures and passions: Sexual culture in contemporary Brazil*. Boston: Beacon Press.
Parker, R. 2003. Changing sexualities: Masculinity and male homosexuality in Brazil in masculinity. In *Changing men and masculinities in Latin America*, ed. M. Gutmann, 307–332. Durham/London: Duke University Press.
Payne, W. 2007. *La violencia de los grupos armados al margen de la ley motivada por homofobia: Una investigación del fenómeno en el contexto del conflicto armado en Colombia*. MA Thesis, La Universidad del Salvador.
Pegg, S. 2008. The dead and the quick. *The Guardian* (4th Nov). [online] http://www.theguardian.com/media/2008/nov/04/television-simon-pegg-deadset. Last accessed Dec 2013.
Perches Galván, S. 2010. *Jorge Michel Grau y el canibalismo familiar de "Somos lo que hay"*. [online] http://revistatoma.wordpress.com/2010/12/01/jorge-michel-grau-y-el-canibalismo-familiar-de-somos-lo-que-hay/. Last accessed Dec 2014.
Pérez, D. E. 2004. *Barrio Bodies: Theorizing Chicana/o Popular Culture as Queer*. Tempe: Arizona State University.
Pilcher, J.M. 2001. *Cantinflas and the chaos of Mexican modernity*. New York: Rowman & Littlefield.
Polan, D.B. 2004. Eros and syphilization: The contemporary horror film. In *Planks of reason: Essays on the horror film*, ed. B.K. Grant and C. Sharrett, 142–152. Lanham: Scarecrow Press.
Potter Engels, M. 1990. Evil, Sin and Violation of the Vulnerable. In *Lift every voice: Constructing Christian theologies from the underside*, ed. S. Brooks Thistlethwaite and M. Potter Engels, 152–164. Maryknoll/New York: Orbis Books.
Pulliam, J. 2007. The Zombie. In *Icons of horror and the supernatural: An encyclopedia of our worst nightmares*, vol. 2, ed. S.T. Joshi, 723–754. Connecticut: Greenwood Publishing Group.
Raed, J. 2000. *The new avengers: Feminism, femininity and the rape-revenge cycle*. Manchester: Manchester University Press.
Ramírez, E.C. 2000. *Chicanas/Latinas in American theatre: A history of performance*. Bloomington: Indiana University Press.
Ramírez Berg, C. 1989. *Latino Images in Film: Stereotypes, Subversion, and Resistance*. Austin: University of Texas Press.
Ramírez Berg, C. 2002. *Latino images in film: Stereotypes, subversion, and resistance*. Austin: University of Texas Press.
Ramirez Berg, C. 2010. *A cinema of solitude: A critical study of Mexican film, 1967–1983*. Austin: University of Texas Press.
Reis, L. 2002. *A Cultura do Lixo: Horror, Sexo e Exploração no Cinema*. Universidade de Campinas. MA Dissertation.
Rheindorf, M. 2007. Split masculinities and homosocial desire in nip/tuck and six feet under. In *Screening gender*, ed. P. Keike, 130–147. Berlin: LIT Verlag Munster.

Rich, A. 1976. *Of woman born: Motherhood as experience and institution*. New York: WW. Norton and Co.
Risner, J. 2011. Killer on the Pampa: Gender, cinematic lansdscape, and the transnational slasher in Adrián García Bogliano's Habitaciones para turistas (2004) and 36 Pasos (2006). *Hispanet* 4: 1–28.
Robson, K. 2002. The female vampire: Chantal Chawaf's melancholic autofiction. In *Women's writing in contemporary France: New writers, new literatures in the 1990s*, ed. G. Rye and M. Worton, 53–64. Manchester: Manchester University Press.
Rocha, C. 2012. *Masculinities in contemporary Argentine cinema*. London: Palgrave Macmillan.
Rodríguez Tapia, S. and Verduzco Argüelles, I. 2008. "La Llorona": Análisis Literario-Simbólico. In T. López Pellisa and F. A. Moreno (eds.). *Ensayos sobre ciencia ficción y literature fantástica*. Madrid: Asociación Cultural Xatafi and Universidad Carlos III de Madrid, 306–318.
Rutherford, J. 1988. Who's that Man? In *Male order: Unwrapping masculinity*, ed. R. Chapman and J. Rutherford, 21–67. London: Lawrence & Wishart.
Sale, R. 1979. *Fairy tales and after: From snow white to E .B. White*. New Jersey: Harvard University Press.
Salles Gomes, P.E. 1997. Cinema: A trajectory within underdevelopment. In *New Latin American cinema, volume two: Studies of national cinemas*, ed. M.T. Martin, 263–271. Michigan: Wayne State University Press.
Salyers Bull, S. 1998. Machismo/marianismo: Attitudes, employent, education and sexual behaviour among women in Ecuador and the dominican republic. *Journal of Gender, Culture and Health* 3(1): 1–27.
Sardenberg, C.M.B. 1994. Clarification: Machismo. *The concept of machismo*. [online] http//userpages.umbc.edu/~korenman/wmst/machismo.html. Last accessed July 2014.
Sargent, D. 2013. American masculinity and homosocial behavior in the bromance era. MA Thesis, Georgia State University. [online] http://scholarworks.gsu.edu/cgi/viewcontent.cgi?article=1099&context=communication_theses. Last accessed Dec 2013.
Schaefer, E. 2009. Foreword. In *Latsploitation, exploitation cinemas, and Latin America*, ed. V. Ruétalo and D. Tierney, ix–xii. London/New York: Routledge.
Schnabl Schweitzer, C. 2010. *The stranger's voice: Julia Kristeva's relevance for a pastoral theology for women struggling with depression*. Berne: Peter Lang Publishing.
Schoell. 1985. *Stay Out of the Shower: 25 Years of Shocker Films, Beginning With Psycho*. Charlottesville: Dembner Books.
Sequeira, D. 2009. *The machismo and marianismo tango*. Pittsburgh: Dorrance Publishing.
Sharrett, C. 1996. The horror film in neoconservative culture. In *The dread of difference: Gender in the modern horror film*, ed. B.K. Grant, 253–278. Austin: University of Texas Press.

Shaw, D. 2003. *Contemporary cinema of Latin America: Ten key films*. London/New York: Continuum International Publishing Group.
Shaw, L. 2007. Afro-Brazilian identity: Malandragem and homosexuality in Madame Sata. In *Contemporary Latin American cinema: Breaking into the global market*, ed. D. Shaw, 87. Lanham: Rowman & Littlefield Publishers.
Shildrick, M. 2002. *Embodying the monster: Encounters with the vulnerable self*. London: Sage.
Smihula, J.H. 2008. *"Where a thousand corpses lie": Critical realism and the representation of war in American film and literature since 1960*. Michigan: ProQuest.
Smith, P. J. 2010. Film of the month: We are what we are. [online] http://old.bfi.org.uk/sightandsound/review/5710. Last accessed Dec 2014.
Smith, A., and D. Wallace. 2004. The female Gothic: Then and now. *Gothic Studies* 6(1): 1–7.
Sontag, S. 1966. *Against interpretation and other essays*. New York: Picador.
Starrs, B. (2008) *'If we stretch our imaginations'; the monstrous-feminine mother in Rolf de Heer's "Bad Boy Bubby" (1993) and "Alexandra's Project" (2003)*. Scope: An Online Journal of Film Studies. [online] http://www.nottingham.ac.uk/scope/documents/2008/february-2008/starrs.pdf. Last accessed January 2016.
Stein, A., and K. Plummer. 1996. 'I can't even think straight': 'Queer' theory and the missing sexual revolution in sociology. In *Queer theory/sociology*, ed. S. Seidman, 129–143. Oxford: Blackwell Publishers.
Stephens, E. 2012. Queer monsters: Technologies of self-transformation in Bulwer's anthropometamorphosis and Braidotti's metamorphoses. In *Somatechnics: Queering the technologisation of bodies*, ed. S. Murray and N. Sullivan, 171–186. Surrey: Ashgate Publishing.
Stern, M. 2010. Dudes, Bros, Boyfriends and Bugarrones: Redistributing the stigma of same-sex desire. *Sprinkle: A Journal of Sexual Diversity Studies* 3: 144–153.
Stevens, E. 1973. Marianismo: The other face of machismo in Latin America. In *Female and male in Latin America: Essays*, ed. A. Pescatello, 89–102. Pittsburgh: University of Pittsburgh Press.
Straw, M.C. 2010. *The damaged male and the contemporary American war film: Masochism, ethics, and spectatorship (doctoral thesis)*. Birmingham: University of Birmingham.
Strikwerda, R.A., and L. May. 1992. Male friendship and intimacy. In *Rethinking masculinity: Philosophical explorations in the light of feminism*, ed. L. May, R. Strikwerda, and P.D. Hopkins, 79–94. Lanham, MD: Rowman & Littlefield Publishers.
Subero, G. 2014. *Queer masculinities in Latin American cinema: Male bodies and narrative representations*. London: I B Tauris.

Sullivan, R. 2010. Falling short of feminism: Why modern retellings of fairy tales perpetuate negative stereotypes of the aging woman. [online] http://hdl.handle.net/1811/45697. Last accessed Jan 2015.
Tarrat, M. 2003. Monsters from the Id. In *Film genre reader 3*, vol. 3, ed. B.K. Grant, 346–365. Austin: University of Texas Press.
Theidon, K. 2009. Reconstructing masculinities: The disarmament, demobilization, and reintegration of former combatants in Colombia. *Human Rights Quarterly* 31: 1–34.
Thomas, K. 2012. Bromance is so passé. In *Robert Downey, Jr's queer paratexts in Sherlock Holmes for the 21st century: Essays on new adapatations*, ed. L. Porter, 35–47. McFarland: North Carolina.
Tierney, D. 2009. José Mojica Marins and the cultural politics of marginality in 'Third world' film criticism. In *Lastploitation, exploitation cinema, and Latin America*, ed. V. Ruetalo and D. Tierney, 115–128. New York/London: Routledge.
Trencansky, S. 2001. Final girls and terrible youth: Transgression in 1980s Slasher horror. *Journal of Popular Film and Television* 29(2): 63–74.
Tyler, I. 2009. *Against Abjection. Feminist Theory.* 10(1): 77–98.
Vermaak, J.L. 2008. Horror versus terror in the body genre. [online] http://dspace.nmmu.ac.za:8080/jspui/bitstream/10948/636/1/Part%20One%20-%20Horror%20Versus%20Terror%20in%20the%20Body%20Genre.pdf
Viveros Vigoya, M. 2001. Contemporary Latin American perspectives on masculinity. *Men and Masculinities* 3(3): 97–116.
Viveros Vigoya, M. 2003. Contemporary Latin American perspectives on masculinity. In *Sex and sexuality in Latin America*, ed. D. Balderston and D. Guy, 27–57. New York/London: New York University Press.
Warner, M. 1993. Introduction. In *Fear of a queer planet: Queer politics and social theory*, ed. M. Warner, vii–xxxi. Minneapolis: University of Minnesota Press.
Webb, S. 1999. Masculinities and the margins: Representations of the Malandro and the Pachuco. In *Imagination beyond nation: Latin American popular culture*, ed. E. Bueno and T. Caesar, 227–264. Pittsburgh: University of Pittsburgh Press.
Welby, L. 2010. The monstrous feminine: Confronting the horror of female fecundity in Angela Carter's the passion of new eve. *Interdisciplinary.net*. [online] http://www.inter-disciplinary.net/wp-content/uploads/2010/08/Welby-paper.pdf. Last accessed Jan 2015.
Whannel, G. 2008. *Culture, politics and sport: Blowing the whistle, revisited.* New York/London: Routledge.
Williams, S. M. 2008. *When the other writes back: "Poaching," "bargain shopping," and rewriting the vampire narrative in Jewelle Gomez's "The Gilda Stories" and Octavia Butler's "Fledgling".* ProQuest.
Wood, R. 2003. *Hollywood from Vietnam to Reagan… and beyond.* New York: Columbia University Press.

Wyatt, J. 2001. 'Identity, Queerness, and Homosocial Bonding: The Case of Swingers' in P. Lehman (ed.) Masculinity: Bodies, Movies, Culture. New York: Routledge, 51–66.

Yates, W. 1997. An introduction to the Grotesque: Theoretical and theological considerations. In *The Grotesque in art and literature: Theological reflections*, ed. J. Luthers Adams, W. Yates, and R. Penn Warren, 1–68. Michigan: Wm. B. Eerdmans Publishing.

Yenerall, K. 2011. Reproductive rights and modern film: Five women, six movies, and the politics of abortion. Paper presented at the American Political Science Association Annual Meeting. [online] http://www.apsanet.org/content_65547.cfm. Last accessed Jan 2015.

Zamorano, A. 2011. La Llorona: Leyenda híbrida en la cinematografía Mexicana. *Actas IV Congreso Internacional sobre Análisis Fílmico: Nuevas Tendencias e Hibridaciones de los Discursos Audiovisuales en la Cultura Digital Contemporánea*. Madrid: Ediciones de las Ciencias Sociales, 1265–1277. [online] http://repositori.uji.es/xmlui/bitstream/handle/10234/31377/Zamorano_ActasIVCongreso.pdf?sequence=1. Last accessed Jan 2015.

Index

A
abjection, 121–2
abortion, 131, 132, 138
Alfredo's monstrosity, 95
A Meia-Noite Levarei Sua Alma, 39, 55
American culture, 97
Amores Perros (2000), 74
anti-abortion laws, 132
Argentina, motherhood in
    female politicians, highest level of, 146
    Habitaciones para Turistas (2005) (*see Habitaciones para Turistas* (2004), motherhood in)
    Madres de la Plaza de Mayo, 112, 129–130
    patriotic motherhood, sense of, 132
    social imposition, 132
Argentina Sc-Fi (2001), 158

B
Baby Shower (2011), femininity and motherhood in, 114, 145
    abjection, 121–122
    anti-mariana femininity, 115, 116, 120
    castration, 123–125
    female emancipation, 115, 120–1, 124
    female mutilation, 115
    female nudity, spectacle of, 116
    female stereotypes, 115
    Latin American sexual culture, 121
    male nudity, spectacle of, 116
    mariana and non-mariana identity, confrontation of, 128
    mariana subjectivity, 126, 127
    masculine aggression, 115
    phallocentric symbolic order, disruption of, 127
    pregnancy and monstrous behaviour, 116–19
    rape, 125–6
    repulsion and empathy, feelings of, 121
    sexualised mariana female gaze, 123
    sociosexual imaginary, 127
    torture sequence, 124

transgression, identification with, 118
Banner machismo, 44
Beau Travail (1999), 100
Billy Bud (1962), 100
The Brain That Wouldn't Die (1962), xvii
bromantic and homosocial narratives
  comedy, 149–150
  fraternal mockery, 150
  Juan de los Muertos (2011) (*see Juan de los Muertos* (2011))
  physical aggression/banter, 151
  Plaga Zombie trilogy (*see Plaga Zombie* trilogy, bromance in)
  romance between buddies, 151
  Shaun of the Dead (2004), 148, 153–4
  toilet humour, use of, 151
The Brood, Alien (1979), 113, 117

C
cannibalism, 83, 91
Caribbean masculinities, 171
Caribbean sexual culture, 165
castration, 123–5
Cine Latino en Nueva York, 86
Cinema do lixo, 65
Cinema novo, 56, 65
Coffin Joe trilogy, 46
Conqueror macho, 44
conquistadores, 111
Cougar Town (2009–2015), 127
Criollo grotesco, 60
Crocodile Dundee (1986), 158
'crypto gay couple,' 158
cultural refinement, 54
The Curse of Frankenstein (1957), xvii

D
28 Days Later (2002), 148
Desperate Housewives (2004–2012), 127
Dos monjes, 2

E
El Espejo de la Bruja (1962), xxiv, 22–6
El Fantasma del Convento (1934), 2
El Lugar sin Límites (1966), 101
El Misterio del Rostro Pálido (1935), 2
El Páramo (2010), 77, 97
El Vampiro (1957), 17–18
El Vampiro Sangriento (1962), 26–30
empathy, 121
Encarnação do Demônio (2008), 39
Esta Noite Encarnarei no Teu Cadaver (1976), 39
The Exorcist (1973), 24

F
farting, 166–167
female castration, 123–5
female emancipation, 115, 120–1, 124
female hysteria, 161
female mutilation, 115
femininity, 4
femininity and motherhood. *See* mothering and motherhood
fertility, 145
Fresa y Chocolate (1993), 168
Funny Games (1997 and 2007), 159

G
gays, 44, 166
gender violence, 125
genital castration, 124–5

gothic horror Mexican cinema
  Diana Films, 1–2
  El Espejo de la Bruja (1962), 22–6
  El Vampiro (1957), 17–18
  El Vampiro Sangriento (1962), 26–30
  femininity, 4
  La Bruja (1954), 18–22
  La Llorona, 7–16
  La Maldición de la Llorona (1963), 30–5
  masculinity, 4
  monster, 1–2
  Producciones Bueno, 1–2
  Producciones Delta, 1–2
  queerness, 4
  Tele Talia Films, 1–2
  transformations and transgressions, 3
  tropicalisation, 2
Grotesco criollo, 57
guerrilla warfare, 98

H
Habitaciones para Turistas (2004), motherhood in
  abortion, unwanted pregnancies, 131, 132, 138
  anti-motherist young women, extermination of, 135–7
  civilization and brutality, notion of, 132, 154, 140
  clinical terminations, illegality of, 146
  contemporary Argentina, motherist politics of, 141
  escaping machismo, 141–142
  gender politics, 133, 143–5
  girls as object of murderous gaze, 135, 136
  illegal abortion, 142–143
  male hegemonic supremacy, 144
  monstrosity and female identity, notions of, 133
  monstrous feminine, transformation into, 138–139
  motherist politics, 143, 144, 146
  national consciousness, 132
  national identity and pride, 133
  national political strategy, 140
  normative femininity, 138
  pro-motherist agenda, 135
  reproductive rights, 134
  rural *vs.* urban life, 132–3
  sex outside marriage, 133
  unborn babies, disappearances of, 139
heteromasculinity, 158, 159, 167
heteronormativity, 45
heterosexual couples, 149
heterosexual masculinity, 150
homoeroticism, 150
homosexuality, 161
homosocial/homosexual, 76
homosociality. *See* bromantic and homosocial narratives
hypermasculine behaviour, 150
hypermasculine sexuality, 89

I
illegal abortion, 142–3
institutionalised homosociality, 77
It's Alive (1974), 117

J
Juan de los Muertos (2011), 150, 164–76
  beta-male, 168
  bromanctic interactions, 165, 166

bromosocial moment, 169
Caribbean masculinities, 171
Caribbean sexual culture, 165
crisis of masculinity, 168
Cuban *compadrazgo*, 165
heteromasculinity, 167
homoeroticism, 166, 168
homosociality, 174
hyperbolic sexual penetration, desire for, 166–7
machismo, 165, 166, 169
melocomedic penis, 173
meta-bodily interaction, 168
overt homoerotic desire, 168
penis/phallus, representation of, 170–1, 173, 174
queer bromance, 172
queer masculinity, 165, 170
same-sex desires, 168
sexual minorities, tolerant attitude towards, 166
social and sexual barriers, 167

L
La Bruja (1954), xxiv, 18–22
La Llorona (1933), xxiv, 2, 7–16
La Maldición de la Llorona (1963), 30–5
La Malinche, 6–7
Latin American masculinity, 42
L.A. Zombie (2010), 149
lesbian, gay, bisexual, transgender (LGBT), 44
LGBT community, 44
Lipstick Jungle (2008–2009), 127

M
machismo, 150, 151
Macunaíma (1969), 91
Madres de la Plaza de Mayo, 112, 129–130

male psychopaths, 131
male-to-male relationships, 149
marianismo
 fecund female, 112–13
 femininity, form of, 111–12
 mother as monstrous figure, 113
 mothering and motherhood (*see* Mothering and motherhood)
 notion of, 111
 pregnancy within horror narratives, 113
 Virgin Mary, 111–12
maricón, 93
Meia-Noite Levarei Sua Alma, 51
mestizo, 111
Mexican sexual culture, 84
military dictatorship, 53
miscarriage, 139
misogyny, 131
monsters, 147
monstrous and murdered machos
 damaged male, 101
 El Lugar sin Límites (1966), 101
 FARC, 98–99
 guerrilla warfare, 98
 homoerotic tension, 107
 homosexual panic, 102
 machismo, 105
 male monster, 75
 monstrous feminine, 106
 Parra moans, 103
 primal uncanny, 101
 real feminine monster, 104
 sexual prowess and conquests, 74
 social discrimination, 100
 Somos lo que Hay (2010); cannibalism, 83, 91; clingy woman, 80; crisis of masculinity, 82; disavows machismo, 85; dog-eat-dog society, 91; fetishistic fascination, 77; hypermasculine sexuality, 89; Julián's behaviour,

79; Julián's machismo, 80; las familias y culturas, 78; machismo, 80; *Macunaima* (1969), 91; maricón, 93; 'masculine' assertiveness, 85; moment of fetishisation, 79; mujeres de la mala vida [loose women], 92; *opera prima*, 77; queer masculinity, 87; sadistic and lascivious gaze, 79; self-loathing and depiction, 94; sexual awakening, 84; socio-sexual national imaginary, 88; socio-sexual relations, 82; transformation, 87
vernacular hypermasculinity, 77
war movies, 96
mothering and motherhood
  in contemporary Latin American culture, 112
  fertility, 145
  heteronormative and Catholic paradigm, 114
  in horror cinema; *Baby Shower* (2011) (*see Baby Shower* (2011), femininity and motherhood in); fecund female subject, 112–13; *Habitaciones para Turistas* (2005) (*see Habitaciones para Turistas* (2004), motherhood in); mother as monstrous figure, 113; pregnancy within horror narratives, 113
  mariana identity, construction of, 112
  as political platform, 112
  as quintessential elements, 111
  self-sacrificing mother, 112, 145
  social and political adherence, 112, 114
  in Southern Cone, 112
  Virgin Mary, 111–112
  womanhood, essence of, 112

N
Night of the Living Dead (1968), 147
normative sexuality, 153
Nosferatu (1922), 40

O
O Cangaceiro (1953), 43
O Ritual dos Sádicos, 55, 59

P
patriarchal domination, 120
Pelado stereotype, 43
Pixote (1981), 43
Plaga Zombie trilogy, bromance in, 150, 176
  bromantic break-up, 155
  bro-zom-com, 155
  compadrismo, 161
  crisis of masculinity, 155, 161–4
  crypto gay couple, 158
  disintegration, narratives of, 163–4
  female hysteria, 161
  hegemonic masculinity, 163
  heteromasculinity, 158, 159
  heteronormative and homosocial paradigms, 158
  homoerotic bromance, 154, 157
  homosexuality, 161
  machismo, 156, 158–63
  male sexual physicality, 162
  queer psychopath, 159
  social and heteromasculine codes, transgression of, 159
  un-macho sequence, 162–3
  'us' *versus* 'them' paradigm, 157
  zombies and humans, battles between, 155, 159–160
pregnancy, 113

premarital sex, 115, 146
Psycho (1960), xvii
Psycho (1960), 159
psychoanalytic theory, 131
Punto y Raya (2005), 97

Q
queer masculinity, 165, 170
  conceptualisation of, 41–6
  definition, 41
  otherness, 41

R
Rebecca (1938), 14
revolutionary Army Forces of
  Colombia (FARC), 98–99
Revolutionary Road (2008), 138
Robot Monster (1953), xvii
romantic zombie comedy (rom-zom-
  com), 148–149
Rosemary's Baby (1968), 113, 117
Rudo y Cursi (2008), 74

S
same-sex desire, 166
Santa Sangre (1989)
  abjection, x
  artificiality of masculinity, xiv
  Concha's submission, xiii
  deculturation of Mexican culture, ix
  drunkenness, xiv
  dystopian, xxi
  El Santo, xxii
  flashback sequence, xiii
  gothic villainess, xxiv
  historisation, xxiii
  horrific nature, xix
  horror genre, viii
  ironic sensibility, xvii

La Santa, xxii
Little White Lies, x
"machismo," xiii
machismo or masculinity, xv
macho phallic investment, xv
masculinity, xxv
meta-transsexualism, xviii
Mojica Marins's films, xxv
Monsignor's reaction, xxi
normativity, xi
normativity and abjection, xi
paradigmatic imagination, xxii
penetration and permanence, xii
perpetuate machista ideology, xx
phallic power, xvi
saint girl Lirio, xx
society regulating normativity, xi
song *La barca de Oro*, xvi
symbiotic relationship, xix
symbolic orders, x
Tattooed Woman, xi
Zé do Caixão, xxiv
zombie narrative, xxvi–xxvii
Santo contra los Zombies (1962), 147,
  152
Satiricon (1969), 61
self-sacrificing mother, 112
Sex and the City, aka *SATC* (1998–
  2004), 114, 115
sex typology, 100
sexual awakening, 84
sexual politics, 127
Shaun of the Dead (2004), 148, 153–4
The Shining (1980), 159
socio-sexual spectrum, 44
Somos lo que Hay (2010), 76
  cannibalism, 83, 91
  clingy woman, 80
  crisis of masculinity, 82
  disavows machismo, 85
  dog-eat-dog society, 91
  fetishistic fascination, 77

hypermasculine sexuality, 89
Julián's behaviour, 79
Julián's machismo, 80
las familias y culturas, 78
machismo, 80
Macunaima (1969), 91
maricón, 93
'masculine' assertiveness, 85
moment of fetishisation, 79
mujeres de la mala vida [loose women], 92
opera prima, 77
queer masculinity, 87
sadistic and lascivious gaze, 79
self-loathing and depiction, 94
sexual awakening, 84
socio-sexual national imaginary, 88
socio-sexual relations, 82
transformation, 87
Soñar no Cuesta Nada (2006), 97
Species II (1998), 113

T
Toy Story (1995), 158
transvestites, 166
trojan zombie, 155
28 Days Later (2002), 148

U
'us' vs. 'them' paradigm, 157

V
vampires, 147
Virgin Mary, 111–112
voodoo practices, in Haiti, 147

W
war movies, 96

The Warriors (1965), 97
werewolves, 147
The Wolf Man (1941), xvii
World War Z (2013), 148

X
X-Tro (1982), 113

Y
Y Tu Mamá También (2001), 74

Z
Zé's queer machismo
  besta-fera (centaur devil), 64
  carnival and grotesque, 53–7
  cinema do lixo, 51
  cinema novo, 65
  homen marinho (merman), 64
  hypermasculinity, 51
  jaracara (vampire snake), 64
  A Meia-Noite Levarei Sua Alma, 51
  O Ritual dos Sádicos, 62–3
  in underworld, 57–62
Zombieland (2009), 148
zombie narratives
  American population, miscegenistic anxieties of, 147
  bromantic and homosocial narratives; comedy, 149–150; fraternal mockery, 150; *Juan de los Muertos* (2011), 150, 164–6; physical aggression/banter, 151; *Plaga Zombie* trilogy (see *Plaga Zombie* trilogy, bromance in); romance between buddies, 151; *Shaun of the Dead* (2004), 148, 153–4; toilet humour, use of, 151
  contemporary monster, 147

as exemplary of Western world, 147
friendships, 150
heteronormativity, 154
heterosexual couples, 149
heterosexual masculinity, 150
homoeroticism, 150
in horror-comedy narratives, 148
in horror-gore narratives, 148
humour in, 154
hypermasculine behaviour, externalisation of, 150
L.A. Zombie (2010), 149
love triangle, 148
macho masculinity, 151
male hero, evolution of, 152
male-to-male relationships, 149
'modern' zombie, 147
Night of the Living Dead (1968), 147
normative sexuality, 153
romantic zombie comedy (rom-zom-com), 148–149
Santo contra los Zombies (1962), 147, 152
traditional zombie narratives, 149
28 Days Later (2002), 148
vampires and werewolves, win over, 147
voodoo practices, in Haiti, 147
World War Z (2013), 148
Zombieland (2009), 148
Zombies of Mass Destruction (2009), 149
Zombies of Mass Destruction (2009), 149

Printed by Printforce, the Netherlands